KILLER CULTS

KILLER CULTS

Murderous Messiahs and their Fanatical Followers

Brian Lane

HEADLINE

For Bela,
without whom . . .

First published in 1996
by HEADLINE BOOK PUBLISHING

10 9 8 7 6 5 4 3 2 1

British Library Cataloguing in Publication Data

Lane, Brian
Killer cults : murderous messiahs and their
fanatical followers
1. Cults 2. Murder 3. Violent deaths 4. Murder -
Political aspects 5. Murder - Religious aspects
I. Title
364.1'523

ISBN 0 7472 1812 9

Typeset by Avon Dataset Ltd, Bidford-on-Avon, Warks

Printed and bound in Great Britain by
Mackays of Chatham PLC, Chatham, Kent

HEADLINE BOOK PUBLISHING
A division of Hodder Headline PLC
338 Euston Road
London NW1 3BH

CONTENTS

ACKNOWLEDGEMENTS

This has been a curious exercise in writing, bringing together as it does the twin passions of homicide and the occult. I might have made research easy by calling upon the huge cuttings library of the former Murder Club and a veritable *library* on magic and off-beat religions. But I have found a new and exciting research tool. It is called the Internet. From modest, and necessarily humble, beginnings, I have come to rely more and more on the wisdom and experience of those far better informed than I on so many subjects. And at the other end of my keyboard, twenty-four hours a day – or so it seems.

In a slight departure from the customary 'Select Bibliography', I have included not only books which have proved useful in checking references, but also the website locations of a number of specialists who can provide extended information on-line. As far as I am aware, this is the first use of such a bibliographical resource in a general reference book. A note on websites is appended to the Bibliography.

World Wide Web aside, a book does not exist without a good publisher. And no good publisher exists without good staff. I consider myself fortunate in having the continued support of what I have come to know, perhaps presumptuously, as 'the team'. I could never write as confidently without knowing that Lorraine Jerram would be clocking my every move, and that Bela Cunha would be checking my every word. And if that weren't enough, I am lucky to have the continued support and encouragement of Headline's Publishing Director, Alan Brooke.

Brian Lane
London, June 1996

INTRODUCTION

While few sane individuals would disagree that killing people is wrong, this book seeks to provide a broad analysis of extreme cult behaviour rather than be an attack on individual cults. Indeed, with some exceptions (such as, historically, the Thugs, and more recently the Japanese Aum Shinri Kyo group) most of the organisations discussed here are more or less respectable with a few rogue members or breakaway factions. It was not the fault of the Mormon church, for example, that Jeffrey Lundgren's Reorganised Church of Jesus Christ of the Latter-Day Saints decided to murder a family of their own disciples.

One of the obstacles to an understanding of cult mania is a lack of adequate definitions. We are asking in effect the fundamental question: 'What exactly *is* a cult?'

Many words are blessed with a single meaning – 'tree', for example, or 'motorcycle'; everybody knows what they are in their own language, and the mind can 'paint' a picture of one. Others have more than one meaning; such as 'bank'. A high-street bank which deals with financial transactions, or the bank of a river? Usually the context will provide information as to the meaning – one would hardly be depositing cash in the river.

Problems arise when a word has so many different, but similar, meanings that it needs pre-definition. 'Cult' is such a word. The following attempt at a list of definitions offers at least a partial key to the ways in which it will be encountered in this work:

Theological: This is the historical use of the word simply to describe a style of worship.

Sociological: Commonly used to describe a religious group which exists outside a nation's dominant religion. The Buddhist community in England might be considered a cult by some, while Christianity might equally be seen as a cult in Tibet.

Fundamentalist Christian: In this case any religious group which does not adhere strictly to historical Christian doctrine (the Creation, Immaculate Conception and so on) is termed, usually negatively, a cult. This effectively dismisses the beliefs of some 70 per cent of humankind.

Evangelical Christian: Like the fundamentalists, the evangelical church regards historically accurate Christianity as the only path. However, it confines its use of the term cult to other Christian collectives (such as Mormons), not to such groups as Hindus, Pagans or Buddhists.

Open Religious: Where the word cult is used to define any small religious group which does not derive from an established religion.

Popular: This is a useful definition in the context of the present book, for it describes cults as being, in the main, small, occasionally malevolent collections of disciples, often led by a charismatic 'messiah'. This leader is not infrequently accused of ensnaring converts and then subjecting them to a form of coercive mind control in order to manipulate them both spiritually and financially. Violence, or the threat of violence, is often endemic to this cult's rationale.

It is only necessary to appreciate the cult's insularity and necessary isolation – spiritually, if not physically – to reach some understanding of its ability to kill. Cults, by their nature are 'islands' existing in a state of tension with the host society, and as such are vulnerable to what they perceive as attack from outside their borders. In much the same way that a nation state will wage war against an enemy which threatens its security, so the cult, sensing threat, will fight back. This was the situation in

1993 when an enclave of the Branch Davidians repelled an invasion by US government agents at Waco, Texas.

This is a dramatic example of cult defence tactics, but modern history is peppered with what we might call revenge attacks against those – either within or outside the group – who attempt to question its beliefs or undermine the authority of its hierarchy. This includes media representatives who try to gather information to discredit the cult leader(s). Such a case occurred in Guyana in 1978, when followers of the Reverend Jim Jones shot dead journalists who had flown in to investigate the People's Temple. This resulted in a mass suicide of around 900 cultists.

Although in the popular conception cults are usually breakaway groups from Christianity, this study includes many religious and social groupings which are not – the Indian and Russian cults, for example, and the Voodoo cults of Africa.

It must be stressed at the outset that the majority of groups are relatively benign, if eccentric. We are concerned here only with those which, either as a result of their beliefs, or in a moment of anger or lunacy, commit homicidal acts upon their own followers or members of the community at large.

There are cults whose very 'constitution' encourages violence for its own sake. Among them are units of the broad category of Satanists, and of the various offshoots of Voodoo, such as Palo Mayombe and Santeria who indulge in blood sacrifice, sometimes human. It is a long time since the various witch covens of the world were accused of 'bewitching to death', but in their day many convicted sorcerers were tortured and burned alive for such crimes.

Political 'cults', such as the Ku Klux Klan, had (and have) very bloody histories of beatings, shootings and lynchings – mainly aimed at the black communities of the Southern States of America. And self-appointed social outcast groups, such as Hells Angels and other biker gangs too numerous to mention, adopt creeds of violence and become involved in criminal activities which often result in 'executions'.

Belief that some forms of behaviour are the result of demonic possession is common to many of the world's religions. Curing such matters requires exorcism. Some cultures use physical harassment of the patient, believing that if the victim's body is made uncomfortable, the evil spirits leave.

Because the motives which result in some cults committing acts of murder are so different, each of the groupings that follow will be discussed separately.

KILLER CULTS
IN HISTORY

JUDAEO-CHRISTIAN CULTS

Christian *versus* Jew *versus* Christian

During the twelfth century the animosity between Christians and Jews reached an unprecedented level, with frequent outbreaks of violence and bloodshed. The conviction of Christian masses that there was a Jewish conspiracy to gradually exterminate them gained ground, and when, in 1179, the dead body of a Christian child was found on the banks of the river Rhine by a boating party, they immediately assumed that the murder had been committed by a group of Jews on another craft just up-river. So they were followed to the city of Boppard, where the Christians set upon the Jews, savagely wounded them and threw them into the water alive. One victim was later recovered from the river and dragged through the local towns and villages as an example of the justice awaiting murderous Jews. This seems to have met with official approval and the Holy Roman Emperor Frederick I, known as 'Barbarossa', went so far as to impose a fine of 500 silver marks on the local Jewish community as punishment for their wickedness.

In a similar incident in Switzerland in 1195, the body of a Christian woman was found in Spires, leading to neighbouring Jews being accused of murder. As a reprisal, the local mob exhumed the recently interred corpse of the daughter of rabbi Isaac bar Asher ha-Levi. She was stripped of her clothing and her body was exposed to ridicule in the town square. As a further humiliation a mouse was put on the dead girl's head. It was only by the offer of a considerable sum of money that the horrified father was able to recover the body from the authorities for reburial. Next morning the rabble gathered at the rabbi's home, killed him and eight other occupants of the house and burned down and looted a number of houses belonging to Jews. The following day it was the turn of the synagogue to be razed by fire, burning the holy texts. However, in this instance Duke Otto, the emperor's brother, insisted the burghers rebuild the synagogue and the fired Jewish houses; but he omitted to act against the fire-raisers.

There was no such justice in the case of the mentally unbalanced Jew who murdered a Christian girl on the street at Neuss, near Cologne, in 1197. The killer was strung up on the spot, along with six other Jews for good measure. A week later the culprit's mother was dragged from her home and buried alive and his brother was broken on the wheel. The final indignity was when the bishop declared all Jews in the community guilty by association and fined them heavily.

Not that the Christians had it all their own way. A document of 1144 states that:

> The Jews of Norwich bought a Christian child before Easter and tortured him with all the tortures wherewith our Lord was tortured, and on Good Friday hanged him on a cross in hatred of our Lord, and afterwards buried him. They supposed that this would stay hidden, but our Lord revealed that he was a holy martyr, and the monks took him and buried him in the church, and through our Lord he performed wonderful and various miracles, and he was called St William.

Another account was handed down by a monk from Cambridge named Theobald:

> . . . in the ancient writings it was stated that without shedding human blood Jews could neither obtain their freedom nor return to their homeland. For this reason they needed to sacrifice a Christian every year.

A tragic affair took place at Blois in May 1171, two months after Passover. It arose from a servant's suspicion that he had seen a Jew drowning a child in a river (though no body was ever recovered). It so happened, to the detriment of the Jewish community, that the business occurred just as news broke that Count Thibauld had taken a Jewess named Polcelina as a mistress. It was not a popular liaison with the mainly Christian population of the French city, and the incident of the drowned child became a catalyst. The accusing servant was immersed in a tank of holy water and when he survived drowning his honesty was established; forty Jews were sentenced to death by burning. Thirty-two were executed (seventeen of them women) after refusing the offer to convert to Christianity.

The incident is immortalised in a verse (more inspirational than literary) by Hillel bar Jacob:

When the order came to take them to the place of burning,
Like brides to their canopies, they went hearts with joy
    astir,
They sang 'Let us praise the Lord', with voices full of
    yearning,
'Behold, thou art beautiful, my love, behold, thou art fair.'

May Jeshurun be inscribed for pardon and salvation,
On this our atonement day, secure us consolation.
May the martyrs' merit help appease God's indignation,
Bring reprieve to the priests and assembled congregation.

The Cretan messiah

And Moses stretched out his hand over the sea; and the Lord caused the sea to go back by a strong east wind all that night, and made the sea dry land, and the waters were divided. And the children of Israel went into the midst of the sea upon the dry ground: and the waters were a wall unto them on their right hand, and on their left.

(Exodus xiv, 21–22)

That is the way it should be done. Sadly it not always is. In around AD 400 a Jew from Crete arrived on the scene claiming to be the messiah that everybody had been waiting for, and announcing that he would lead his people to the promised land. He called himself Moses and, like his namesake, planned to part the sea in readiness for their exodus. Followed by hundreds of disciples, who had hastily packed their few possessions for the journey, Moses II stood on the seashore and, with arms raised aloft to heaven, in a booming voice commanded the waves to part. When, after several such exhortations the water still stubbornly lapped at his feet, the messiah ordered his followers into the sea anyway. Obediently they strode into the briny. A great many were drowned, but when the survivors looked round for mad Moses, he was nowhere to be found. It is assumed that either he had drowned with the others, or he had considered the potential delicacy of his position and opted for a tactical retreat. At any rate he was never heard of again.

Margaret Peter, some nails and a couple of floorboards

One of the significant observations to be made about cult killings is the frequency of 'overkill', the extent to which the victim or victims are subjected to quite disproportionate levels of brutality. This may be the result of calculated savagery, coldly and ruthlessly applied – as in certain kinds of exorcism; or it may be for ceremonial effect, as happens in some forms of blood sacrifice. Another reason for the overkill effect is a state of 'religious' frenzy, during which participants in a ritual no longer have regard for their victim's basic right to life or their own culpability before the law. Occasionally this violence is turned on the celebrants themselves – one thinks of the flagellants of the Middle Ages, or certain voodoo ceremonies.

The power of group hysteria gripped the small band of disciples who followed a young prophetess called Margaret Peter in 1823 in the Swiss/German border town of Wildisbuch. The house was occupied by John Peter, a widower, and his family of five daughters and a son. Margaret was the youngest of the girls and had been born on Christmas Day. She soon became a precocious Christian and even before she had entered teenage her word was law in the household. Far from being simply a member of the family, Margaret Peter came to be seen as teacher, guru and saint. In her twenties Margaret took to the road as a peripatetic preacher, attracting considerable attention. By the time she returned to Wildisbuch, two sisters had married and their husbands had taken up residence; in addition there were two maids, Ursula and Margaret Jaggli, and Heinrich the odd-job boy on the farm.

In the spring of 1823, around Easter time, Margaret announced to her faithful that she had been graced with a revelation from God. Revelations have always played an important part in religions, and particularly in cults. Whether the receipt of these snippets of news from the future (usually centred around Armageddon) is genuine or the result of obsessive wishful thinking is a psychological debate without end. The cynical view might be that revelations are a device for maintaining power over the cult. After all, who would dare to be disloyal to a leader in direct contact with God (or Krishna, or Kali or Baron Samedi . . .)?

Margaret Peter's revelation was that Satan had taken up residence in a nest under the roof of the house. If the world were to be saved and the devil put in his place then she, Margaret, would have to die.

Following a week of fervent prayer the plan was hatched. The congregation was led upstairs to the room beneath the attic, and Margaret immediately received a vision of Satan floating in the air. Quick as a flash, she commanded the congregation to go and fetch cudgels and axes to help in the forthcoming battle against evil. When they returned armed, Margaret insisted they 'strike everywhere – on every side, wall, floor; lose your lives if need be'. And, obediently, that is exactly what they did. So enthusiastically did the disciples apply themselves to their task that before long the room and its contents had been wrecked. In fact, so brutally had the external walls been attacked, that there were holes in them through which bewildered neighbours could view the proceedings. Then Margaret prepared to make the supreme sacrifice. Not only would she have to die, she would have to suffer crucifixion. Well. Everybody was shocked. Margaret was the centre of their very existence. Not the least distraught was Margaret's sister Elizabeth, who interrupted to offer herself as a holy sacrifice.

'You are not ready to die,' Margaret might have said.

'I am, I am!' Elizabeth might have replied.

'You are not ready to die.'

'I am!' And to emphasise her point, Elizabeth picked up a heavy mallet and delivered herself a resounding thwack to the head.

'She is ready!' exulted Margaret. 'It has been revealed,' and gave her sister another thwack on the head.

Presumably sensing their duty in a moment of intense spirituality, the half-dozen or so disciples joined in, savagely beating poor Elizabeth with any implement that came to hand. Not unexpectedly she succumbed to his brutal attack, and with Margaret assuring her flock that her sister would shortly return from the dead, Elizabeth's bloody corpse was carried to a bed in the corner of the room.

'Crucify me!' insisted Margaret, and hit herself on the forehead with a hammer. She then handed it to a brother-in-law, and he thumped her with it too – but not very savagely. The congregation looked shiftily at each other and shuffled their feet. Perhaps they were a little less euphoric after their martyrdom of Elizabeth.

'Crucify me!'

Well, she was their leader; and that sounded a bit like an order. There was no ready supply of crosses for crucifixion in Wildisbuch at the time – probably there still isn't. But with

12

commendable pragmatism the faithful ripped up a couple of floorboards and laid them one across the other. Margaret Peter climbed aboard and insisted on being nailed through her arms and breasts, all the while comforting her by now very anxious followers and assuring them that she would return in three days. With that promise the servant Ursula attempted the *coup de grâce* by driving a knife into the prostrate woman's heart, but the blade snapped against a rib. In the end one of the men, out of compassion, cracked Margaret on the head with a crowbar and put her out of her suffering.

Three days later the household gathered around the decomposing remains of Margaret and Elizabeth Peter. It was clear that neither of the sisters had returned from the other side. Yet. Prayers were chanted . . . then some more. Still there was no sign of life in the sisters save the flies buzzing around the mouldy flesh. More prayers . . .

By this time the strange goings-on among the cult of Margaret Peter had reached the notice of the police. When they arrived it was to the sound of almost hysterical praying as Margaret's followers attempted to make the impossible possible. As it was, Margaret and Elizabeth were given Christian burials and put into the earth, while the disciples were given fair trials and put into prison. So loathsome had the house at Wildisbuch become to the minds of the local people that it was torn down and the land levelled. It was forbidden ever to build on the site again.

Appendix: Crucifixion

Because of the extensive international publicity given to the incident that took place at Golgotha almost two thousand years ago, it is not fully appreciated how widespread and common torture and execution by crucifixion were in the ancient world. It was widely used by the Assyrians, Carthaginians, Egyptians, Greeks, Persians, Phoenicians, Scythians and of course the Romans who, at the insistence of the Jewish Sanhedrin, executed Jesus Christ.

The customary form of crucifixion, though there were many variations, was to tie or nail the victim to a stake (with or without a cross-beam). However, despite the widespread use of this method of execution, very few detailed descriptions of crucifixion have survived.

The prisoner was first scourged (though this was a preliminary to many of the Roman capital punishments) and then, if a cross-beam was to be used, he would be made to carry this heavy wooden member to the place where an upright post was already securely fixed in the ground – usually alongside a main road to ensure maximum exposure of the body after death. The victim was then stripped and forced to lie face up on the ground with his arms outstretched while the executioner nailed or bound his hands to the cross-beam; sometimes both methods were used so that the weight of the body did not cause the flesh of the hands to tear away from the nails. The beam, with its victim suspended from it, was then hauled to the top of the upright. Again to prevent the hands tearing away from the nails, a wooden peg protruding from the upright between the captive's legs gave some measure of support. The preparations were concluded by nailing both feet to the upright. In this position the victim suffered a slow, agonising death, aggravated by whatever supplementary torments the executioner and the mob might indulge in – breaking his legs with clubs, tearing his skin with combs like metal rakes, stoning . . . In the case of the execution of Christ, the executioners had already exhibited uncommon ingenuity in fashioning the crown of thorns.

Other novelties were effected by changing the position in which the victim was attached to the cross – upside down was a popular variant. Josephus described a Roman mass execution of Jews, where 'They nailed those they caught in different postures to the crosses, by way of jest'.

For the Romans, crucifixion was rated above burning and decapitation as the most common penalty for severe crimes such as treason, desertion from the army, murder, the practice of 'magic' (particularly if it involved making predictions concerning the welfare of the emperor!) and incitement to rebellion. Initially it was a punishment for slaves and foreigners (prisoners of war, etc.), though later it could be invoked in cases of aggravated crime committed by Romans of the lower class. This is in direct contradiction to the attitudes of the Carthaginians and Persians, for whom crucifixion was a punishment appropriate only for high-ranking officials and military commanders.

Self-crucifixion

Among the penitents of New Mexico there are incidents recorded of a form of self-crucifixion where the subject is bound by the arms to the cross-member of a huge wooden cross which he is obliged to drag over ground littered with broken glass and sharp stones. A refinement involved the tying of a sharp spear to the body with its point touching the arm, in such a position that should the penitent stumble or fall, the weapon would pierce his flesh.

MIDDLE EASTERN CULTS

Order of Assassins

The Assassins, or 'hashisham' from their fondness for the drug hashish, were, ultimately, a sect of the Ismaili founded in Alamut, Persia by Hasan bin Sabbah around 1090. In common with many secret societies, the precise history and development of their practices have become the subject of myth and folk-legend.

Hasan bin Sabbah was an Ismaili *da'i*, or preacher, of Persian nationality. The Ismailis were in turn a sub-sect of a sub-sect of Mohammedanism, which suffered schism on the death of Mohammed in 632. Legend tells that Hasan bin Sabbah attended the University of Nishapur along with Omar Khayyam and was later given a position at the same court where the poet was the official astrologer. He visited Egypt in 1086, and became a loyal supporter of the Fatimid Ismailis – named after Mohammed's daughter, Fatima, who had been murdered. Under Nizar, successor to the Fatimid Caliphate, Hasan bin Sabbah returned to Persia where he continued to be active in the Fatimid branch of the Ismailis. However, when Nizar was imprisoned and his brother replaced him, Hasan bin Sabbah broke with the Fatimid faction and, in 1090, seized the fortress of Alamut (known as the Eagle's Nest) in the Elburz mountains. Here he remained true to a kind of Ismaili faith, though he elevated himself to the supreme position of Imam – God's personal representative on earth. He also began the risky business of meddling in politics.

Having surrounded himself with a band of followers so fanatically loyal that they were prepared to kill for and to die for their Imam, Hasan bin Sabbah set about disposing of his enemies. He would dispatch his Assassins to infiltrate the ranks of his prospective victims. Some Assassins could be in the service of a high-ranking officer or Sultan for several years before the opportunity arose to commit murder. The deed was usually carried out with a knife, following which the Assassin would wait calmly until he was seized and put to death. Many Sultans found it preferable to give in to the whims of the Old Man of the Mountains than to be constantly looking over their shoulder.

Many of the more romantic and extravagant legends of the Assassins of Alamut derive from the writings of the Venetian traveller Marco Polo. The incidents he recorded are clearly not first-hand observations, because the mountain strongholds of the Assassins had been destroyed by Mongol raiders in 1256, some twenty years before Marco Polo's visit. One of the most enduring of these myths, and one that may have some small vestige of truth, concerns the fabled Garden of Paradise built by the Old Man of the Mountains to encourage his followers. When a job of killing needed to be carried out, selected Assassins were induced into a stupor with hashish and taken to the Garden, where they would come round to the tender ministrations of beautiful houris. Over the next few days the young men wanted for nothing: sex, fine food and wine, soothing music; then they were drugged again and returned to the fortress where they were told they had been given a glimpse of paradise. The paradise that they would immediately enter when they had carried out their task and died for the cause.

Another illuminating tale of the power of the Old Man of the Mountains was told by the scholar Arkon Daraul in his *History of Secret Societies*. In the year 1102, Hasan bin Sabbah was entertaining an ambassador from the Persian emperor at the Eagle's Nest. Pointing to a devotee standing on a distant rampart, the leader of the Assassins told his guest to watch the man. Then he made a signal. The robed figure held his arms in the air in salutation, and threw himself 2,000 feet down the mountain. 'I have 70,000 followers,' said Hasan bin Sabbah. 'Every one willing to sacrifice themselves for me. Can your master, Malik Shah, command such loyalty? And he expects me to accept his sovereignty. This is your answer. Go!'

Although Alamut was sacked by the Mongols, it was retaken by the Egyptians several years later and returned to the Assassins. Their power went into decline however, though small pockets survived in Persia and Syria. There are still descendants of the Order living among the tribal people of the Elburz mountain range.

It should be said that although the word Assassin is generally believed to have originated in the use of hashish, another explanation has been offered. That is that it derives from the Arabic 'assasseen', meaning 'guardian'.

INDIAN CULTS

Thugs, or Phansigars

There is little corroborative evidence as to the origin of the cult of the Indian Thugs (pronounced 'tugs', their cult 'tuggee'). Some say that their ceremonies were depicted in the stone carvings in the caves at Ellora in the province of Bombay. This, though, is retrospective research. The first that Europeans learned of this fanatical group of 'religious' killers was through the writings of Robert Sherwood in the journal *Asiatic Researches*, at the beginning of the nineteenth century. Sherwood was a military medic working in Madras and had been introduced to individuals involved in this secret society which combined ritual killing, in the name of the goddess Kali, and robbery, to line their own pockets. Sherwood's article came to the attention of Captain William Sleeman, an officer in the British Army, who had served his country in India since 1809. Sleeman determined to find out more about the elusive Thugs and over the ten years up to 1829 caused a sensation with his regular dispatches about the depredations of this strange cult. The following account of their practices derives partly from Sleeman and partly from official Indian Government documents of the first half of the nineteenth century.

In different parts of India, these ruffians assumed various names derived either from the mode in which they dispatched their victims, or from the arts by which they inveigled their prey to destruction. In the more northern parts of India, these murderers were called Thugs, the name by which they are

19

most generally known among Europeans. This term signifies 'deceiver'. In some provinces to the south, they went under the name of Phansigars, or 'stranglers', from the Hindustani word *phansi*, or 'noose'. In the Tamil language they were called Ari Tulucar, or Mussulman 'noosers'. In Canarese, they were Tanti Calleru, implying 'thieves who use a wire or cat-gut noose'; and in Telagu, Warlu Wahndlu, or Warlu Vayshay Wahndloo, meaning 'people who use the noose'.

A gang might consist of from ten to fifty people, or sometimes an even greater number – occasionally two or three hundred – though in these instances they usually followed each other in smaller parties. Different groups frequently acted in concert, apprising one another of the approach of travellers whose destruction promised valuable booty. They assumed the appearance of ordinary inoffensive travellers, sometimes pretending to be traders. If already enriched by earlier robberies they might ride on horseback, with tents, and pass for wealthy merchants. Thugs were accustomed to wait at choultries, caravanserais on the high roads or near towns where travellers rested. They arrived in straggling parties of three or four, appearing to meet by accident. On such occasions some members of the gang were employed to collect information, to learn if any persons with property were about to undertake a journey. They were often accompanied by children of ten years of age and upwards who, while they performed menial tasks, were gradually initiated into the horrid practices of Thuggee, and served to prevent suspicion of their real character. Skilled in the art of deception, they would enter into conversation, and insinuate themselves into the confidence of travellers, to learn whence they came, where and for what purpose they were travelling, and most important what property they possessed. When the Thugs decided to attack a traveller they usually proposed to journey with him for mutual protection (against Thugs!), or for companionship. Otherwise they would follow the traveller at a short distance and at the appropriate opportunity, attack.

Many variations exist in the manner of perpetrating the murder, but the following seems the most common. While travelling along, one of the gang suddenly throws the rope or strangling cloth (*ruhmal*) round the neck of the prospective victim and retains hold of one end. The other end is seized by an accomplice. This instrument of death, crossed behind the neck, is then drawn very tight, the two Thugs who hold it pressing the head of the victim forwards. A third villain, who is in readiness behind the traveller, seizes him by the legs, and he is thus thrown to the ground. In this situation there is little opportunity for resistance. The operation of the noose is aided by kicks inflicted in the manner most likely to cause vital injury, and the sufferer is thus quickly dispatched.

Extreme precautions were taken to prevent discovery or surprise. Thus before the murder some of the gang were sent on in advance and some left in the rear to prevent intrusion or to give warning. If any person should unexpectedly appear before the body was buried, some deceit was practised such as covering it with a cloth, and wailing loud lamentations to give the impression that a comrade was sick or had died.

The corpse of the unfortunate victim was usually placed face downwards in a hole dug three or four feet deep. Though death had brought a termination of suffering, it had not put an end to the outrages of the murderers. Long and deep gashes were made in various parts of the body; sometimes the limbs were disjointed or dismembered, and the figure distorted into unusual and grotesque positions. This desecration arose from a variety of motives. The intention generally was to defy identification and to speed decomposition of the body and prevent it inflating with body gases, which might disturb the sand and attract the attention of jackals, thus leading to the discovery of the remains. Sometimes, however, these depredations were the result of disappointment and represented a petty revenge. When the amount of plunder was less than had been expected, the villains frequently vented their displeasure in wanton indignities upon the remains of the dead.

If, after the murder had been perpetrated, there was no convenient place nearby to bury the body, it was either tied in a sack and transported to a convenient spot, or dropped into a well.

Sometimes a shallow grave was dug into which the corpse was put until a better resting place could be found. In instances where they feared to be observed, the Thugs erected a screen, like a tent, and buried the body within it. If anyone should inquire they were told that there were women within the screen. It was at this point that, before the cult became corrupted into a mere network of vicious thieves, the religious part of the scene was played out, the part known as *tuponee*. The Thugs sat in a circle around the grave while their leader intoned prayers to Kali to bless them with wealth and success. Then, in a form of holy communion, each of the participants ate a sliver of special sugar, called *goor*.

As an example of the thoroughness of the Thugs, if the dead traveller had a dog, it too was killed, lest the affection of the animal should lead it to draw attention to the burial site of its murdered master. The job of mangling the body was usually the responsibility of one particular member of the gang, and they always carried concealed knives and the ceremonial pickaxe (*kusee*) to dig the grave.

The indiscriminate slaughter in which the Thugs indulged was to some extent tempered by superstition. It was considered unlucky to kill certain castes and classes of people. The most general exception was women. Thugs who had any real regard for the principles which they professed to respect never took the lives of women. However, this rule was frequently violated. One Thug was reported as saying: 'Among our group it is a rule never to kill a woman; but if a rich old woman is found, the gang sometimes get a man to strangle her by giving him an extra share of the booty, and persuading him to take the responsibility upon himself. We have sometimes killed other prohibited people, particularly those of low caste, who we should not even have touched.'

These other 'prohibited people' are a mixed bunch indeed, counting among them 'washermen and poets, professors of dancing, blacksmiths and carpenters, musicians, oil-vendors and sweepers, Ganges water carriers (if they are carrying water with them), Madaree Fakirs and, in some districts Sikhs'. The maimed and leprous were also avoided, though more through fear of contamination than on humanitarian grounds.

On account of their sacred position among the Indians, cows were also covered by the Thugs amnesty, as were people travelling with the beasts. One story tells of a group of fourteen travellers which numbered among them several women and a cow. The Thugs were prepared to dispatch the women with little enough reservation, but there was the problem of the cow. Pragmatic as ever, the gang persuaded the travellers to sell the cow to them in order that they might make it a sacrifice at the nearby temple. Reluctantly the cow's owner parted with it and, the obstacle removed, the band of travellers was quickly disposed of and their possessions reallocated.

So familiar had he become with the ways of the Thugs, that the British Government gave Captain William Sleeman the task of eradicating the cult. Records show that more than 4,000 active members of the cult were arrested and put on trial. Many were hanged for their crimes, others imprisoned, and by 1850 the Thugs had been all but suppressed.

Thugs on the water
The following is a first-hand account by one of a band of land Thugs, taken from *Illustrations of the History and Practices of the Thugs* (1837):

About fourteen years ago, I had been on an expedition from Chupra to Moorshedabad. We were twenty-two Thugs under Sewbuns Jemadar, who was a Rajpoot. Two of our gang, Khoda Buksh and Alee Yar, had often served with the river Thugs, and used to interest us by talking about their modes of proceeding. On the other side of Rajmahul we fell in with two of these Thugs. They had two bundles of clothes, and pretended to be going on pilgrimage; and had with them five travellers whom they had picked up on the road. Sewbuns recognised them immediately, and Alee Yar and Khoda Buksh found them old acquaintances. They got into conversation with them, and it was agreed that Sewbuns, I, and Dhorda Khormee should go with them, and see how they did their work, while the rest of the gang went on along the bank of the river. We embarked at Rajmahul. The travellers sat on one side of the boat, and the Thugs on the other; while we three were all placed at the stern – the Thugs on our left, the travellers on our right. Some of the Thugs, dressed as boatmen, were above deck, and others walking along the bank of the river, and pulling the boat by the goon, or rope, and all, at the same time, on the look-out. We came up with a gentleman's pinnace and two baggage-boats, and were obliged to stop and let them go on. The travellers seemed anxious, but were quieted by being told that the men at the rope were tired and must take some refreshment. They pulled out something and began to eat. And when the pinnace had got on a good way, they resumed their work, and our boat proceeded. It was now afternoon and when a signal was given above that all was clear, the five Thugs who sat opposite the travellers sprang in upon them and, with the aid of others, strangled them. They put the ruhmal round the neck from the front, while all other Thugs put it round from behind: they thus push them back, whereas we push them forward. Having strangled the five men, they broke their spinal bones, and then threw them out of a hole made in the side of the boat, into the river. They kept on their course, the boat being all the time pulled along by the men on the bank. The booty amounted to about two hundred rupees. We claimed and got a share for all our party; and Sewbuns declared that we were twenty-nine, while we were really only twenty-three, and got a share for that number – he cheated them out of the share of six men. We landed that night and rejoined our gang. We operated on the roads leading along the river Ganges till we got to the Mormakeya ghat, where there is an invalid station . . . the other side of Bar. Here we fell in with the same party of *Pungoos*, or river Thugs, who had three travellers with

24

them. I did not join them this time, but Sewbuns, with two other members of our gang, went on board and saw them strangled.

RUSSIAN CULTS

Khlysty

Being a secret, underground sect, followers meet on one of the official Russian feast days when a gathering will be less likely to attract police attention. They assemble in a long whitewashed hall with benches along two opposite walls, one side for men the other for women. In the centre stands a table on which have been placed loaves of bread and a pitcher of water; these represent the Eucharist of the Khlysty. The celebrants, men and women, remove their shoes and outdoor clothing to reveal uniform white flowing robes. Each member carries a white handkerchief which will be waved above the head during dancing; they represent the wings of angels.

The meeting is presided over by a 'Christ' or a 'Mother of God', and the faithful file past and prostrate themselves before this leader. A brief 'sermon' reminds the faithful that they must retain the cult's secrets even unto death; it has been said that traitors are rewarded with execution. Then the dancing and hymn singing begins. Often the meeting opens with the Prayer of Jesus:

> Give us, Lord,
> To us, Jesus Christ!
> Give us, Son of God,
> Light; have mercy upon us!
> Ruler, Holy Spirit,
> Have mercy upon us!
> Lady Ruler, our little Mother!

Ask, Light, for us
The Light, thy Son,
The Spirit of God, the Holy one!
Light, by thee are redeemed
Many sinners on the earth,
Unto the little Mother, unto our Lady Queen,
Light, unto her that cherishes us.

At first members of the congregation hold hands and dance in a circle which gets faster and faster and the singing gets louder and louder as they fill with the ecstasy of the Spirit. This is followed by a frenzied rendering of a hymn to the same Spirit:

Past us in paradise a bird is hovering,
It flies amain,
To yonder side it glances,
Where the trumpet's blast is heard,
Where God himself is speaking:
O God, O God, O God,
O Spirit, O Spirit, O Spirit!
Float down, down down!
Oi Yega! Oi Yega! Oi Yega!
It floated down, it floated down,
The Holy Spirit, the Holy Spirit!
'Twill blow where it will, where it listeth,
The Holy Spirit, the Holy Spirit.
O I burn, O I burn,
The Spirit burns, God burns!
Light is in me, Light is in me,
The Holy Ghost, the Holy Ghost!
O I burn, burn, burn,
Ghost! Oi Yega! [repeated four times]
Yevoye! Host Yevoi! [repeated three times]

Now individual members detach themselves from the circle and spin around with ever increasing speed until they drop insensible to the ground. Others begin to leap about, stamping and shrieking, waving their arms and foaming at the mouth. More collapse to the floor. Some begin to gibber in tongues – all are filled with the Spirit; they believe themselves to be in paradise, at home with the angels.

When a man or woman becomes a member of the Khlysty they are obliged to take a spiritual spouse, rejecting their 'worldly' marriage. Established wives – called 'gifts of the Devil' – may still sleep in their husband's bed (along with the spiritual partner) but must remain celibate. Any children are referred to as 'sins' and treated with spite or indifference; they are not permitted to call their parents 'mother' and 'father'. Chastity is highly prized among the Khlysty, who believe that if a virgin is meant to conceive then she will be impregnated by God. This distaste for the sexual act carries over into the diet of the Khlysty, which forbids meat on the grounds that it is a product of copulation. There are a number of other taboo foods, such as onions and garlic (because they taint the breath) and potatoes (because it is believed that it was with the potato that Eve tempted Adam).

The origin of the Khlysty is lost in time, though it is reasonably thought to be a development of Bogomilism, a tenth-century Bulgarian dualist cult, who believed that Christ had entered the Virgin Mary's right ear and emerged as a phantom. The great upsurge in interest in the cult followed the schism in the Russian church. Nikin Mordvinov was a peasant who took to religion and, in 1645, visited Moscow and met Tsar Alexis. So impressed was Alexis with this zealous man that in a short time he was appointed patriarch, one of the most powerful men in Russia. The problem was that Nikin couldn't resist interfering in the running of the church. This so angered many priests that a breakaway faction was established known as the Old Believers. It was a time of considerable bloodshed and frequent mass execution. Many of the Old Believers committed suicide by burning themselves on huge funeral pyres (this is dramatically depicted in Mussorgsky's opera *Khovanshchina*).

One of the most characteristic Khlysty beliefs is that Christ did not ascend to heaven with his earthly body, but that his corpse remained entombed and his spirit entered another living man. One sinister recommendation was that for greater salvation members of Khlysty should themselves actively seek crucifixion.

The leading Khlysty 'Christ' was Danila Philippovich who, when he died, became the spiritual father of the movement and his relics were venerated as sacred. Danila was a peasant born during the reign of Alexis Michailovich (1645–76). Despite his humble origins, Danila could read and write and was considered something of a teacher. However, his real brush with the Spirit took place as he was standing on the high hill called Gorodina. Here the great God Zebaoth (or Sabaoth) descended from the sky in a chariot on fiery clouds, accompanied by a host of angels, seraphim and cherubim and took possession of Danila's body. So he became the earthly incarnation of Zebaoth, a living God.

Danila Philippovich started preaching in the village of Staraya where he began to attract a following. He next moved on to Kostroma which he and his sect called the New Jerusalem. In a moment of exultation, Danila hurled all his religious books into the river Volga except the Khlysty hymn book, the *Dove Book*. For this open blasphemy the living God was imprisoned in a miserable cell. With a little help from his followers Danila escaped, and in gratitude presented the world with his Twelve Commandments:

1. I am God, foretold of the prophets, and am come down to earth a second time to save men's souls. There is no other God than I.
2. There is no other teaching but mine. Seek ye none other.
3. Whereunto ye are appointed, abide therein.
4. Keep God's commandments, be ye fishermen of the world.
5. Drink no intoxicant, commit no sins of the flesh.
6. Marry not. He that is married shall live with his wife as a sister, as is declared in the old scripture. Let the unwedded wed not, the wedded separate.

29

7. Utter not foul words nor black speeches [invocations of the Devil].
8. Go not to weddings or baptisms, nor frequent drinking resorts.
9. Steal not. If a man steal but a single kopeck, it shall in the dead judgement be laid on his skull, and when the coin melts in fire on his head, and not before, shall he gain remission of his sin.
10. Keep these rules in secret, reveal them not even to father or mother, and even if men scourge thee with whip or burn thee with fire, bear it. So doing the true shall after the pattern of the old martyrs win heaven, and on earth spiritual satisfaction.
11. Visit one another, practice hospitality, practice charity, keeping commandments, pray to God.
12. Have faith in the Holy Spirit.

At about this time, Danila Philippovich adopted a spiritual son, Timofeyevich Suslov. It was his destiny to take over the role of Christ. After receiving the Godhead in his thirty-first year, Suslov selected twelve disciples and a Mother of God and set about spreading the gospel of Danila along the Oka and the Volga. As his influence spread, so Tsar Alexis became concerned. In the end Suslov found himself on a rack in the torture chamber of the boyar Odoyevski. Despite the agonising treatment he received Timofeyevich Suslov stuck to the tenth commandment and kept his mouth shut. For which he was crucified. However, like the Christ before him, Suslov rose from the dead. Unlike the Christ before him, he was again seized by the Tsar's guards and flayed alive before being crucified again. An angel held on to his skin for him till Suslov was resurrected and able to slip it back on. Just in time to be crucified for a third time. Things were becoming rather tedious, and either as the result of a large bribe, or, as some versions tell it, the intervention of the wife of Peter the Great, Suslov was left alone the next time he rose from the dead. In fact he continued for the next thirty years preaching and teaching in Moscow.

On 1 January 1700, Danila Philippovich died, it is said at the age of one hundred and, before a huge congregation, ascended bodily to heaven. Three years later his 'son' died, though only his spirit went to heaven.

In 1733 more than 300 Khlysty were rounded up in Moscow as the result of a purge. Five were executed, the rest suffered knouting (see Appendix, below), having their tongues cut out, or being set to hard labour. Ten years later there was a fresh inquisition in the capital, where Khlysty were put on the rack and burned with red-hot irons. This time five more were publicly burned alive, and some 450 others subjected to the knout, exile and having their noses cut off.

Appendix: The knout

According to the American George Ryley Scott in his *History of Corporal Punishment*, 'In no country in the world is whipping so widely practised, so savagely and so vindictively inflicted, as in the Russia of the Tsars.' The special instrument of flagellation uniquely favoured by the Russians was the fearful knout:

> it was a wooden-handled whip usually consisting of several thongs of raw hide twisted together and terminating in a single strand projecting some eighteen inches farther than the body of the knout. In some cases wire was plaited with the hide, in others rings or hooks were attached to the ends of the thongs; in other instances, the barbaric sadism of the individual wielding the whip caused him to harden the raw hide by dipping it in water or other liquid and allowing it to freeze.

The use of the knout was prescribed for a wide range of crimes, and in the time of Peter the Great the maximum sentence was 101 lashes. It was applied without favour both to men and women, and even the aristocracy was not exempt. Found to have been involved in a treason plot, a Madame Lapuchin, attached to the court of

Elizabeth, was publicly stripped to the waist and savagely whipped with the knout before having her tongue cut out and being sent into Siberian exile. It is even fabled that Peter the Great knouted his own son to death.

However, there is one apparently authentic description of the knouting of a man and a woman relayed in the *Anecdotes* (1820–23) of the historians Reuben and Sholto Percy. The eyewitness was none other than the great English philanthropist and prison reformer John Howard:

When Howard was in Petersburg, he saw two criminals, a man and a woman, suffer the punishment of the knout. They were conducted from prison by about fifteen hussars and ten soldiers. When they had arrived at the place of punishment, the hussars formed themselves into a ring round the whipping post; the drum beat a minute or two, and then some prayers were repeated, the populace taking off their hats. The woman was first taken, and after being roughly stripped to the waist, her hands and feet were bound with cords to a post made for the purpose. A servant attended the executioner and both were stout men. The servant first marked the ground, and struck the woman five times on the back; every stroke seemed to penetrate deep into her flesh; but his master thinking him too gentle, pushed him aside, took his place, and gave all the remaining strokes himself, which were evidently more severe. The woman received twenty-five blows, and the man sixty. 'T', continues Mr Howard, 'pressed through the hussars, and counted the number as they were chalked on a board for the purpose. Both of the criminals seemed just alive, especially the man, who had yet strength enough remaining to receive a present with some signs of gratitude. I saw the woman in a very weak condition some days after, but could not find the man any more.'

The use of the knout was abolished in 1845.

Skoptsy

Sister 'religion' to the Khlysty, the Skoptsy came into being around 1700 as an off-shoot of a group of Khlysty comunities, called 'ships', in the industrial town of Tula, south of Moscow. What distinguished these groups was their veneration of a Mother of God – a leader of the local cult – named Akulina Ivanova. The hierarchy below her consisted of a number of male and female prophets, chief among the latter being Anna Romanova. At the time the 'ships' did not have their own Christ, and it was through Anna's prophesies that the congregation came to recognise their messiah in the person of a man named Selivanov. This Christ figure immediately set about imposing rigorous restraints on what he saw as the lax morals of his followers. This met with strong disapproval which would eventually lead to his being informed against to the government, and his spiritual 'son' being murdered.

Although he had been given the name Andrei Ivanov at birth, the new leader changed it to Kondrati Selivanov. He also called himself Simeon on occasion and passed himself off as a monk from Kiev. A peasant from the Ukrainian village of Stolbov, he was described as being fifty-three years of age, of middle height and pale complexion, with a sharp nose and closely shorn reddish-yellow hair. He had emasculated himself with a red-hot iron sometime before 1772 (though Selivanov claimed the operation was performed when he was only fourteen). It was this extraordinary procedure that was to characterise the new sect that he led called Skoptsy.

In July 1772, Catherine II, residing in Moscow, came to hear of the sect and ordered Prince Volkov to eliminate it. The leaders were to be arrested, knouted and exiled to Nerchinsk in Siberia. The preachers were to be beaten with sticks and sent to work on the fortifications at Riga. The gullible congregations were sent home to their masters if they were private serfs, or to the crown estates if they were royal serfs. Selivanov was taken into custody and shortly thereafter found himself transported to Siberia, where he claimed that he was Peter III. Peter had in fact been murdered by his wife Catherine II on 19 July 1762. (Actually, pretending to be Peter III was a fashionable exercise at the time. A Don Cossack called Pugachev was even able to raise a peasants' revolt by using the ruse, for which he was publicly executed; and a Serb going by the name of Stephen the Little posed as Peter and laid claim to the principality of Montenegro.)

For his own deceit Selivanov was dragged back to Moscow and interned in a mental hospital. However, at the request of wealthy and influential Skoptsys, Alexander I released him back into the community. At liberty once more Selivanov went back to his old ways and with his own hands baptised as many as one hundred people with his individual method of mutilation. For some extraordinary reason the beliefs of the Skoptsy raged around Russia like wildfire, and individuals from all walks of life made pilgrimages to Selivanov's front door. When they returned home it was clutching some personal souvenir of the Leader – nail parings, hair from his head – all of which were fervently believed to possess magical powers. As a reminder of his 'incarnation' as Peter III, the congregation was obliged to carry around a silver rouble with the portrait of Peter embossed on it.

The Skoptsy communities were formed into 'naves', or 'Korablya', presided over, like the Khlysty, by Christs. They never ate meat, and senior male members eschewed the company of women. It is this disdain for the process of procreation that partly explains the insistence on emasculation. As Selivanov preached to his disciples:

For behold the days are coming in which they shall say, blessed are the barren and the wombs that never bore and the paps that never gave suck . . . For there be some eunuchs which were so born from their mother's womb, and there be those eunuchs which were made eunuchs by men; and there be eunuchs which have made themselves eunuchs for the Kingdom of Heaven's sake. He that is able to receive it, let him receive it.

34

Another of the cult's firm beliefs was that when the number of conversions reached 144,000 it would signal the millennium, and only this group of faithful would ascend to heaven. It was not as it turned out such a fanciful figure, for whole areas of the country turned to Skoptsy, one mass 'baptism' consisting of 1,700 souls. Clearly with such a workload, and many mutilations being performed by individual members on themselves, some were rather hit and miss affairs, and many women had to be content with a couple of cuts on their breasts; a number of them became prostitutes to fill the coffers of the church. As the sect expanded a new two-tier system of mutilation was introduced: the Greater Seal, where complete emasculation was carried out, and the Lesser Seal, which involved only castration.

The religious ceremonies of the Skoptsy were held in secret, and anybody daring to breathe a word about them was executed. Children who had been born to Skoptsy parents and ran away to avoid mutilation were tracked down and killed. In the spirit of ecstasy that characterised both cults, the Skoptsy frequently indulged in the most brutal treatment of each other and, like the Khlysty, engaged in mutual flagellation.

One particularly sickening piece of ritual was the 'manufacture' of a Christ child. The 'Mother of God' was a girl of fifteen or sixteen years of age, who was put naked into a tub of water whereupon the older women would cut off her left breast. The breast was sliced into tiny pieces and distributed around the congregation to be eaten. The girl was then mauled and sexually molested by such of the male members who still had anything to molest with, which usually resulted in a pregnancy. On the eighth day of the resulting infant's life its left side was pierced with a lance and the blood sucked from the wound by the celebrants. The body of the child was then dried, pounded into powder and made into cakes to be eaten at Easter.

TWENTIETH-CENTURY CHRISTIAN CULTS

FOUNTAIN OF THE WORLD
WKFL

Francis Pencovic + Divine Light = Krishna Venta

Francis Heidswatzer Pencovic was born in San Francisco in 1911. In his formative years he made a rudimentary study of theology and eked out a living from a series of lacklustre menial jobs – shipyard labourer, dishwasher, that kind of thing. And when he couldn't work, or wouldn't, he resorted to crime of an equally lacklustre nature – petty larceny, cheque fraud . . . He came to the notice of the police in Arizona after posting a threatening letter to President Roosevelt. Using the name 'Frank Jensen' he accumulated a few more convictions, for burglary and theft.

It was while Francis Pencovic was playing his part in the Second World War (as a conscientious objector) that he was showered with Divine Light and emerged from it as Krishna Venta, 'Son of God'. Clearly this was a revelation to be shared, so the Son of God put on the robes of a holy man and set about collecting a group of disciples who were prepared to pay for the privilege of following him; the price was all their worldly possessions. Krishna Venta told his followers that he had been born in a valley in Nepal long ago, that he had been in Rome more than a thousand years previously and in America in the 1930s. Whether Krishna Venta believed it is doubtful in the light of his previous 'activities', but his adherents clearly did, and that was all that mattered.

All cults need a name to identify with, and Krishna Venta came up with the slightly immodest 'Fountain of the World' followed by the letters WKFL, which stood for Wisdom, Knowledge, Faith and Love. Being a communal sect they also needed live-in headquarters. Thanks to a particularly generous 'donation', the Fountain of the World bought a two-storey stone and timber building in Ventura County, California, not far from Box Canyon.

During the years they were established there, the colony earned a local reputation as gentle, honest people who were conspicuous helpers at several neighbourhood disasters, such as brush fires and even an air crash. Other than these charitable appearances, the disciples in their distinctive blue and green robes, the men bearded and long-haired, were rarely seen about town.

What went on behind the helpful smile was something quite different.

It was Krishna Venta's belief, or so he claimed, that 1965 would see a revolution in which the forces of Communism would overthrow the American Government. He also preached that he and his 144,000 disciples (actually at the time there were only one hundred) would govern America. The Communist take-over never happened, and Krishna Venta and his faithful never got the chance to take over either.

On Wednesday 10 December 1958, two disaffected former cult members, Ralph Muller and Peter Kamenoff, paid a visit to the Fountain of the World WKFL. There was some kind of altercation with Krishna Venta at the door, and the Leader was heard to shout: 'What do you think I am, a hypocrite?' One of the disciples then told Muller and Kamenoff that they no longer had any right to be on the premises.

There was a moment's silence and then a huge explosion ripped apart the Fountain of the World headquarters. In the blast nine members of the cult, including Krishna Venta and the two bombers, were killed. The other victims were named as 'Cardinal Gene' Shanaflet, his wife Jane and their eleven-month-old son, Martin Baker (called 'Priest Paul'), Ethel Ray ('Priest Elvira') and Anna Noga. Of the fifty members in residence several, including three children, suffered various degrees of injury. The tragedy would have been worse but for the fact that Krishna

Venta's wife, Ruth, had earlier led forty-three other disciples into Alaska to found a new colony.

Although it was not clear at first why the cult had been bombed, a tape recording found in a vehicle near the scene of the explosion offered a number of clues. One accusation levelled at Krishna Venta was his fondness for taking his disciples' wives to bed – including those of the two men who eventually killed him. Certainly this excessive sexual zeal plus the Leader's undisguised pursuit of the good things in life were beginning to reveal him as a very tarnished saint indeed – especially in the eyes of a community which had been taught the virtues of abstinence and frugal living.

YAHWEHS

'Out of the wilderness of white domination . . .'

On 7 November 1990, FBI agents raided Yahweh Ben Yahweh's hotel room in New Orleans at 3.30 a.m. According to his own account, the self-proclaimed Messiah, despite offering no resistance, found 'pump shotguns, M-16s and a variety of handguns' pointed at his 'head, neck, heart and other vital organs'. (Other reports indicate that the time of the incident was five in the morning and that Yahweh Ben Yahweh left his luxury suite, in which he was 'assisted' by a team of bodyguards, and voluntarily surrendered.)

Yahweh Ben Yahweh (or 'God, Son of God', or

יהוה בנ יהוה

in the Hebrew which he affects) lays strong claims to having risen from the dead to act the role of Messiah to members of a black American tribe of Israel.

This particular messiah was born Hutton Mitchell Jr in 1935 in the town of Kingfisher, Oklahoma, the eldest of fifteen children. In 1979 he relocated to Miami, after a spell with the Black Muslims in Chicago, to take up his duties as spiritual leader. And if Mitchell could change his name (as he had several times), then he insisted his followers took on a new handle too – in future they would all replace their family (or 'slave') name with 'Israel'. They would also exchange their everyday clothing for white robes, sandals and turbans. (The device of a 'uniform'

42

is a common bonding theme with cults – such as the Solar Temple's robes and the Hells Angels' leather 'n' denim.)

While the arrest was progressing in New Orleans, Yahweh Ben Yahweh's deputy, Judith Israel (formerly Linda Gainer and now the sect's financial brains), was picked up driving a group of the faithful to a meeting in Texas. Other members of the sect were arrested around Miami by the local police force supplemented by SWAT teams and Drug Enforcement Agency officers.

The 'lost tribe', which predictably calls itself the 'Nation of Yahweh' (or simply 'Yahwehs'), claims to have thousands of followers waiting to be led out of the wilderness of white domination. However, the sect is nothing if not businesslike, and since they opened their 'Temple of Love' in a former Miami supermarket around 1980, the Yahwehs have accumulated businesses and real estate worth in excess of $250 million; in fact this extraordinary enterprise was rewarded by Miami's mayor, Xavier Suarez, declaring a 'Yahweh Ben Yahweh Day'; it was on 7 October 1990. I recall somebody once saying that no one got rich by being honest. Ironically, the Leader claims that his success is due to following the scripture's teaching that 'It is more blessed to give than to receive'. It is more likely that his owning one of the biggest egos in the Sunshine State was responsible for his delusions . . . Yahweh Ben Yahweh once announced to a meeting of Florida business chiefs: 'Egypt has the pyramids; India has the Taj Mahal; France has the Eiffel Tower; Rome has the Pope; Orlando has Disneyland; Miami has the son of Yahweh. The world's greatest attraction is in your midst. I'm here!'

Initially Yahweh Ben Yahweh and sixteen of his followers were taken into custody on Federal racketeering charges. By the time they reached court they faced a huge twenty-five-page indictment which included fourteen killings and two attempted killings. The string of murders in the indictment included several members who allegedly disagreed too publicly with the sect's administration – one man, Aston Green, was decapitated. Other cases were said to result from an enthusiastic response to Yahweh Ben Yahweh's chilling instruction to his flock to 'Kill a white devil and bring me an ear!' In fact, according to one recollection, the bodies of eight white vagrants were found around Miami minus their ears. It was also claimed that Yahweh Ben Yahweh kept the resulting lugs as souvenirs, to be displayed on special occasions just for the fun of it.

In one incident, acting supposedly on the Yahwehs' behalf, Robert Ernest Rozier Jr (cult name Neariah Israel), a former professional football player with the St Louis Cardinals and the Oakland Raiders, murdered two tenants in a broken-down housing complex who had refused to move out when the sect wanted to purchase it. He also apparently turned in his quota of white devils' ears. It is in great part due to the testimony given by this repentant disciple that other crimes came to light and charges were brought.

According to the Messiah: 'The allegations stem from and hinge entirely upon the testimony of Robert Rozier, a former disciple and an admitted serial killer.' He remarks wryly that Christ was also betrayed by one of his disciples.

In an Informational Profile published by the sect this, in part at least, is what they claim happened next:

The United States government falsely charged Yahweh Ben Yahweh and His followers with operating their religion as a racketeering enterprise under the Racketeering Influenced Corrupt Organizations statute (RICO). These charges included murder, attempted murder, arson and extortion. In the five-month-long federal trial (costing the taxpayers over $4 million), none of the defendants were found guilty of any charges by the federal jury. In fact, Federal District Judge Norman Roettger found the defendants charged with extortion not guilty. However, Yahweh Ben Yahweh and six of his co-defendants were 'wrongly' convicted of conspiring to commit racketeering.

This, in a loose sense, was true. The trial did last a long time, and it did cost a lot of money. Judge Roettger was accused of being lenient. In one account he is said to have reduced Yahweh Ben

Yahweh's sentence because the Nation of Yahweh, 'under the direction of the defendant, cleaned up its act – or acts – and tried to be a good citizen'. All of which prompted Assistant State Attorney Richard Scruggs to observe: 'There are literally hundreds of victims in this case. Some died in pain, others will have to live in pain. This man [Yahweh Ben Yahweh] is a classic con man, a classic megalomaniac. This is a man who used religion as a shield to amass power and money and commit horrendous crimes.'

Despite the overall acquittals in the federal court, the state of Florida rearrested Yahweh Ben Yahweh and a couple of his followers to stand trial in the matter of the same first-degree murder charges. The evidence was all but a rerun of that given at the federal trial, and the Yahwehs were again found not guilty of murder. This leaves the Messiah serving an eighteen-year stretch in the Lewisburg Penitentiary in Pennsylvania on the conspiracy to commit racketeering charges, and six of the faithful also with lengthy terms of imprisonment for conspiracy.

As this is being written, the Yahwehs are fighting their convictions with funds collected through what they call The Abraham Foundation, Inc. (it appears that it is clearly better for Yahweh Ben Yahweh to receive than to give). They have also distributed through various media a curious document headed 'Judicial Murder', which opens with the words: 'The Crucifixion of Yahweh Ben Yahweh. How is the Son of Almighty God identified? The Son of Yahweh is identified by suffering and persecution.'

Unlike many messianic cults, the Yahwehs do not seem unduly worried by the coming of the millennium – perhaps it is the thought of all that money going to waste. Besides, they have just invested in 'The Wonderful World of Yahweh' catalogue, a costly Internet site where 'a selection of most cherished offerings' can be found. In fact it comprises solely seven books written by none other than Yahweh Ben Yahweh, who describes himself as 'the Blessed and only Potentate, Grand Master of the Celestial Lodge, Architect of the Universe'. Quite a journey for the boy who was born Hutton Mitchell Jr in Kingfisher, Oklahoma.

CHRISTIAN SCIENTISTS (CHURCH OF CHRIST SCIENTIST)

Death by faith, the Twitchell trial

A case that had far-reaching consequences for the continued inviolability from prosecution of cults of faith and religions under the United States Fifth Amendment was heard in the Suffolk County Courtroom, Boston, during April and May 1990. On trial were the fundamental beliefs not of some marginal hippie sect, but of the powerful Church of Christ Scientist, and in the very city of its establishment at that.

On the night of 8 April 1986, two-year-old Robyn Twitchell died from a bowel obstruction. It was a tragic death that could easily have been prevented if at any time during Robyn's five-day illness his parents had bestowed the benefit of medical treatment. Extraordinary as it seemed to the shocked city of Boston, David and Ginger Twitchell had offered their child nothing by way of relief but prayer.

Devout Christian Scientists, the Twitchells – undoubtedly loving and caring parents – were following a teaching as important to them as their Bible, a Christian Science manual on *Parents, Children and God's Omnipotent Care*, which instructs: 'Christian Scientists turn resolutely to God, as the Master [Jesus Christ] did, to effect the needed healing . . . disease hath no basis in God's kingdom.' In other words, 'Harmony is the fact . . . and sickness a temporal dream.'

So instead of a doctor, David Twitchell and his wife summoned the Practitioner, a Christian Science 'specialist' in prayer who, after a mere two weeks' training, is qualified to offer his or her services as a spiritual healer for a remuneration. They also availed themselves of the ministrations of a Christian Science Nurse, whose entitlement to that status ends with the name. Neither the Practitioner nor the Nurse have any training in medicine or even in the most rudimentary anatomy. As one Practitioner explained: 'Anatomy to a Christian Science Practitioner is a very different thing than for a medical practitioner; the anatomy of a man as a spiritual being comes into play. The completeness and the wholeness in the way that God made him: yes there is anatomy, but not the physical body; we do not turn to that to define man totally.'

Nevertheless, so strong is the Christian Science lobby in America that medical insurance companies, such as Blue Shield and Blue Cross, are obliged to meet the costs of Christian Science Practitioners and Nurses who, furthermore, enjoy protection from malpractice suits.

So David and Ginger Twitchell found themselves sitting in a tense, crowded courtroom facing a charge of manslaughter relating to the death of their infant son. On the face of it, it was just two calm, sincere Christians who sat attentively in the dock; effectively, it was the whole of their religion that had been put on trial.

There was no dispute as to the facts – the child had died as a direct result of the failure to treat medically a condition which had not, in itself, been life-threatening. What was in question was whether parents were constitutionally immune to prosecution for, in the simplest terms, 'sacrificing' their children to their own religious beliefs.

In common with another forty-seven states in America, Massachusetts retains a statute on its books, passed in 1971, which ensures that: 'A child should not be deemed to be neglected or to lack proper physical care for the sole reason that he is being provided remedial treatment by spiritual means alone in accordance with the tenets and practice of a recognised church.'

However, in the interpretation of District Attorney Flanagan, responsible for presenting the prosecution case to the court, the statute applies only to child abuse: 'The parents are being tried for manslaughter; it is up to the jury to decide if there are sufficient facts to find that the parents' failure to get medical care for their child was wilful, wanton and reckless conduct . . . We are not going to allow parents to make their children martyrs.'

It was obvious that the case was set to become a landmark for the Church of Christ Scientist, and one that would have a potentially far-reaching influence on its recruitment drive. A massive publicity campaign was therefore launched around America through the medium of double-page advertisements in the major newspapers asking: 'Why is prayer being persecuted in Boston? Selective prosecution of Christian Science is of grave concern. Today it is the prayers of Christian Scientists, tomorrow it may be the prayers of the established religions – perhaps *your* religion.'

As for the Twitchells themselves, having lived not only with the sorrow of losing their child, but also having endured four years of uncertainty leading up to their trial, the couple were reticent in talking to the media, and had gone so far as to move home to a secret location in order to avoid unwanted publicity. Nevertheless, David Twitchell has, throughout his ordeal, publicly maintained that he was *not* careless of his son's life: 'Our spiritual understanding of God's laws told us we were behaving in an acceptable manner. It has been tough; some people might call it a severe test of your faith. There will be some people who will say we didn't care enough, but what is neglect? We used extreme measures to try to save Robyn – extreme Christian Science measures.'

This defence would be elaborated in court by the couple's lawyers led by Rikki Klieman. Ms Klieman would emphasise the legal and statutory aspects of her clients' rights, and attempt to dispel the emotionally charged atmosphere that must inevitably obscure the situation where a child is apparently left to die unnecessarily: 'The first and most important issue is whether the Constitution permits parents to be subject to criminal prosecution if there is a statute that explicitly allows for the care and treatment of a child through spiritual healing. The second issue is whether we will permit or tolerate the commonwealth to place itself in a very special relationship between a parent and a child, and to substitute its own judgement for the parents' judgement.'

From the 'other side' of the court it would be argued by observers like Wendy Mariner of the Boston University of Public Health: 'The issue of First Amendment rights for religious freedom does not extend to the freedom to endanger the life of someone else. You are allowed to believe anything you want, but you cannot allow your kids to die for the sake of your religion.'

And that, for most Americans at least, was what this trial was about.

A judicial dilemma
When the trial opened in April 1990, the events leading up to Robyn Twitchell's death were presented to the jury as a pathetic chronology. On 5 April 1986, the Twitchells were aroused in the middle of the night by their son's evident pain and distress, though they had no clear idea at that time what the symptoms might indicate. The parents' automatic response was to pray, and, so David Twitchell testified, the child began to improve. Over the following four days and nights, Robyn alternated between extreme discomfort and apparent recovery, indicating to the parents that their prayers were beginning to produce some beneficial result – that it was working so slowly and intermittently they took as a celestial criticism of their own weakness of prayer. Twitchell further testified that it was only on the first night that Robyn had been in what he would call 'severe' pain. On the second day of the child's illness, Ginger Twitchell called in the Practitioner, who began the process of 'healing' by prayer, which included praying with the child, with its parents and in isolation. This treatment was reinforced by the assistance of the Christian Science Nurse, whose responsibility was to assist in the practical – though non-medical – comfort of the patient and family. Questioned as to whether at any time he considered the necessity of summoning medical help, David Twitchell insisted: 'We are

not against calling medical doctors, it is just that what we have been taught and what I have experienced is that turning to prayer, turning to God, is a better, a more complete and more thorough healing solution of a problem than turning to other systems . . . If I didn't think prayer was the better solution, if I didn't think it was *safer* for my children and myself, I'd turn to medicine.'

Which was strange; because it would later be revealed that both David Twitchell and his wife had at various times sought conventional medical treatment for themselves, and had taken prescription drugs. David, for example, had visited a dentist and was given the pain-killer Novocaine: Ginger Twitchell received pain-deadening Xylocaine when giving birth to the very child to whom she later denied medical aid.

Nevertheless, when attorney Rikki Klieman presented her defence of the Twitchells, it was on the primary premise that her clients *truly believed* that their son was responding positively to healing by the power of prayer: 'These parents did not choose, or think, or consider about *martyring* their child, they didn't think about sacrificing their child, they did not think that one day they would meet their child in Heaven and therefore martyred their child. They loved their child. He was their son.'

According to Klieman, it was only on the very last day of his sickness that Robyn Twitchell took a 'dramatic turn for the worse', from which sadly he did not recover.

Quite predictably, this was to be at variance with prosecution evidence which quoted the pathologist's report that the child had been suffering from an abdominal 'twist', and although for the first few days the pain would have come and gone irregularly, at least during the last thirty-six hours of the child's life he would have been suffering severe cramps and frequent, if not continuous, vomiting of material that looked like faeces. In short, it could only have been, the medical experts advanced, the parents' blinding faith in the power of their own prayers that prevented them acknowledging the serious extent of their child's suffering; a total inability to recognise even the possibility of Robyn's death.

In presenting the state's case, special prosecutor John Kiernan laid emphasis on the fact that through the act of summoning the Practitioner and the Nurse, the Twitchells were acknowledging that Robyn's condition was more serious than they pretended: 'If your child is vomiting his own excrement, wouldn't you think that that child was at grave risk? If that child was screaming and clutching at his belly, isn't that child at grave risk; somebody who has not slept or eaten for five days, whose parents move into a small room to sleep next to him, obviously indicating a recognition that the child is seriously ill. Everything they did was an acknowledgement that the child was seriously ill . . . that child looked at the source of his care, his nutrition, his warmth, his love, his food, his shelter, his clothing, and he had a name for his god – and the name of his god was "mother and father"; and his mother and father abandoned him.'

Perhaps the most controversial aspect of the Twitchell trial was whether – according to the Massachusetts statute of 1971 – Christian Scientist families like David and Ginger Twitchell were exempt from prosecution. In a move for which she was sub- sequently severely criticised, Judge Sandra Hamlyn declined to instruct the jury on the matter, preferring instead to give her own interpretation of the law: 'The reliance on spiritual healing alone, in other words the exclusive reliance on spiritual healing alone, without medical care, may not be permitted under the cir- cumstances the child was exposed to the risk of serious bodily injury or death.'

In effect this wholly incorrect interpretation of the statute *as it stood* left the jury little option but to find David Twitchell and his wife guilty as charged. The Twitchells, who faced a possible twenty years' imprisonment, were sentenced to ten years' probation, during which period their other three children were required to submit to regular medical examination.

It was only after conviction and sentence that members of the jury became aware through newspaper reports of the true wording of the Massachusetts law on which the defence had rested, and which was denied to the jury at the time of the trial. At least two very vociferous jury members – one their forewoman – made both public protests through the media and private representations to the judge, claiming that if they had been fully aware of the *legal* defence offered by the defendants then they would have declared them not guilty.

So what fundamental issues were at stake, and how, if at all, did the prosecution of David and Ginger Twitchell clarify those issues? Both sides of the case quite naturally invoked that bastion of the American Constitution, the First Amendment, which establishes the rights of freedom of speech, freedom of the press and free exercise of religion. Their interpretations, equally naturally, were at strong variance.

The Christian Scientists and their supporters (including other unorthodox religions like the Jehovah's Witnesses) see a threat to the freedom of their religion by establishing a precedent that it is perfectly acceptable for a person to believe what he or she chooses, but not to practise it. For Rikki Klieman, the trial exhibited a clear example of religious persecution.

On the other hand, the message coming from the opposite camp – the state prosecutor's office – is that the First Amendment is alive and very much enriched by the trial and the verdict: 'It [the First Amendment] accommodates all our views ... Our values are found there and our values include both the freedom to believe and the protection of our children ... This is not restrictive on anybody's religion, it is just a restatement of the law, that you may believe as you wish, but when your child is at risk of death, you had better make sure you use all available means, including medical science, and prayer if you so wish.'

Appendix: The cult of Christ the Healer

The Church of Christ Scientist was founded in 1879 by Mary Baker Eddy, herself a life-long victim of frail health. It was in 1866 that Mary Eddy was walking in her native town of Lynn, just north of Boston, when she fell on an icy pavement and sustained serious internal injuries. It was while she was nursing herself through this illness, fortified by regular doses of biblical texts, that Mary Eddy devised the system of spiritual healing which, through her book *Science and Health with Key to the Scriptures*, became Christian Science.

It has grown to be a powerful organisation worldwide. It publishes the prestigious *Christian Science Monitor* and also broadcasts its own television show.

The most controversial of the Christian Scientists' beliefs is that people properly attuned to God's spirit are free from sin and disease. Although this is such a fundamental principle of the faith, it was not until the Twitchell case that the Church decided to address itself to a systematic study of the efficacy of spiritual healing covering a multitude of physical complaints not commonly considered psychosomatic – from gangrene to glaucoma, from cancer to multiple sclerosis.

POSTSCRIPT:

Christian Ethiopian Orthodox Church

Lest it be imagined that only Christian Scientists have a faith which requires the non-medical treatment of adults and children, sometimes leading to their untimely deaths, one of the largest organised religious groups in the world – the Jehovah's Witnesses – are similarly careless of their members' lives. For the Witnesses it is the abhorrence of blood transfusions which puts them into constant conflict with the medical and caring services.

Another, much smaller group made a certain degree of news in 1993. They call themselves the Christian Ethiopian Orthodox Church, a cult about which little is known. Two zealots from this faith, Dwight and Beverly Harris of Nottingham, found themselves arraigned in a Crown Court, charged with the manslaughter of their daughter. Nine-year-old Nahkira was admitted to the Queen's Medical Centre,

Nottingham, where she was diagnosed as suffering from diabetes. The Harris couple refused to allow doctors to treat their sick daughter with insulin. The reason appears to be that at one time the drug was derived from pigs – an animal the Christian Ethiopian Orthodox Church have deemed 'unclean'. Little Nahkira was discharged from the hospital by her father, *after he had been told she would die without treatment*, and taken home. Two days later a social worker was asked to seek out the family and try to persuade them to allow treatment. Unfortunately the Harrises had by then moved in with friends and the social worker was left with no alternative but to leave a note in the hope that they would receive it. They did receive it, but felt that they did not want to discuss the matter. Just over a month later Nahkira Harris died of her illness.

At their trial Dwight and Beverly Harris were convicted on the manslaughter charge.

ARMAGEDDON CULTS

The world's religions have been punctuated throughout their development by fanatics who mesmerised groups of followers in large or small numbers into becoming detached from the mainstream belief, or who have laid down their own unique sets of rules and beliefs not based on any existing faith.

Christianity does not have a monopoly of such cults, but as a major international religion whose fundamental beliefs are simple enough to be open to widely varying interpretation, it has seen its share of charlatans, madmen and the misdirected. Christ figures – Messiahs – have come in all shapes and sizes, exerting a greater or lesser degree of malevolence over their disciples and camp-followers.

Many of the more off-beat beliefs of Christian breakaway groups centre around apocalyptic visions of the end of the world – these are the so-called 'Armageddon Cults', who look forward to sooner or later being embroiled in a literal realisation of the battles between Heaven and Earth, between Good and Evil, predicted in the sixteenth chapter of the biblical Book of Revelation of St John the Divine:

> . . . And the seven angels came out of the temple, having the seven plagues . . . and one of the four beasts gave unto the seven angels seven golden vials full of the wrath of God, who liveth for ever and ever . . . And I heard a great voice out of the temple saying to the seven angels, 'Go your ways, and pour out the vials of the wrath of God upon the earth. And the first went and poured out his vial on the earth; and

there fell a noisome and grievous sore upon the men who had the mark of the beast, and upon them which worshipped his image. And the second angel poured out his vial upon the sea; and it became as the blood of a dead man; and every living soul died in the sea. And the third angel poured out his vial upon the rivers and fountains of waters; and they became blood . . . And the fourth angel poured out his vial upon the sun; and the power was given unto him to scorch men with fire. And the men were scorched with great heat, and blasphemed the name of God, which hath power over these plagues: and they repented not to give him glory. And the fifth angel poured out his vial on the seat of the beast; and his kingdom was full of darkness; and they gnawed their tongues for pain. And blasphemed the God of heaven because of their pains and their sores, and repented not of their deeds. And the sixth angel poured out his vial upon the great river Euphrates; and the water thereof was dried up . . . And I saw three unclean spirits like frogs come out of the mouth of the dragon, and out of the mouth of the beast, and out of the mouth of the false prophet. For they are the spirits of devils, working miracles, which go forth unto the kings of the earth to gather them to the battle of that great day of God Almighty . . . and he gathered them together in a place called in the Hebrew tongue Armageddon. And the seventh angel poured out his vial into the air; and there came a great voice out of the temple of heaven, from the throne, saying, 'It is done.' And there were voices, and thunders, and lightnings; and there was a great earthquake, such as was not since men were first upon the earth, so mighty an earthquake, and so great. And the great city was divided into three parts, and the cities of the nations fell: and great Babylon came in remembrance before God, to give unto her the cup of the wine of the fierceness of his wrath. And every island fled away, and the mountains were not found. And there fell upon men a great hail out of heaven, every stone about the weight of a talent:

and men blasphemed God because of the plague of the hail;
for the plague thereof was exceeding great . . .

The coming of the Messiah to lead his faithful out of the jaws of sorrow, pain and oppression was fundamental to the Jews since the time of the Exile. It was around 700 BC when the Jewish tribes were driven from their lands by the conquering Assyrians, and the prophet Isaiah boosted morale by declaring that 'Unto us a child will be born' – in Hebrew, the Messiah ('the anointed one'), the reincarnation of King David. There was no shortage of candidates over the centuries, men and women – most of them self-proclaimed, the majority either fanatical or deluded. Finally, one of these Messiahs unaccountably became adopted by more than the customary handful of local believers, and within centuries was on his way to becoming a dominant world religion – his name was Jesus Christ ('Christ' is the equivalent Greek word for 'Messiah').

It should not be thought that Christianity was ever a cohesive, unifying influence. Like the pagan religions which it to some extent displaced, Christianity was (and still is) interpreted in many different ways, and cults were formed. Among them the various Millennarians. In the Book of Revelation (Chapter 20) it is said that an angel bound Satan for one thousand years, and later that the martyred dead would rise from their graves and 'live and reign with Christ for a thousand years' – this, according to St John was the Millennium – when Christ would return to earth.

Although very clearly the Second Coming and the attendant Armageddon did not take place in the year 1000, it did not stop speculation as to when that Second Coming might be expected. Among the more recent sects holding such a belief are the very powerful Mormon Church, the Irvingites (known as the Catholic and Apostolic Church) and the Adventists. Most of these cults wisely prefer not to be too specific about the date of Armageddon – most of them favouring a simple 'The End of the World is Nigh' approach.

Nevertheless, some of the early Adventists did make predictions. William Miller, leader of the 'Millerites', was one of them.

59

By a process of exceedingly complex mathematical calculations, prophet William determined that Christ would return to earth and the world would end at precisely midnight on 22 October 1843. In their readiness for the ascent to heaven the faithful gathered on a hilltop in Massachusetts and waited . . . and waited. The world failed even to wobble, let alone rip asunder, and many who had sold or given away all their worldly possessions as an extra spiritual insurance were left destitute. Then William went back to his sheafs of scribbling . . . what a FOOL he had been! Miller had been calculating the end of the world on the Christian calendar – it should have been based on the Jewish year! Deliverance would have to be postponed until 22 March 1844, the following year. And there they all were again; on the hilltop; at midnight. They were still there at five minutes past the hour . . . ten . . . fifteen . . . William Miller had got it wrong again. What is most illuminating about this incident – and highlights humankind's desperate need for 'answers' – is that although Miller left his ministry and died five years later a sadder but wiser man, many of his followers simply licked the wounds of their embarrassment and regrouped. The remnants of the Millerites became the Seventh-Day Adventists in 1863, retaining a strict fundamentalist adherence to the scriptures and an abhorrence of alcohol and tobacco.

BRANCH DAVIDIANS

David Koresh and the siege of Waco

Few individuals with access to the world's news can have failed
to sit up and take notice of the American tragedy which became
notorious as the Waco Massacre. In the early light of Sunday 28
February 1993 US federal agents attached to the Bureau of
Alcohol, Tobacco and Firearms approached a rambling cluster of
fortified buildings on the outskirts of Waco, Texas. The compound was owned by a religious cult calling themselves Branch
Davidians; the headquarters they called the 'Mount Carmel
Center'.

The reason for the raid was information received that the
Davidians had been stockpiling huge numbers of firearms –
enough, some said, to start a war. Officers now had a warrant to
search the premises for weapons and another for the arrest of the
cult's leader on breaches of gun-control law. The thirty-three-
year-old self-styled Messiah, christened Vernon Howell but since
1991 calling himself David Koresh, had become disillusioned
with the Seventh-Day Adventist Church, defected, joined the off-
shoot Branch Davidians in 1980 and become their leader in 1984.

It had been reported in the Waco *Tribune-Herald* that Koresh
had at least fifteen 'wives', the only legal one of which – Rachel
Jones – he married when she was fourteen years old; he was also
known to have fathered numerous children and was not entirely
platonic in his relations with several other younger members of
the sect. On the controversial subject of his divinity, Koresh told
an interviewer: 'If the Bible is true, then I'm Christ. But so what?

What's so great about being Christ? A man nailed to the cross. A man of sorrow acquainted with grief. Being Christ ain't nothing, know what I mean? All I want is for people to be honest this time.' The leader's belief in his reincarnation as the Messiah was rooted in his conviction that he was the 'lamb' referred to in the Book of Revelation:

And I saw in the right hand of him that sat on the throne a book written within and on the back side sealed with seven seals . . . And no man in heaven, nor in earth, neither under the earth was able to open the book, neither to look thereon . . . And I beheld, and lo, in the midst of the throne and of the four beasts, and in the midst of the elders, stood a Lamb, and it had been slain, having seven horns and seven eyes, which are the seven Spirits of God sent forth into all the earth. And he came and took the book out of the right hand of him that sat upon the throne. And when he had taken the book, the four beasts and four and twenty elders fell down before the Lamb, having every one of them harps, and golden vials full of odours, which are the prayers of saints . . . And I beheld, and heard the voice of many angels . . . saying with a loud voice: 'Worthy is the Lamb that was slain to receive power, and riches, and wisdom, and strength, and honour, and glory, and blessing.'

It was the opening of the seals which unleashed upon the world war, pestilence and the wrath of God – and ultimately the elevation of the faithful followers of the Lamb to heaven. However, although there are estimated to be between two and three hundred members of the sect in the United States, it is only the children fathered by Koresh himself who will inherit the earth after the non-believers have been eliminated – and other male members of the cult would have to wait until they got to heaven to enjoy sex; it was apparently forbidden to them on earth.

The cult had already been involved in one gunfight at Mount Carmel, with members of a rival sect, in 1983. Several of the

Branch Davidians – including Koresh – were accused at the time of attempted murder but the case ended in a mistrial. The astonishing fact in retrospect is that the authorities who took charge of the Waco siege had learned nothing, either from the past record of the Branch Davidians or from recent history. It might have been thought that criminologists and law enforcement agencies would have taken note of other, parallel Armageddon cults which had begun to arm themselves in readiness for their own Apocalypse: Charles Manson's 'Family' stockpiled weapons for the promised 'Helter Skelter'; the Reverend Jim Jones ruled his cult as a military dictatorship before leading more than 900 faithful followers to mass 'revolutionary suicide'. David Koresh had exactly this kind of power over his followers, and in the days to come there would be more than one occasion on which the siege negotiators had reason to fear a multiple 'suicide'.

At Mount Carmel, at 9.30 that Sunday morning, one hundred Bureau officials and federal agents backed up by three helicopters drove into the fenced compound in cattle-carriers towed by two pick-up trucks. Then the invasion force began a lightning assault on the main building. Without warning, the officers found themselves under heavy automatic gunfire from inside the building. During the forty-five-minute gun-battle which followed, four agents were killed and a further sixteen received gunshot wounds. When the dead and injured had been removed from the compound, troops in armoured vehicles moved into a siege position. What was not known at the time but became evident over the following days was that the law enforcement officers and troops had claimed lives among the cult followers. Some hours after the initial fighting, three members stormed out of the main building firing off guns; one was killed instantly, one was wounded and the third captured.

According to the Davidians, one of their number, Wayne Martin, had called the 911 emergency telephone number at 9.48 and pleaded with the officers to stop shooting. There is no official record of the call.

But for all that they were surrounded by the authorities with awesome firepower, the besieged cultists were relatively secure. Short of blowing the buildings apart with rockets, the officers and National Guardsmen who arrived later were frustratedly helpless. One of the main reasons was that the original operation had been planned by the BATF for months and somehow news had reached Mount Carmel, giving Koresh time to secure his boundaries and mobilise an armed defence of the main administration block. Inside the compound there were an estimated seventy-five people, including women and children. Another reason for the besiegers to sit on their hands for a while.

Clearly at this time talking was a better plan, in the short-term at least, than shooting. As early as 11.00 a.m. on the day of the siege FBI agents requested a negotiator; three hours later Agent Byron Sage arrived. As a result of the discussions Koresh was allowed to broadcast a radio message through a phone link. He opened by reminding the media that Vernon Howell was now David Koresh, and should be referred to as such in all bulletins (though his mother continued affectionately to call him her Vern). Then he insisted that it had been the Davidians who were aggressed by federal agents as the result of which he, the Messiah, had been wounded 'in my guts and arm', and a child had been killed. Then Koresh began negotiating, gradually releasing children from the compound in ones and twos in exchange for the broadcast of his sermons over local radio.

While David Koresh was preaching his gospel over the airwaves, the authorities were surrounding Mount Carmel with 300 ground personnel backed up by armoured vehicles and helicopters.

But all that was being fired at the moment were words – and it was David Koresh who was shooting his mouth off with thinly veiled threats that he and what he called 'God's marines' would rather die than surrender: 'We know our lives have been spared in heaven.' Koresh's mother couldn't resist a display of maternal pride when she told a reporter: 'My Vernon is a nice boy. People have got him all wrong – he doesn't mean any harm.' Others took a less benevolent point of view, and one English national daily described David Koresh as a 'beer-swilling night-club musician'.

The third day after the shoot-out dawned, and the atmosphere was tense among the official personnel now surrounding the farm compound. In the days which followed it became obvious that there was not going to be a speedy negotiated settlement. Senior Davidians were only prepared to speak with one negotiator. Then Koresh made a half-hearted promise to surrender. Instead two mothers and two children were turned loose bearing another sixty-minute cassette of the Messiah's tedious rhetoric. Such was the state of pessimism that a fleet of ambulances had taken up position like white ghosts behind the armoured troop carriers at the perimeter fence.

There was a growing sense of unease. *Nothing was happening*. Then, just as the stand-off at Waco had begun to be pushed out of the headlines, David Koresh released two more children. With his talent for psychological manipulation it was becoming less surprising that Koresh was the Messiah and everybody else was . . . well, the rest.

The FBI thought about cutting off mains electricity to the buildings, but as the cult had an emergency generator there didn't seem much point. Then later they cut it off anyway, just for the nuisance value. The cultists also had a topped-up water tower, plenty of food and a huge collection of guns.

The date was now Saturday 6 March 1993; in Britain there was some comfort to be drawn from the few morning papers that still thought David Koresh and the 'Wackos of Waco' were worth writing about: 'Cult Leader Rejects Idea of Mass Suicide'. Well, that was a turn-up for the books! What was more, Koresh was still waiting for a message from God. Could the world hold its breath much longer? The Branch Davidians began to serenade the countryside loudly with a selection of songs written by the 'Son of God' himself, including an early hit entitled *There's a Mad Man in Waco*. No, you are not dreaming. Only a few years before, the Mad Man in Waco had recorded a song called *There's a Mad Man in Waco*!

Then Koresh followed up by calling negotiators on the phone

with the threat: 'We are ready for war, let's get it on. Your talk is becoming vain. I am going to give you an opportunity to save yourself before you get blown away.' This sufficiently alarmed the FBI into bringing in the Abrams M1 battle-tanks, and pointing out that they had 'sufficient firepower to neutralise the situation at any moment'.

By the tenth day, negotiations were not getting any easier, and over the following week there were only a few half-hearted press stories to be found, but these were mostly personal accounts by relatives of the besieged Davidians, or quasi-analytical reports on the psychological state of the twenty-one children who had so far been released. A seven-year-old girl and her four-year-old brother were said to be like 'zombies', so confused that they did not realise that they were still in America.

In an attempt to undermine the psychological stability of the cultists, the FBI launched measures to render day-to-day activity inside the compound unbearable: powerful lights were trained on the windows to interfere with the occupants' sleep, and plans were laid to blare heavy rock music at the walls – a tactic used successfully by the US Army to flush General Manuel Noriega out of his hideaway in Panama City. Officers also refused to listen to any more of David Koresh's sermons preached over the telephone. It didn't work.

Then, three weeks to the day after the attack which started the siege, people began to leave the cult headquarters. They were quitting at last! Or some of them were. The exodus began with the release of a fifty-nine-year-old British woman suffering from heart trouble; she was accompanied by three other sect members. Five more followed, including Livingstone Fagan, one of the heavily armed ringleaders – or 'Mighty Men', as they called themselves. When asked whether David Koresh was coming out, Fagan grinned and replied: 'God will decide when he comes out.'

As they left the compound, each of the new defectors was searched by federal agents for weapons and then taken into custody as witnesses to the murders of four ATF officers. On 23 March the detainees, dressed now in the distinctive orange boilersuits of the county jail and wearing handcuffs, were taken before a federal magistrate.

That, though, was the last of the voluntary surrenders. It was now obvious that those remaining at Ranch Apocalypse (as it was called locally) were there because they wanted to be. Now there was earnest talk of suicide pacts; each of the ninety-three Branch Davidians had pledged to stay till the death, and as a symbol of solidarity they all changed their name to Koresh. Meanwhile, Koresh himself was becoming daily more irrational, more delusional – more likely to lead a mass suicide.

The above words were written on the last day of March 1993. From then on only occasional small paragraphs about the Waco incident found their way into the international press. The possibility was there that soon all interest would vanish. But it might be different; it was suggested that, as the Messiah, David Koresh might choose an appropriately religious date for Armageddon – Easter perhaps. There were less than two weeks to wait.

The end of the world is nigh: diary of a disaster

4 April 1993

Well it wasn't Easter, but that was close enough. Just as the world and his wife had forgotten what was going on down there in Waco, David Koresh made an announcement. He told members of the cult that the up-coming Passover holiday would be the last they would celebrate. Passover is a Jewish festival which commemorates the deliverance of the Israelites from the Angel of Death, the exodus from Egypt. The fact that Passover did not feature on the Branch Davidian calendar seemed not to cause Koresh much of a problem. Another development was that two lawyers, one of whom was Koresh's champion, Mr Dick deGuerin, were now having frequent meetings with the cultists inside the compound. Much of this talk seemed to revolve around the size of advance payments for a book and film deal.

10 April 1993

Despite some anxiety that the new Messiah might revert to the Christian calendar and stage some sort of spectacle on Good Friday to celebrate the first Messiah's crucifixion, the holiday came and went without dramatic incident – of the apocalyptic kind anyway. Now all minds were refocused on the end of Passover on 14 April. Even so Easter did have its moments. The FBI were still shattering the peace of the Texan countryside by blasting recordings of brass instruments and klaxons at the cult's compound, and this was accompanied by strobe lights and hovering helicopters. Keeping up his end of the burlesque, Koresh ordered a banner to be hung from the compound windows: 'FBI – God sees your lies', and a four-page letter was sent out 'under the signature of God' – in reality just another of the Lamb's rhetorical exercises in religious gobbledegook, but with the timely reminder from the Book of Jeremiah that 'A sound of great battle is in the land'.

The Easter holiday also brought out other weirdos, such as the Texas-based 'Women for Hebrew Disciples', who arrived at Ranch Apocalypse bearing large wooden crosses and a 'message of peace' for David Koresh. Another crazy who turned up for Easter was an itinerant fruit-picker from California who rejoiced in the name Jesse 'Lord Lightning' Amen. Unlike the lady disciples, 'Lord Lightning' managed to embarrass FBI officials by ambling unchecked and unnoticed across the compound to the cult's front door to offer himself for the Messiah's work. Koresh, in a typically Saviour-like gesture, bathed the man's feet and bade him welcome. Just days later Jesse was pushed back over the threshold he had so recently crossed. He was, Koresh decided, too mad!

In fact the only people who didn't seem to be having a ball were the politicians, who settled for accusing each other of bungling incompetence, risking the lives of children, and anything else they could think of. Even the new President, Bill Clinton, had stepped in to insist the FBI avoid any more 'unnecessary' bloodshed and loss of life. However, there was also another agenda.

The stand-off at Waco had already cost the taxpayer more than

$13 million – and that isn't the sort of thing that wins the hearts of voters. It was time to scale down the police and military presence, reduce the more than 1,000 personnel surrounding Mount Carmel. Which is why one morning when the cultists awoke – if they were getting any sleep at all with the *son et lumière* going on outside the windows – they found their seventy-seven acres encircled by a high fence of barbed wire. Cheaper by far than armoured cars and tanks, barbed wire has a long history in the state of Texas, having been introduced in 1871 to corral cattle.

13–16 April 1993

As the deadlock continued, David Koresh delivered a second letter, or 'message from God', couched in much the same belicose language as the first, threatening that enemies of the Lamb of God would be 'devoured by fire and destroyed'. It was a phrase to be remembered.

But if the FBI had repeated its hope for a non-violent settlement of the situation, it was not giving up on its full-frontal attack on the Davidians' sensibilities. It had replaced the sound of blaring trumpets and trombones, and the Tibetan chants known to be loathed by Koresh, with the whine of a dentist's drill which officers hoped he would loathe even more. To break the monotony, the drill would be accompanied by the vocal sounds of a number of farmyard animals, the squealing of rabbits being slaughtered and, horror of horrors, Nancy Sinatra singing *These Boots Are Made for Walkin'*. But David Koresh had more personal problems to ponder and worry about. His mother had pipped him to the post and sold the film rights to his story for a reported $75,000; they were already building a replica Mount Carmel on a farm somewhere in Oklahoma ready for filming 'In the Line of Duty: Assault on Waco'. The Lamb of God was very peeved indeed.

19 April 1993

These shall make war on the Lamb (Revelation xvii, 14)

Shortly before dawn on 19 April, the FBI loudspeakers crackled into action as they had countless times over the fifty-one-day 'Siege of Waco'. Negotiators announced to the sect members behind the barbed-wire fence that this was their last chance to surrender. At the same time an M-60 A1 armoured combat engineering vehicle rumbled up to the perimeter gate. FBI agents got David Koresh on the telephone line, made it quite clear that one way or another the siege was going to end, and urged him to move the children to a place of safety. By way of reply, the Messiah hurled the telephone hand-set through the window.

By these three was the third part of men killed, by the fire, and by the smoke, and by the brimstone which issued out of their mouths (Revelation ix, 18)

As the M-60 reached the walls of the building a hail of gunfire poured from inside. It was a few minutes after six in the morning, and with the helicopter buzzing the compound from the air the first blow was struck at the corner of the building by the vehicle's special hydraulically operated battering ram.

Agents tried one more time: 'This is not an assault. Do not shoot. We are not entering your compound.' Still the crack of gunfire from within the building, and the chink and whine of bullets as they ricocheted harmlessly off the vehicle's armour. Now another CEV trundles up and starts punching holes in the walls, breaking windows . . . another target. 'Do not shoot. You are responsible for your own actions. Come out now and you will not be harmed.' Still the heavily armed cultists responded with everything they had; 'God's marines' were now seeing a bit more real active service.

But even the firepower of a Kalashnikov automatic assault rifle pales into insignificance in the face of the armoury ranged against the Davidians. Tanks with specially adapted cannons were pumping non-lethal tear-gas into the building – toxic enough, so they claimed, to flush out the cultists, but not to kill the children. There was always the hope at this stage that David Koresh, or at least enough of his followers to overrule his authority, would opt for the safety of themselves and their children and surrender. They did not. As FBI negotiator Bob Ricks said: 'Apparently they don't care about their children, and that's unfortunate.' It was.

The federal agents were intending, as they phrased it, 'to continue to gas them and make their lives as uncomfortable as possible until they come out'. Few people could have predicted what happened next.

Then the angel took the censer and filled it with fire of the altar and cast it into the earth (Revelation viii, 5)

It was obvious the CS gas was not going to persuade the Davidians to surrender any more than the threats and promises of the previous seven weeks had. If anything their comradeship in adversity had strengthened the cultists' resolve to stay put until the end. At this stage it is difficult to know what exactly was going on inside the compound, but the cultists must certainly have had gas-masks as part of their huge military arsenal, and in theory at least they could have survived for days wearing them – longer if they could change the filters. For six hours the FBI pumped in gas without noticeable effect. Just once during that time a tank modified with a battering ram returned to the compound and smashed in the main door to the building, drawing more frantic gunfire from cult members inside. At noon the assault started again in earnest, and armoured vehicles began to demolish the already weakened walls of the complex, at one point causing a section of the roof to cave in.

Then it happened.

A small trickle of grey smoke could be seen filtering out from a punched-in window in one of the side towers. Soon orange flames were licking their way around the timber-framed main building fanned by a 30 mph wind blowing off the Texas plains into a blaze which seemed to eat the structure away before one's eyes. Suddenly a huge explosion sent up a fireball and threw blazing wreckage high into the sky – the ammunition dump had blown. There was now no chance at all of saving any part of the building – even had there been any fire engines on stand-by, which there weren't. As soon as the first flames had been sighted, a horrified Bob Ricks shouted out: 'Oh my God, they're killing themselves.' The fire had engulfed the whole complex within minutes. Was this what Armageddon would be like?

Later Special Agent Ricks gave his reconstruction of events to the press: 'Massive amounts of [CS] gas were poured into the compound. Their gas masks by that time had to be failing. They had come to a decision. They were facing either death or having to come out and answer for their crimes. David Koresh gave the order for them to commit suicide and they all did.'

His name that sat on him was Death, and Hell followed with him (Revelation vi, 8)

But did they? Was the promised 'end' of the siege a mass suicide? Because if it wasn't, then the conflagration which by now had razed Ranch Apocalypse to the level of the flatlands which surrounded it must either have been a terrible accident or the direct result of the six-hour tactical attack launched by the FBI. At the height of the fire a few survivors came stumbling out from the inferno, some with their clothes aflame, screaming . . . but all too few. Of the ninety-six Branch Davidians thought to have been trapped in the complex, only nine survived Apocalypse. Reports varied as to how many died – 88, 87, 86, 80, whichever was the true figure, if it was ever known, it was too high.

With a familiar tragi-comic inevitability the villains were suddenly transformed, cleansed by fire, into angels. Gone were the monsters who destroyed families and engaged in perverse sexual relations with children; or at best a bunch of wackos the world could do without. Now they were reborn as innocent God-fearing men and women exercising their right to follow their chosen religion and to raise their children as they thought right. Some observers could even be seen shaking their heads and invoking the time-honoured right of the American people to bear arms, and use them to protect themselves and their land – even against the might of the US authorities. Heads would roll for this.

There was a glimmer of a theory in the early days to support the accusation that the FBI attack had caused the fire at Ranch Apocalypse. The few cultists who managed to survive the blaze by getting out early were beginning to talk. According to one of them, the cult had been using oil lamps to provide light, and, when the army tanks had begun to batter down the walls, a lamp was knocked to the ground and started a fire. Almost simple enough to be true.

But nothing is ever that simple, and when the numbness and shock had begun to evaporate and hard information started to be gathered and analysed, a very different story began to see the light of day. A number of FBI agents keeping the final showdown under surveillance reported seeing a man dressed in black and wearing a gas mask making throwing motions just before the fire started; the implication being that he might have been hurling a burning torch. It was a theory which gained some credence when one of the surviving cultists, a twenty-nine-year-old British man named Renos Avraam said that while he was in the compound he heard someone he thought was David Koresh shout, 'The fire has been lit, the fire has been lit.' Another survivor told how, as the flames began to engulf the building, Koresh told his disciples: 'Stay put. Just sit back and wait until you see God. God is coming.' Then it was announced that by a supreme irony two of the surviving nine cult members were the very disciples who had set the fires. It was beginning to look as though the FBI was in the clear; at least as far as the charge of fire-raising was concerned.

The finger was now pointing at David Koresh. People were beginning to have eerie recollections of previous threats. Remember his 'second message from God', the one that promised the enemies of the Lamb of God would be 'devoured by fire and destroyed'? Well, there had been fire and destruction all right – shame it was the faithful who had been destroyed. Now a magazine had found a former cult member with an even more chilling tale of prediction: way back, Koresh had told Mark Breault, 'When I die, the world will watch. Man, when I die it's gonna be the biggest thing anyone has ever seen – it's gonna be a blaze.' According to Breault, the reasoning behind it all was that 'by dying in the flames, [members] would see the Devil, then pass through the flames and be cleansed; he said he gave us a chance to visit Hell – and then pass through to Heaven.'

But this strength of conviction – on David Koresh's part at least – that fire cleansed, and opened the gate to paradise, raised another question that no one really wanted to contemplate: what if it were not a suicide pact; what if reluctant disciples had wanted to get out, to save themselves and their children? Would Koresh have made the decision to emigrate to Heaven for them? Mass suicide or mass murder?

20 April 1993

'Cult leaders shot people trying to flee', according to one headline; 'How we fled the maniac's bullets', yelled another. It was known that during the course of the fifty-one-day siege the FBI and special forces had been at work installing some very sophisticated electronic gadgetry around the Mount Carmel compound. One of these was a parabolic microphone system, the Vendo-Dyne 1800, used for acoustical penetration; in other words a highly sensitive bugging device which could pick up conversations from inside the cult headquarters. It was now revealed that one of Koresh's murder plans had been to strap grenades to his body, walk out of the compound and when FBI agents came to arrest him pull the pins and blow himself and them to smithereens. One senior federal agent in charge of the Waco operation revealed that, according to information received over the listening devices, the cultists were at first very calm after they fled from the tear-gas attack down into the concrete bunker beneath the watchtower in the middle of the compound. However, when the siege tanks with their battering rams pierced the bunker, Koresh ordered the mass suicide, shouting, 'We are on our way to God!' There were also reports of the sound of gunfire during the time the fire was spreading; this was subsequently quoted as confirmation that reluctant martyrs were shot by Koresh and his élite guard.

One of the obstacles to such speculation becoming established scientific fact was the state of the burned-out compound. For a start the rubble was still far too hot for the vital fingertip search for bodies and clues. And there was the ever-present danger to search teams posed by explosions of live ammunition. It was therefore decided to leave the site to cool down overnight before any scientific and medical experts were allowed in.

Meanwhile, on the political front the Clinton administration was coming in for increasingly vociferous criticism over the FBI's handling of the whole Waco affair. They may have been exonerated from torching the cultists, but the question everybody wanted answered was why, with an unpredictable, unstable madman inside there, no one had thought he might just be crazy enough to start his own Apocalypse. After all, there had been enough indications over the days of the stand-off that Koresh might do just that. The FBI, though, had gambled on the likelihood that under such pressure as the tear-gas assault and the possible danger to the children, cult members would leave the compound. President Clinton's newly appointed Attorney General, Janet Reno, was under special pressure to explain why she and FBI chief William Sessions had condoned this course of action rather than continue the waiting game, as many seasoned hostage negotiators had suggested. They could always add the aggravation factor with nothing more deadly than the dentist's drill and Nancy Sinatra. Why was tear-gas used at all, and why were there no fire engines anywhere near the scene of the fire? The answer to the last question was easy: nobody had told the local fire chief at Waco what was going on. It was only when they received a regular 911 emergency call that firefighters knew there was a fire. By the end of the night Janet Reno had offered her resignation, and the FBI was offering a low-key apology for 'misjudging' the situation. As for President Clinton, he was fulsome in his support for his Attorney General, telling her: 'You should sleep well. You did a great job.' Needless to say, the President declined to accept Ms Reno's resignation, preferring instead almost to take responsibility himself: 'It is not possible,' he said, 'for the President to distance himself from things when the federal government is in control.'

One of the most vociferous critics of the 'final solution' to the Waco problem was an almost hysterical Mrs Bonnie Haldeman, Koresh's mother. 'The FBI pushed him too far,' she sobbed. But Jeff Jamar, FBI senior agent in overall control of the siege was adamant: 'These people did not die because of our actions. They died because Koresh had them killed. What if we had gone another ninety days and had children dying of hunger and disease? As horrible as it was, I think Koresh always had the same end in mind.'

21 April 1993

And the devil that deceived them was cast into the lake of fire and brimstone, where the beast and the false prophet are, and shall be tormented day and night for ever and ever (Revelation xx, 10)

As dawn broke over the still-smouldering ruins of Ranch Apocalypse, FBI teams formed up in the still acrid, smoky morning air, and medical experts began to arrive from Fort Worth two hours away. They were about to undertake the preliminary search for bodies. Compared with the job which was to come later – identifying the corpses – this was the easy part. As with all mass disasters where visual identification is impossible, heavy reliance would be placed on the skills of the forensic odontologist, or dentist, in comparing surviving dentition with ante-mortem dental charts. By the end of the day forty bodies had been lifted from the charred debris; and there was a rumour that three of the corpses had suffered gunshot wounds. According to Justice Department spokesman Carl Stern: 'The head of one victim was virtually blown away'; another had a bullet wound in the forehead. Whether this proved that potential escapees were shot or whether individuals preferred the speed of the bullet to the slow agony of roasting to death was a matter for speculation.

Meanwhile, the much publicised made-for-TV film 'Assault on Waco . . .', the story of David Koresh's life and rise to notoriety, as sold by his mother, was taking shape just north of Texas in the state of Oklahoma, where the replica of Ranch Apocalypse was receiving its last lick of paint. 'Hot, hot, hot!' was the way the story was described by the show's producer; perhaps not the best choice of phrase in the circumstances! The actor who got to play the late wacko from Waco is Tim Daly (no, nor had I, he is the younger brother of 'Cagney and Lacey' star Tyne Daly – and he is the spitting image of David Koresh).

22 April 1993

As though the whole Waco affair were not already turning into a black comedy, the British tabloids had been doing a bit of in-depth research of their own. 'Koresh Guns Bought with British Dole Money', squawked *Today*, in what it described as 'Another Exclusive'. The story read, in part: 'Social Security Giro cheques were regularly mailed to the Britons inside the Waco compound in Texas. The money was confiscated by Koresh and used to buy the guns with which the Branch Davidians held FBI agents at bay for 51 days.' Not all the guns, surely? Another popular daily had already told us that 'The Deadly Arsenal' included '123 AR-15 and 44 AK47 assault rifles, 26 M1 rifles and two huge Barrett .50 calibre "Manstoppers" ' (like those used by the IRA to shoot squaddies in Ulster), as well as the hundreds of grenades, handguns, rifles, rocket launchers and so on stocked by any self-respecting group of Christians. And so, in the desperate attempt to share the blame around, the British Department of Social Security found itself in the frame and promising an investigation into the allegations.

There was also mounting controversy over the alleged 'executions' which took place inside the compound on that fatal day. While one report claimed that a 'Pathologist rejects claims that Koresh ordered shootings', another upped the scandal stakes by insisting that 'Crazed cult leader David Koresh herded 17 children into a room and shot them one by one.' Curioser and curioser! But there was more to come, as one 'exclusive' followed another, and counterclaim followed claim. 'Koresh shot dead before flames destroyed our ranch.' The source was Derek Lovelock, one of two Britons to have escaped the flames, and who was now languishing in the county jail awaiting charges. According to Lovelock, he didn't actually see his Master being shot, but assumed that the FBI had done the shooting. Preposterous? Well, not entirely; medical evidence later emerged that supported the story of Koresh being shot before the flames reached him. But the FBI did not pull the trigger.

23 April 1993
An official obituary to David Koresh appeared in only one British newspaper, the *Independent*. Compiled by Malise Ruthven, it began: 'David Koresh, who died in the fire that engulfed the Branch Davidian compound in Waco, Texas, on Monday – survivors' accounts indicate that he was caught in the fire, although it now appears his body may never be identified – presents the almost classic case of the doomsday prophet in a culture that produces them with catastrophic regularity...'

It was a fact that identifying the badly burned bodies was going to present a problem to the medical teams. To the accompaniment of the tolling of local church bells, investigators poked amid the debris for corpses which were then wrapped and zipped into body bags. The authorities had driven refrigerated trailer units to the scene to act as impromptu mortuaries, and to transport the remains up to Fort Worth. In many cases, it would be beyond even the most modern miracles of forensic medicine, such as DNA, to lead to identification.

Dr Rodney Crow, a leading forensic odontologist, said at a

press conference: 'There are no faces on some of [the victims]. They have turned to powder. Hopefully, the teeth, taking much higher temperatures to destroy, will be in this debris.' At the same time, Dr Crow confirmed that the bunker beneath the watchtower where many of the bodies were found was 'thigh high' with weapons and ammunition. Some of the ravaged bodies were reportedly still clutching on to fire-blackened guns with which they intended to repulse the federal invaders. A constant threat to the masked searchers as they moved painstakingly through the charred rubble were the tens of thousands of rounds of unstable live ammunition still scattered around the blockade area of the compound, which at any moment could be heat-activated. A bizarre effect was now being created on the soot-covered ground by the incongruously cheerful-looking orange flags dotted over the compound to mark the spots where bodies too badly burned to be salvaged lay.

24 April 1993

On Saturday, forensic dentist Rodney Crow was back in the news. Autopsies had suggested that there was medical evidence for the theory that some of the Waco victims had been 'executed'. Dr Crow said post-mortem examinations carried out on two of the bodies recovered from Mount Carmel showed that a single bullet had entered the back of the victims' heads and exited through the front. This forensic evidence was important not only because it established shooting as a fact, but because it excluded, in these cases at least, the suicide theory – nobody shoots themself through the back of the head!

The tanks and armoured vehicles had gone now. There was a memorial service for the dead of Ranch Apocalypse, but hardly anybody turned up. One woman was quoted as saying: 'Don't cry for David Koresh – I'd hang him.' Too late. Anger, frustration, fear, hatred . . . all the emotions had served their turn here in Waco over the past seven weeks; and as the brisk, warm Texas winds began to clear the air of the acrid smell of burning, a new emotion skulked in – embarrassment. Almost ninety people had died needlessly, seventeen of them children. Faces were red – right up to the White House. Everybody wanted to know WHY? Why didn't the FBI just sit it out, as hostage negotiators the world over would, in hindsight, have advised. After all, they had nothing to lose. Nobody was going anywhere. One thing was certain, the FBI's 'psychological profile' assuring the ground troops that David Koresh was not the sort to commit suicide was way off the mark. Murray Miron, a specialist in offender profiling, had suggested that Koresh was too cowardly to risk physical pain and too egotistical to die a martyr. It was also reported that Mr Miron thought the Davidians were unlikely to surrender and that the FBI should take 'positive action sooner rather than later; further delays would increase rather than reduce the danger'. Retrospectively Murray Miron defended his analysis of the situation by insisting that Koresh must have thought he would be miraculously shielded from the flames. Well, they were both wrong.

26 April 1993

Bicker amongst themselves as they might, neither the FBI and the authorities on one hand, nor the surviving cultists and their supporters on the other, had so far explained what *exactly* had happened. In other words, who was to *blame*? Some came right out with it: 'FBI Responsible for Waco Massacre' (on one side), or 'Cult Started Fire' (on the other).

But most of the media was uncomfortably aware of what it called 'Unforgivable Mistakes'. For example: even assuming that official investigators were right and the fire was set from inside the compound by cultists themselves, then where were the firefighters to cope with the blaze once it started? They were back in the sleepy little fire station at Waco; according to the experts David Koresh was just not the sort to commit suicide, so they didn't bother to alert the fire chief. But while Houston's assistant chief fire inspector, Paul Gray, was telling the press that the fire was started simultaneously in at least two places using flammable liquids after the last FBI assault on the compound, lawyers representing the surviving Branch Davidians were crying 'Cover-up'. 'Until I see the evidence from an independent, impartial expert, I choose to believe the first-hand account of witnesses who were in the centre, who said there was no fire started by the Branch Davidians,' said Jack Zimmermann.

1–4 May 1993
By now the whole Waco business had become rather stale news; the world had other disasters to feed on. What once might have made banner headlines in the international press, was now relegated to a small paragraph in the *Daily Telegraph's* 'World in Brief' column on 1 May: 'Gun wounds to 12 Waco bodies'. The number of those shot through the head had risen to five. The total number of bodies recovered according to the medical examiner was seventy-two, though identification was proving all but impossible.

However, one piece of identification was given priority. There had been rumours circulating ever since the fire that somehow, miraculously of course, David Koresh had escaped – just as a Messiah might. With remarkable skill and tenacity a group of forensic anthropologists pieced together a shattered skull found in the kitchen area of Mount Carmel compound. Comparisons of the dental remains of this skull with David Koresh's dental records proved a positive match. The skull was his. But there was an even more startling revelation: the skull had a bullet entry wound in the centre of its forehead. David Koresh *had* been shot before the flames reached him; the question was, who pulled the trigger?

Details also began to emerge of the way the Branch Davidians treated their children – or, rather, the way David Koresh treated *his* children. According to their own accounts, the surviving offspring of ages ranging between a few years and teenage had endured, apparently without question but with considerable fear, an almost cruelly authoritarian regime under Koresh. Minor 'misdemeanours' – such as spilling some milk – were punished by beating with a stick called 'the helper'; physical evidence of this, in the form of weals and marks on the children's buttocks, was available to the child-care workers. But the most sinister finding of all was that girls as young as eleven were made to wear a yellow plastic Star of David badge – a sign that they were ready to indulge in sex with Koresh. By comparison, the boys had it easy: they were just endlessly trained in the use of guns and explosives.

And so, for a while at least, the matter rested. A United States Justice Department inquiry was set up under Deputy Attorney General Philip Heymann: 'To undertake a generalised assessment of what can be learned from the incident.'

With the blessing of hindsight, perhaps this was, after all, a very American tragedy – a combination of gurus, guns and gung-ho quite unrepeatable on another continent. Jeff Jama, the FBI operational chief at Waco told reporters after the holocaust: 'In England you would have ended it two days after it had begun, in Germany two hours after. The Israelis would have done the same. But we live in a country where everyone second-guesses everything you do. We were in a no-win situation.'

And nobody did.

THE PEOPLE'S TEMPLE

Jimba, murder and mass suicide at Jonestown

James Warren Jones was born in the small mid-western town of Lynn, Indiana on 13 May 1931. His first sermon was preached to a group of children when Jones was just twelve years old. When his parents separated in 1945, Jimba went to live with his mother until he married at the age of eighteen. Although he dropped out of Indiana University after just a year, Jones earned a degree at night school while preaching hellfire-and-damnation during the day. When he left the Methodist Church over doctrinal differences (truth to tell, the Methodists were beginning to find Jim a mite too weird), Jones determined to found his own church.

In order to raise money to purchase a building, he entered the extraordinary trade of selling spider monkeys door-to-door. Clearly more people wanted these strange pets than one might have thought, because in 1951 Jones opened his People's Temple Church in a broken-down black district of Indianapolis. At the same time he affiliated to the Disciples of Christ, a mainstream Christian group, which entitled him to be ordained as a minister. From the beginning Jones was very much the poor people's preacher, and his church became a haven for the homeless and hungry of the neighbourhood ethnic community. He opened two care centres for the sick and elderly, and to prove there was no hypocrisy in his actions, Jones and his wife adopted three ethnic children themselves.

By the mid-1950s, the Reverend Jim Jones was beginning to display some disturbing psychological behaviour. He added reincarnation to his collection of beliefs, and unaccountably took against the Bible. Despite this he still referred to himself as 'God's Heir on Earth', and attracted large crowds with his bogus 'healing' services.

In 1964 Jones had a revelation and announced to his congregation that the end of the world was nigh, that planet earth would be destroyed by a thermonuclear explosion on 15 July 1967. Of course, those that followed the Reverend Jim Jones would be saved. So they followed him, out of Indiana to a 'safe' spot in Northern California. Where he bused his congregation to a new church – another haven for the oddballs, the disadvantaged and the impoverished ethnic minorities. In 1975 Jones's influence among black voters was recognised when the mayor of San Francisco elected him on to the city housing authority.

By now Jones had introduced an unhealthy sexual element into his meetings and was enjoying intercourse with a large proportion of his congregation. But something more sinister than all this Bible-thumping mumbo-jumbo was afoot. The People's Temple had a hidden agenda. In 1976 Jones began elaborating on the use of mass suicide as an expression of political dissidence – 'revolutionary suicide' he called it. At a New Year's Day meeting, Jones decided to put the loyalty of his followers to the test – he wanted them all to drink poison, or so he said. For those who were hesitant, the Reverend Jones staged a little charade acted out by members of his 'élite guard', his 'inner circle': a plant in the congregation would refuse to drink the liquid and make as if to run away, then one of Jim's guards would 'shoot' him. So everybody ended up taking a swig of this quite innocuous drink. But Jim Jones had proved his point.

Although his prophecy of Armageddon embarrassingly failed to come true, Jones's credibility was not diminished, nor indeed was his bank balance. With proceeds given by the faithful (in fact, all their worldly possessions), Jones invested $1 million in a tract of Amazon rain forest in Guyana. 'Utopia'.

Once the faithful had made the one-way trip to what was officially, if immodestly, known as Jonestown, and had constructed a few rudimentary buildings, the Reverend and his band of élite, and armed, guards put the screws on. Defection was forbidden, and most of those who did manage to escape Jones's clutches mysteriously ended up dead. Jones and his cronies also began to indulge in some even more bizarre sexual activities, with Jones taking the pick of both genders. Any perceived misdemeanours, such as nodding off during one of the Reverend's interminable rambling sermons, were punished with public beatings and torture. With such strength Jones himself was becoming more than a little unbalanced; the power he once controlled was now controlling him; in short, he was on his way to becoming a card-carrying psychopath. One report stated that electrodes were attached to children who failed to smile at the mention of the Leader's name.

Although news of these goings-on did gradually leak out of Jonestown and find ears in the United States, they were deaf ears, and nobody paid much attention to what a lot of hippies and weirdos were up to in the South American jungle. Good riddance seemed to be the general sentiment. One man who did pay attention to the rumours was Congressman Leo Ryan. Ryan collected together a fact-finding party of lawyers, journalists and a few concerned relatives of cult members and, on 17 November 1978 they boarded a chartered aeroplane bound for Jonestown, Guyana.

The trip looked to be a great success, the cult members were on their most civilised behaviour, and the guests were treated royally, graced by a guided tour from Reverend Jim Jones himself. Then towards the end of the visit, the scouting party saw the other side of cult life. A reporter made the mistake of pressing Jones on the purpose of the heavily armed guards; Jones had to be restrained from attacking him. Then an elderly woman approached Congressman Ryan and begged him to take her back to the United States with them. This started a stampede and before long Ryan was surrounded by disaffected cult members wanting to make the trip back home. In the middle of this commotion, one of Jones's enforcers tried to stab Leo Ryan.

When he was pulled off, the visiting party regrouped and took to their heels. Or rather, piled hastily into their jeep and made for the airstrip where their plane was waiting. Before they reached safety, however, Ryan and his group were overtaken by gun-toting goons from Jonestown, and in the shoot-out which followed, three journalists, three fleeing cult members and Congressman Ryan were left dead on the tarmac.

Meanwhile, back at Jonestown, the tannoy system was blaring out an order across the compound: 'Alert, alert, alert!' Jones gathered the faithful around him and warned that it was only a matter of time before the military and the CIA parachuted down from the sky into their camp. 'If we can't live in peace, then let us die in peace . . . Take the potion as they did in ancient Greece. This is a revolutionary act . . .'

At shortly after 5.30 p.m. on 18 November 1978, 913 members of the cult known as the People's Temple, including 260 children, drank Kool-Aid laced with cyanide. Mothers began feeding it to their babies through syringes; children and adults drank the lethal liquid from paper cups. Those who showed a lack of enthusiasm to join the 'political dissent' were encouraged to do the right thing by armed guards. Then the guards drank. Within five minutes of taking the poison they lay dead where they fell. Reverend Jim Jones, one in a long line of mad messiahs, was among them.

At least, that is one version of events. Attorney Mark Lane, who was with the fact-finding team headed by Congressman Ryan, addressed a press conference on 20 November at Georgetown, Guyana. He told representatives of the world's media that while the population of Jonestown gathered to commit 'suicide', he counted eighty-five bursts of fire from automatic weapons. Reverend Jones called out: 'Mother, mother, mother!' Then, according to Mark Lane's statement, 'there were the first bursts of gunfire'. He and fellow attorney Charles Garry fled into the jungle from where they heard 'lots of gunfire and people screaming, including children'. Suicide or murder? Or a bit of both?

Of course no human tragedy of this magnitude would be complete without its conspiracy theories. The strongest was that

Marina Tsvygun in her cult costume. (*Popperfoto*)

The charred remains of Joseph Di Mambro's Morin Heights home. (*Popperfoto*)

The scene at the Solar Temple's headquarters in Cheiry, Switzerland, on 5 October 1994. (*Popperfoto*)

The Great Seal of the
Knights Templar.

Luc Jouret. (*Popperfoto*)

The underground chapel at
Cheiry. (*Popperfoto*)

Matthew Hopkins,
Witchfinder-General.
(*Mary Evans Picture
Library*)

¶ The Apprehenſion and confeſſion
of three notorious Witches.

Arreigned and by Iuſtice condemned and
executed at *Chelmeſ-forde*, in the Countye of
Eſſex, the *5.* day of *Iulye*, *laſt paſt.*
1 5 8 9.

¶ With the manner of their diueliſh practices and keeping of their
ſpirits, whoſe fourmes are heerein truelye
proportioned,

IOAN PRENTIS
& hir Bid.

TACKE

GILL

Public executions following
Matthew Hopkins' investigation of
the Chelmsford Witches.

Jones photographed shortly before the events leading to his sect's mass suicide. (*Topham*)

The seat used by Jim Jones in Jonestown's main temple. (*Popperfoto*)

THOSE WHO DO
REMEMBER THE P
ARE CONDEMNE
TO REPEAT IT

An unsuspecting
traveller falls victim to
a gang of Thugs.

Preparation for 'squassation', the torture undergone by burgomaster
Johannes Junius.

Charles Manson. (*Topham*)

Three of Manson's 'Family':
(*left to right*) Patricia Krenwinkel,
Susan Atkins and Leslie Van
Houten. (*Popperfoto*)

Jeffrey Lundgren.
(*Associated Press*)

Weapons seized by
Federal agents in
connection with the
Lundgren case.
(*Associated Press/Topha*

the massacre was a plot by the American Government working through the CIA to destroy the People's Temple. It was certainly a fact that Reverend Jones was a known Communist and that, as the result of what he called 'persecution' by the US Government, he was considering transferring Jonestown to the Soviet Union. He had already made firm contacts with the Soviet embassy. However, what was being alleged was even more fantastic. Claims were made that the CIA's mind-control programme, MK-ULTRA (the notorious 'LSD in your coffee' episode in which, it was alleged, unknowing subjects were fed the drug lysergic acid diethylamide to test its hallucinogenic properties), had been used at Jonestown, despite assurances that the experiments had ceased in 1973. In their *50 Greatest Conspiracies of All Time*, Vankin and Whalen state that one of Congressman Leo Ryan's aides, among others, suspects that the MK-ULTRA programme had not been disbanded, but adapted for continued use against cults such as the People's Temple.

Appendix 1: '. . . a feeling of freedom . . .'

The following quotations are taken from a publicity booklet with the above title published by the People's Temple in about 1978, shortly before the massacre. It is a collection of photographs and comments about the Jonestown community by residents and visitors.

My impressions are, having just experienced our visit there that this is a beautiful, heroic, creative project. It is absolutely miraculous. There are excellent medical services, excellent educational services, and it's a community of caring and sharing with an added dimension, and this dimension, I would say, is Love – if you want to use that term. In a sense it reminds me of a New Testament community in the purest sense of the word, in the love and concern for all, that we observed. And with complete freedom for creativity! Those who want to farm are

87

farming; those who wish to teach, teach; those who like to cook, cook. They have an excellent nutritionist who is working scientifically all the time to discover new uses for the indigenous plants and growths there, and is in contact with the Guyanese experts to discover new and useful uses for these various crops. It was most impressive to see the elderly people, the older folks, who had their neat little yards, their white picket-type fences, and their opportunity to take classes if they wished to, or just to sit . . . One of the reporters asked a resident: 'Would you think it's rather Utopian here?' She replied: 'Oh yes, a lovely Utopia.'

Barbara Moore (wife of the Reverend John Moore, United Methodist Church)

I was impressed by the medical center particularly. All of the older citizens live around the medical compound. The medical compound is something you have never seen and you probably won't see unless you go there. It's almost a miracle. This young doctor, who was trained by the temple, graduated with high honours from the University of California at Irvine, has performed miracles. Every morning at eight o'clock, someone knocks on the door and asks: 'Did anybody have any difficulties last night?' Can you imagine the feeling of security that these folks have, to feel that somebody cares for them, is interested in them, and will do things for them?

Charles Garry (attorney who subsequently defended survivors against murder charges)

I have changed my last name. I am now Tobi Mtendaji. My middle name is Chekevu. Put together these two words mean Happy Worker in Swahili. I am now on the construction crew building these beautiful cottages the family lives in. I guess I am just now bringing out my talents here.

Tobi Mtendaji (resident of Jonestown)

Appendix 2: 'Jonestown'

The following is an extract from a ditty said to be popular among the up-state New York rugby clubs. It is sung to the tune of 'Downtown'.

When you're down and you're broke, and your religion's a
    joke,
Why don't you go and see
Jim Jones.
When your life's incomplete, there's only one man to meet,
Why don't you go and see
Jim Jones.

Refrain
Watch him mix the Kool-Aid in the vat so lethal,
Listen to the anguished cries of all the dying people.
Everyone dies.
The Rev's the most gracious host,
So, lift up your glasses, the ultimate toast,
(So, lift up your glasses, the dirge of the masses),
You're in Jonestown.
Drink with the Reverend Jim.
Jonestown.
Chances are mighty slim.
Jonestown.
People are dropping like flies.

Congressman Ryan, on a mission of spyin',
Would not drink with
Jim Jones.
Such a public disgrace, they had to blow off his face,
'Cause he would not drink with
Jim Jones.

Refrain

First you cough and you wheeze, then you drop to your
  knees,
From drinking Kool-Aid, with
Jim Jones.
You arrive back in the States, decomposed in your crates,
From drinking Kool-Aid, with
Jim Jones.

Refrain

Jonestown, Jonestown, Jones . . . (*repeat in diminuendo*)

AUM SHINRI KYO
(SUPREME TRUTH SECT)

Shoko Asahara, the Tokyo subway and the 'poor man's atom bomb'

It would be difficult to conceive of a more horrific nightmare. Imagine, if you can, rush-hour on one of the world's busiest underground railway systems. Trains, as usual, are packed so tight that it is all but impossible to breathe. Without warning a deadly cloud of choking poison gas begins to spread through the carriage. Within minutes the station is swarming with a panicking mass of nauseous, asphyxiating passengers desperately trying to locate the exits. They leave behind the dead and the dying.

That was the scene when, at just after 8.00 a.m. on 20 March 1995, terrorists planted twenty-one containers of nerve gas on five trains of the Teito rapid transport system which serves Tokyo city. The lines hit were the Hibya, Marunouchi and Chiyoda which converge on Kasumigaseki main station below most of the city's legal and governmental centres. An act described by the authorities as 'indiscriminate murder' left ten people dead and at least 5,000 others in need of hospital treatment, many with serious respiratory illnesses. Further thousands of commuters suffered lesser symptoms such as dizziness, temporary eye dysfunctions and coughing. In all sixteen stations were closed as chemical warfare specialists descended into the subway.

The poison gas, later analysed as the nerve gas sarin, had been disguised in lunch boxes and soft-drinks cartons. The gas, which has been called 'the poor man's atom bomb', had been developed by German scientists during the Second World War and stockpiled by all the major powers at the time of the Cold War. It is claimed that the United States military is sitting on 15,000 tons, with 400,000 rockets with nerve gas warheads. In fact it is absurdly easy, if dangerous, to manufacture sarin, and a minute droplet could kill. It certainly worked for Adolf Hitler in 'clearing' the Nazi death camps; and it worked for Saddam Hussein when he needed to 'clear' Kurdish villages. The reason why the Tokyo subway incident did not result in more fatalities was due solely to its distribution as a vaporous gas, not exploded into wide-spreading droplets. Still, the result in Tokyo was ghastly enough.

Within hours of the attack the ruthlessly efficient Metropolitan Police Department had drafted in 10,000 officers. Nor did it take long to identify a likely suspect. Or, rather, a large number of suspects collected under a single name – Aum Shinri Kyo, a cult led by one Shoko Asahara.

Stunning as it was to the world, let alone the terrified commuters of Tokyo, this was not the first incident of its kind. Forget Adolf Hitler; forget Saddam Hussein. It was a repeat on a major scale of an incident in Japan less than twelve months previously. On 27 June 1994 Yoshiyuki Kouno and his wife Sumiko were spending a quiet evening at their home in the resort town of Matsumoto. Quite suddenly Mrs Kouno became ill and was seized with convulsions. Checking the back yard because the dogs had been barking, her husband found one of them dead and the other with fatal spasms. Meanwhile, the emergency services were dealing with hundreds of other cases in which people were suffering breathing difficulties, nausea and problems with their eyesight. In total, eight patients died; Sumiko Kouno remains in a coma with irreversible brain damage. By 3 July traces of isopropyl methyl phosphonofluoridate (sarin) had been identified as the cause of the poisoning. Although the case was never satisfactorily solved, it did not escape notice that among the deaths were three judges involved in a case centring around land purchase by the Aum Shinri Kyo.

In common with most religious cults Aum Shinri Kyo is a

patchwork of scraps of other faiths. Aum relies heavily on Hindu and Tibetan ritual practices, and venerates Shiva, god of destruction and renewal. Its founder, 'Guru' Shoko Asahara (real name Chizuo Matsumoto) was born the fourth of seven children in Kumamoto in the south of Japan in March 1955. Partially sighted, Asahara received most of his schooling at an institution for the blind. He claims to have achieved enlightenment while on a trip to the Himalayas, and shortly after his return founded the cult. He purports to be able to levitate – a state of grace which is offered to disciples in return for drinking the Leader's blood and semen. And handing over all their worldly possessions. Devotees believe that the world will end in 1997, but not for them. They will be spared destruction in order to rule.

Five years after establishing Aum Shinri Kyo, Asahara applied for, and got, recognition as a religious foundation from the Tokyo metropolitan government – with all the tax benefits which go with it. The faithful then set about building a headquarters complex at Kamikuishiki close to Mount Fuji. Signs that the cult might not be as benign as they would have the authorities believe began when residents of the village demanded Aum's expulsion from the area.

Early in 1990 Shoko Asahara and a couple of dozen of his followers contested seats for the Lower House of Parliament – with signal lack of success. This might in part have to do with the candidates campaigning wearing masks with Asahara's face painted on them. Toward the end of the year, in October, Aum was back in the national news when seven leading members were arrested on charges of violating land-use laws.

One of the extraordinary successes of Aum's evangelism was its spread to Russia. Asahara opened a branch in Moscow in 1992, and by the time of the Tokyo attack it was 300,000 strong – three times the number in Japan. The move was not entirely altruistic on the Leader's part: Russia was the origin of the stockpile of firearms held by the cult. There is also some reason to believe reports that Asahara had his eye on nuclear and bacteriological weapons from the same source.

In 1994 the mysterious poisoning at Matsumoto occurred, followed in twelve months by the discovery of sarin residue in the Aum compound at Kamikuishiki. Unsurprisingly the cultists protested that it was the local people trying to murder *them*. But the Supreme Truth sect had been attracting unwelcome attention for other lapses of good citizenship. A hotel manager accused five members, including his own daughter, of trying to extort money from him. A Tokyo notary was abducted when his sister attempted to leave the sect. And on 19 March 1995 – the day before the subway attack – three Aum followers were arrested in connection with the abduction of a student.

In the days which followed the underground gassing, thousands of police officers and detectives nationwide raided buildings maintained by the Aum Shinri Kyo. Although a number of the sect's followers were detained and charged with minor misdemeanours, Shoko Asahara had wisely gone into hiding, abandoning several of his luxury cars at a Tokyo hotel. What had been an obscure quasi-Buddhist apocalyptical cult was now the most talked about subject in Japan. For their part, Aum Shinri Kyo insisted that the government had been responsible for the gas attack in order to discredit the cult's followers.

The police raids were beginning to tell a different story. Dressed in bright orange safety suits and carrying caged canaries so familiar to miners throughout the world, officers entered the Aum headquarters to test for poisonous fumes. The birds lived to tell the tale, and the search teams removed vast quantities of toxic chemicals and laboratory equipment. Enough, one report claimed, to kill ten million people. That was not all they found. Police were able to release half a dozen people who had been forcibly detained, and arrange medical treatment for a further fifty who were suffering from malnutrition after not being allowed to eat for a week.

There was still no trace of the elusive Shoko Asahara, though he did broadcast a message via Japan's Radio Press Agency: 'Followers, the time to arise and help me is now. When facing death you must do it with no regrets.' He also took the opportunity to accuse the government of plotting to kill sect members and pass it off as a suicide pact. Like many another mad messiah, Asahara was demonstrating an alarming level of paranoia.

Although this was not officially ratified, reports were beginning to leak out that forensic scientists had confirmed that the seized chemicals could have been used to manufacture sarin. Furthermore, with the use of gas chromatography it had been possible to link those chemicals with the gas used at Matsumoto and Tokyo. Still the sect denied involvement. In fact a lawyer representing Aum Shinri Kyo proclaimed that the substances were part of a self-sufficiency drive aimed at providing such items as plastic containers, toothpaste and fertilizer for their agricultural programme. Tactfully, the authorities were avoiding use of the word 'murder', but were arresting cultists on charges relating to the illegal imprisonment of individuals at the Mount Fuji compound. Even by the middle of April there were no homicide charges, though in Japan's biggest post-war alert 100,000 police were assigned to security operations. This was a direct reaction to Aum's threat that another 'horrible event' was looming, one 'that will make the Kobe earthquake seem as minor as a fly landing on your face'. As it turned out, Tokyo was spared a further atrocity, though police confirmed that Shoko Asahara was quoted in a diary found at the scene of a raid as saying: 'Making sarin is a very risky business; when doing it you must have a lot of courage.'

The 'horrible event' did not take place in Japan's capital, but in Yokohama on 19 April, on the city's underground system. At 12.45 p.m. a sulphurous gas was released on to the concourse, though more than 300 passengers requiring hospital treatment did not report symptoms similar to those caused by sarin. Nevertheless, rumour abounded that Aum Shinri Kyo was responsible for this fresh outrage, though the cult, as ever, strenuously denied it.

While the people of Japan were reeling from the most recent attack, children taken into protective care during the police raids on Aum's headquarters were beginning to describe their bizarre life-style. They received scant nourishment and were only allowed about four hours sleep at night. The day was mostly spent learning the sect's religious theories. In order to help this process along, the youngsters were obliged to wear battery-operated headsets which sent electronic pulses to the brain. Apparently this was to enable them to share the same brainwaves as the 'Venerable Master'. One inexplicable feature was that some of the children had their eyebrows dyed green.

At the beginning of May the police located Shoko Asahara in one of the cult's buildings. Shortly afterwards Masami Tsuchiya admitted to being in charge of Aum Shinri Kyo's chemical experiments, and to making sarin gas. On 15 May, in one of a series of dawn raids across Japan, police officers arrested Shoko Asahara. He had been hiding in a small secret chamber in the Mount Fuji commune. Despite his continued protestations of innocence and refusal to answer questions, police felt they had sufficient evidence in the form of confessions by cult members to charge the guru with murder and attempted murder. The indictments related to the Tokyo gas attack. Other leading members of Aum will be joining him in separate trials.

The trial of forty-year-old Shoko Asahara was scheduled to open on 26 October 1995. However, in a deliberate delaying tactic, the cult leader dismissed his lawyer. The charges were eventually heard in June 1996, too late for inclusion here. However, on 19 June Shoko Asahara announced, through his daughter, that he had handed the leadership of Aum Shinri Kyo to his two sons. They are aged three and two.

CHURCH OF JESUS CHRIST OF LATTER-DAY SAINTS (MORMONS)

The Mormon Church provides the perfect example of many basic cult characteristics. For a start it demonstrates the way in which a belief can be at direct variance with a host government and its citizens. In the case of the Mormons it was the practice of polygamy. It also shows how, as the result of this conflict, the faithful will feel persecuted, leading to a sense of deep resentment and a climate in which violence might erupt. This last point will in some cases also explain the need some cults feel to cut themselves off physically as well as spiritually in order to build their own communities.

Joseph Smith had, since childhood, laid claims to visionary experiences but his major coup came with the publication in 1830 of the *Book of Mormon*. According to Joseph Smith, he had a few years previously encountered an angel named Moroni who directed him to the hiding place of a sequence of inscribed gold tablets. (For those interested in geographical detail, they were inside a hill at Palmyra, New York State.) With the aid of instructions from the angel and encouragement from his wife, Smith translated the oracle. The *Book of Mormon* purports to contain divine revelations given to the eponymous prophet telling of the history of a 'chosen people' who arrived in America from Jerusalem before even the official native Americans. It is not surprising, then, given such a storyline, that Joseph Smith decided to spread the word by establishing a Church.

In 1860 the Church divided into two factions: the 'old' Mormons and the 'new'. The new radical cult was called the Reorganised Church of Latter-Day Saints with its headquarters in

Independence, Missouri. By this time poor Joseph Smith was beyond caring. He and his brother Hyrum had been arrested on conspiracy charges in 1844 and while confined to the local jail they were murdered by a lynch-mob. In 1847 Brigham Young, who with his apostles led the first Mormon mission to Europe, had taken the major part of the faithful to the Valley of the Great Salt Lake in Utah.

It was not long after the founding of the Church that its leaders began to experiment with polygamy; certainly by the year 1843 Smith could boast of seven wives. The practice was finally made official at the 1852 General Church Conference. The effect of the American Civil War from 1861 to 1865 was to give the government and its now warring population more to think about than how many wives the Mormons had.

However, in the decades following the war, the bogey of polygamy returned with a vengeance. As a result of passing the Edmunds–Tucker Act the authorities had the power to annex the Church's property; Mormons were refused enfranchisement, and wives as well as children were labelled illegitimate. So uncomfortable did things become that in 1890, under very great pressure, Wilford Woodruff, fourth president of the Church, signed a Manifesto ending polygamy. This simply succeeded in driving a number of Mormons from the mother Church and into fundamentalist cults – communities were the old faith was retained. The breakaways now had two enemies, the government and their own Church.

But the fundamentalists were hanging on to more than their wives. They wanted their prophets too. When one considers the origin of the Mormon Church it is hardly surprising that they believe strongly in heavenly visitations. These prophets are thought to be *direct* instruments of God – that is, they speak with God's voice. Thus those who deserted the Church insisted on taking their spiritual guides with them.

Another concept that the breakaway groups clung on to was Blood Atonement and Oaths of Vengeance, two doctrines guaranteed to earn them fear and mistrust. Joseph Smith first gave the Church the doctrine of Blood Atonement, and very simple it was too. Any individual who committed a serious act against a Mormon must shed blood for their sins. When Orrim Potter Rockwell attempted to assassinate the Missouri governor he used Blood Atonement as his defence. Oaths of Vengeance also originated with Smith, or rather with his murder in 1844. The oath is a prayer to God to strike down anybody who harms the prophets. It reads:

> You and each of you do solemnly promise and vow that you will pray and never cease to pray and never cease to importune High Heaven to avenge the blood of the prophets on this nation and that you will teach this to your children and your children's children until the third and fourth generation.

(The dangerous aspect of these pieces of doctrinal mumbo-jumbo is that if violence does result then it is shrugged off as 'God's will'. This recurs again and again in cases of death during exorcism.)

The vast majority of Mormons are peaceful, law-abiding citizens with no violence in them. It is the close-knit fundamentalist cults who are predisposed to aggressive thought, and sometimes deed. It might have been some comfort if this had been a phenomenon that died out with the early turbulent days of the Church. It did not.

Appendix: 'Vision of Destruction'

Wilford Woodruff, a man remarkable for his learning and his piety, lived between 1807–98. He was a leading elder of the Mormon Church and eventually became its fourth President. It was while he held this position that Woodruff was obliged, in 1890, to sign the Manifesto prohibiting polygamy. A dozen years earlier he was allegedly responsible for penning a revelation that came to him while in bed.

99

This document, titled 'Vision of Destruction', was dated 1878 and provides a remarkable, if grotesque, example of the Mormons' (along with many other cults') preoccupation with Armageddon (or Day of Judgement, Apocalypse, Millennium, call it what you will).

There is a slightly different version of the 'Vision' attributed to another highly respected senior churchman, John Taylor (1807–98). The following (much abbreviated) compilation, in the spirit of ecumenism takes passages from both, a pot-pourri of doom and gloom.

[*Note*: In the following text, in the interest of clarity, some of the archaic punctuation and spelling (such as Taylor's 'every whare') have been altered. The grammatical construction, however, remains true to the originals.]

I went to bed at my usual hour, half past nine o'clock. I had been reading the Revelations in the French language. My mind was calm, more so than usual if possible to be so. I composed myself for sleep, but could not sleep. I felt a strange stupor come over me and apparently became partially conscious. Still I was not asleep, or awake, with strange far-away dreamy feelings.

The first thing I realised was that I was in the Tabernacle at Ogden, Utah, sitting in the corner for fear they would ask me to preach – which, after singing the second song, they did . . . I said: 'Yes, I have something to say, it is this: some of my brethren present have been asking me what is coming to pass. I will tell you what will shortly come to pass.'

Then I was immediately in Salt Lake City, wandering about the streets in all parts of the city, and on the door of every house I found a badge of mourning, and I could not find a house but was in mourning. I passed by my own house and saw the same sign there, and asked 'Is that me dead?' Something gave me the answer: 'No, you shall live through it all.'

I continued eastward through Omaha and Council Bluffs

which were full of disease, and women everywhere. The states of Missouri and Illinois were in turmoil and strife. Men killing each other, and women joining in the fight, family against family, cutting each other to pieces in the most horrid manner.

I was next in the city of Baltimore, in the square where the monument of 1812 stands. The dead were everywhere. I saw their bodies piled up, filling the square. I saw women cut the throats of their own children for the sake of their blood. I saw them suck it from their veins to quench their own thirst and then lie down in the streets and die.

I next found myself on Broadway in New York. There it seemed as if the people had done all they could to overcome the disease. But in wandering down Broadway I saw the bodies of beautiful women lying, some dead, others in a dying condition, on the sidewalks. I saw men crawl out of the basements and violate the persons of some who were alive, then kill them and rob their dead bodies of the valuables they had on them. Then, before they could return to their basements, they themselves rolled over a time or two in agony and died. On some of the back streets I saw mothers kill their own children and eat raw flesh, and then in a few minutes die themselves. Wherever I went I saw the same scenes of horror and desolation, rapine and death. No horses or carriages, no omnibuses or street cars, but death and destruction everywhere.

I then went to Central Park and, looking back, I saw a fire start and just at that moment a mighty east wind sprang up and carried the flames west over the great city. And it burned until there was not a single building left standing whole; even down to the water's edge. Wharves and shipping – all seemed to be burned and swallowed up in common destruction. Nothing was left but desolation where a great city stood a short time before. Stench from the bodies that were burned was so great that it was carried a great distance across the Hudson River, and it spread disease and death wherever the fumes penetrated.

I supposed this was the end, but I was given to understand that the same horrors that were here enacted were all over the world, east, west, north and south. That few were alive; still there were some.

Immediately after I seemed to be standing on the west bank of the Missouri River opposite the city of Independence; but I saw no city. I saw the whole states of Missouri and Illinois and part of Iowa were a complete wilderness with no living human being in them. I then saw a short distance from the river twelve men dressed in the robes of the Temple standing in a square, or nearly so. I understood it to represent the twelve gates of the new Jerusalem, and they were with hands uplifted consecrating the ground and laying the corner stones. I saw myriads of angels hovering over them and around about them, and also an immense pillar of cloud over them and I heard the singing of the most beautiful music, the words 'Now is established the Kingdom of our God and His Christ, and He shall reign for ever and ever, and the Kingdom shall never be thrown down, for the Saints have overcome.' And I saw people coming from the river and different places a long way off to help build the Temple, and it seemed that the hosts of the angels also helped to get the material to build the Temple. And I saw some come who wore their Temple-robes to help build the Temple and the city. And all the time I saw the great pillar of cloud hovering over the place.

Later, I found myself in the Ogden Tabernacle, where I was calling upon the people to listen to the beautiful strains of music from the angels, as the building seemed to be filled with them, and they were singing the words I heard before: 'Now is the Kingdom of our God and His Christ established for ever and ever.'

I rolled over in my bed and heard the City Hall clock strike midnight.

It is the belief of historian Richard E. Turley (*Victims*, pp. 16–17) that, quite innocently, the attribution to Woodruff may be false. In fact we know that during Woodruff's time as Church archivist he had the 'Vision' copied by a clerk, and subsequently wrote in his journal: 'Had a very strange vision copied.' One clue may be in the first paragraph, where Woodruff describes reading the Book of Revelations in French. Wilford Woodruff had no French. John Taylor, however, oversaw the translation of the *Book of Mormon* into that language. Or perhaps there is an entirely different explanation.

Mark Hofmann and the Salt Lake City bombings

For something that contributed to two brutal murders, the postcard-sized piece of paper printed with close-set, slightly battered type does not look terribly impressive. That is until you learn that 'The Oath of a Freeman' is the oldest printed document in North America; and that it is the sole survivor of only fifty copies. And that it is worth around $1 million. At least it would be if it were genuine. But it is not.

The oath was taken by the first citizens of Massachusetts, and this examplar was faked by a rare-document dealer named Mark Hofmann. Hofmann was a devout Mormon, and the intrigue which resulted in death was closely linked to that Church.

Steven Christensen was a Mormon; in fact he was one of the Elders of the Temple at the very heart of Mormonism, Salt Lake City. At 7.00 a.m. on 15 October 1985 Christensen was standing in the doorway of his office when a parcel he had picked up from the floor exploded, killing him instantly with a burst of shrapnel and masonry nails. Less than three hours later a similar packet blew up killing Mrs Kathy Sheets. She was the wife of Mormon bishop James Gary Sheets. As Sheets was a former business colleague of Steve Christensen, it seemed reasonable to assume that the bomb was meant for him.

On the afternoon of the following day a bomb exploded as

Mark Hofmann unlocked his car, causing him serious injuries. Hofmann had been born in Salt Lake City in 1954, and from early youth became an enthusiastic collector of Mormon currency and literature. One of the greatest treasures on his bookshelf was an early edition of the King James Bible, and between the cover and the flyleaf a folded paper had been slipped. The manuscript document purported to be a copy of the mystical characters on the gold tablets which were the *Book of Mormon*. According to the paper, the signs had been written by Joseph Smith himself and given to Martin Harris, a friend and disciple. Mormon experts validated the paper, and the Church gave Hofmann $20,000 worth of books and other items for it.

This success led to others and Mark Hofmann made a steady living from Church funds and a select group of collectors. He also borrowed heavily from fellow Mormons in order to purchase stock. Indeed by the time his career was brought to an abrupt halt he owed close on $1 million.

When detectives interviewed Hofmann after the explosions there was a general, though inexplicable, feeling that all was not right; perhaps his story was just a little *too* plausible, smug even. A search of the trunk of Hofmann's car revealed a length of metal piping similar to the fragments recovered from the two murder scenes. There was also a broken light fitting, marked 'Radio Shack'. With remarkable persistence a team of police visited all the local 'Radio Shack' outlets; and were rewarded. The object had been sold to 'M. Hansen'. Which was not a lot to go on.

The first serious break in the case came when detectives searching Mark Hofmann's house found a piece of paper on which was written the name Mike Hansen and a telephone number. The address associated with the number proved to be that of a firm of engravers in Denver, Colorado – and they remembered Mr Hansen. They had made a set of printing plates of rare Mormon banknotes for him. It looked very much as though Hofmann had been forging at least some of the documents he had sold to the Mormon Church. And the Church's financial advisers in these deals were none other than Steve Christensen and James

Sheets. If the pair had smelled a rat and threatened to expose him, did this prove an incentive to Hofmann to murder them? Or had there been rumblings of resentment at the sums of money he had borrowed? At least a connection had been made.

Then the celebrated 'Oath of a Freeman' was subjected to close scrutiny. Hofmann claimed that he had come across it quite by chance in a dump-bin of cheap prints in an antiquarian print-seller's. If it were true, then it was remarkable luck indeed. In fact one might almost say that to discover America's rarest piece of printed ephemera in such circumstances was unbelievable luck. Even so, the 'Oath' was authenticated and Hofmann offered it to the American Antiquarian Society for $1 million. A second copy of this 'unique' document was used as security for a loan of $400,000 from the Mormons.

Ted Cannon, the County Attorney, was no scientific expert, but he had been a first-class letterpress printer. When the 'Oath' came under his eagle eye he declared instantly that it was a fake. Cannon knew that the metal type of the kind purportedly used to print the document was cast on a 'body' larger than the face of the letter, so creating a gap between the lines. Hofmann's lines were too close together!

When Mark Hofmann eventually confessed to murder and fraud on 7 January 1987, he described the method he had used. First he had several pages copied from a facsimile of a book printed in 1640, a year after the 'Oath'. He then painstakingly cut and pasted individual letters and words on to a blank sheet, from which an engraved plate was made. Police later identified the engraver. Making 'authentic' ink was simple, if clever. Hofmann burned paper from a seventeenth-century book and mixed the ash with linseed oil. The next ingredient was ash from a strip of leather from the binding of a book of the correct age and then some beeswax was added. The use of the paper and leather ensured that if carbon dating were employed it would indicate the age of the ink 'correctly'. The final stage was to remove the blank flyleaf from a book of the same period as the 'Oath' and print the plate on to it.

In his confession Mark Hofmann admitted making and planting the Christensen/Sheets pipe bombs and then blowing himself up to avert suspicion. It is impossible to put a figure on Hofmann's fakes, but following an examination at Arizona State Crime Laboratory, document expert William Flynn estimated that of almost eighty items sold to the Mormon Church more than twenty were suspect.

Hofmann confessed again at length in court, and made a half-hearted attempt at claiming temporary insanity. It failed, and Judge Rigtrup sentenced him to two terms of life imprisonment.

POSTSCRIPT:

'The Oath of a Freeman'

How significant the 'Oath of a Freeman' was to the deaths of Steve Christensen and Kathy Sheets was revealed during Mark Hofmann's confession in court to prosecuting attorney David Biggs. Had the American Antiquarian Society voted on 15 October 1985 to purchase the 'Oath' for $1 million, Biggs asked Hofmann, 'what would that have done to the financial hole you had dug yourself in by that time?'

'It would have relieved me from it. Hence, I guess you want me to say the bombings would not have taken place.'

'I don't want you to say that unless it is true.'

'I'll say it, since it's true.'

Jeffrey Lundgren and the Kirtland massacre

Known simply as the Temple, it stands in the centre of the small community of Kirtland in the mid-west state of Ohio. The slightly sinister gothic revival edifice was built in 1836 by Joseph Smith in celebration of his recently founded Church of Jesus Christ of Latter-Day Saints.

In 1986 Jeffrey Don Lundgren, a thirty-five-year-old member of the mother Church at Independence, Missouri, was appointed as a guide for visitors to the Kirtland Temple. With his wife Alice Elizabeth and their four children, Lundgren moved into the small house provided by the Church for his use. Jeffrey Lundgren was by all accounts an unmitigated disaster as a guide. So much of a disaster that in 1987, without much ceremony, he was kicked out of home and job and obliged to rent a modest farm at Chardon Road on the edge of town. There was also some vague and unspecified suspicion that Lundgren was embezzling Church funds.

Not, you may think, an entirely promising start for a self-proclaimed prophet of God. For that is the way Jeffrey Lundgren had come to see himself, a prophet like the great founder Joseph Smith 150 years before him. Surprising as it may seem in hindsight – that is, with the certain knowledge that Lundgren is a multicide – the prophet (or 'Father', as he insisted on being addressed) began to attract a steady stream of converts from the Kirtland Temple. In no time at all he had turned the fifteen-acre farm into his very own religious community. Although it was clear that Lundgren was a persuasive dominator of a weak and gullible flock which was desperate for leadership, the cult grew. Among the dozen or so families which attached themselves to the commune were Dennis and Cheryl Avery with their daughters Trina, Rebecca and Karen, though they did not live on the farm. And in the absence of any overt misdemeanour the cultists were left pretty much to their own devices by neighbours and local authority.

Later it emerged that the Reorganised Church (Jeffrey's version of it) was engaged in some quaintly bizarre sexual practices. It has been written that Lundgren himself enjoyed nothing better than for his wife to rub excrement on to his body.

At the beginning of 1988, the *official* Reorganised Church of Latter-Day Saints in Kirtland set in motion a procedure which would excommunicate Lundgren the usurper, Lundgren the poacher of their flock, stripping him of his lay ministry credentials. At about the same time Jeffrey began to receive visions and hear voices; there was going, it seemed, to be a cataclysmic earthquake. All this he revealed to his awestruck congregation. However, he pointed out, Divine Salvation would be with them and them alone, if on 3 May 1989 (coincidentally Lundgren's birthday) they were to break into the Kirtland Temple and expel the 'infidels'. Then they were to just sit around and await the imminent return to earth of Jesus Christ.

Such a crackpot scheme could not have hoped to remain secret for very long, and before the predicted Day of Judgement arrived the police had already paid a visit to the Lundgren encampment and made it clear that it was under close surveillance.

Doom did not crack on the third day of May, nor did the earth quake; and Jeffrey Lundgren did not sack the Kirtland Temple. Instead he set about remodelling his community in something more like a troop of warriors of the Lord than a flock of His sheep. At any rate they began to stockpile an arsenal of weapons and put themselves through some serious paramilitary training. They also began to drink quite a lot.

As it happened, just prior to Jeffrey's birthday on 3 May he had another revelation. The long and the short of it was that in order for the group to be cleansed in preparation for 'a journey into the wilderness in search of the Golden Sword' some members must be sacrificed.

On the morning of 17 April 1989, Dennis Avery and his family packed up the last of their modest belongings and prepared to move from the small house they had been renting to the farmhouse. Here they were to join the rest of the sect to embark on the Great Journey. What they did not know was that, as they were joyfully looking forward to a Golden Future, Lundgren, his family and close cronies were adding the last details to their plan for murder. Richard Brand took a trip to the Galco Army Supply Company to buy some rope and a stun gun, while Ron Luff put the finishing touches to a 3½-foot-deep pit that he had been digging in the earth floor of one of the barns. At six-thirty in the evening the Averys sat down to eat their last meal with the people they looked on as their fellow servants of God. When they finished Jeff Lundgren left the table followed, as previously arranged, by Brand, Greg Winship, Danny Kraft, Ronald Luff and Lundgren's eldest son, Damon. While Jeffrey affectionately fondled his .45 Colt Combat Elite, the others were swearing allegiance for a final time before going about their respective 'duties'.

First Dennis Avery was lured from the farmhouse kitchen to the barn, ostensibly to help pack equipment for the wilderness trip. Once he was inside Luff and Lundgren attempted to use the stun gun on him. When this failed to immobilise Avery the whole gang jumped him and bound the luckless fellow with parcel tape before dragging him to the pit. Here, in the half-light, Dennis Avery was pushed into the hole and shot twice in the head by Jeffrey Lundgren. Next it was Cheryl Avery's turn to follow her husband into the mass grave. She too failed to respond to the stun gun so they taped around her ankles, wrists, eyes and mouth, and shot her once. The three Avery children posed less of a problem thanks to the cynical plan devised by Lundgren. They were brought out of the house one by one on the pretence that they were all going to play hide-and-seek, or some such game which required them to be blindfolded, gagged and bound. First Trina was carried to the pit and shot; then Becky; then six-year-old Karen. When killing time was over, the bodies were covered with lime and the grave was filled with rocks and rubble topped with a layer of earth.

On the night of 18 April, under the watchful eye of the local police, the commune, their goods and chattels on their backs, left the farmhouse for the 'wilderness'. Or at least for Missouri and Kansas City. They left behind their 'sacrifices'. Kirtland had not had a murder for a dozen years – now it had five.

It was not until 5 January 1990 that seven members of Jeffrey Lundgren's cult were taken into custody by Kansas City police. Six were still missing as the group had split apart the previous

December over 'sexual indiscretions'; among the members temporarily at large were Jeffrey Lundgren and his wife. It was two days later, on Sunday the 7th, that agents of the Federal Bureau of Alcohol, Tobacco and Firearms, in collaboration with members of the San Diego Sheriff's Department, arrested Lundgren and his family at the Santa Fe Motel, National City. Officers had been keeping a watchful eye on the motel since the previous evening to make sure that the fugitives did not slip across the nearby border into Mexico. As well as Lundgren, Alice and nineteen-year-old Damon were placed under arrest; the three younger children, Jason, Kristen Michelle and Caleb were taken into protective custody. Federal agents seized from the motel room an AR-15 assault rifle, three handguns, assorted knives and items of survival equipment. From a locker used by Lundgren officers removed three more handguns and a quantity of smokeless powder.

The senior Lundgrens were later indicted along with eleven of their disciples by a Lake County grand jury. The charges were variously murder and conspiracy; Jeffrey Lundgren himself faced five counts of aggravated murder.

A jury at the Lake County Common Pleas Court deliberated for three hours and fifteen minutes on 31 August 1990; then they returned to court to deliver verdicts of guilty on five counts of murder and five of kidnapping against Jeffrey Lundgren. It was only two days earlier that the same court had convicted Damon Lundgren on four counts of murder and four of kidnapping. Alice Lundgren had also been sentenced to five consecutive life terms for the murders which she consistently blamed on her husband. She gave evidence that Lundgren had criticised the Avery family for their want of zeal, and regretted that they might have to be disposed of.

At his sentencing trial on 21 September, forty-year-old Jeffrey Lundgren displayed no sign of emotion as Judge Martin O. Parks, acting on the jury's recommendation, sentenced him to death. Clearly Lundgren's defence that he was acting on instructions from God did not enter the jury's calculations. The execution was scheduled to take place on 17 April 1991, but mandatory appeals will inevitably delay matters – perhaps for a decade. Besides, the state of Ohio has not executed anybody since 1963; Lundgren will simply have to wait his turn with the other hundred or so prisoners on Death Row.

In their exhaustive study of the Lundgren case,* Cynthia Stalter Sasse and Peggy Murphy Widder state:

> It is a terrible thing to hear another person sentenced to die. I believe in the death penalty and I believe that if anybody ever deserved the death penalty, Jeff Lundgren does . . . [he] has never shown any evidence of a broken heart or a contrite spirit. More, he is dangerous, and he is evil, and no civilised society that is obliged to protect itself from evil should allow him to survive.

*The Kirtland Massacre, Zebra True Crime, Kensington Publishing Corp., New York, 1991

ANT HILL KIDS COMMUNE

Roch Theriault, alias 'Dr' Moses

Canadian Roch (pronounce it 'Rock') Theriault was a Messiah in a rather small way of business, though there is little doubt that he aspired to greater congregations on whom he could inflict his own bizarre version of Armageddon.

Roch Theriault was born in the village of Rivière-du-Moulin in Quebec province on 16 May 1947, one of seven children. It was a brisk community, and before the family moved to Thetford-Mines Roch had picked up the rudiments of the local trade of woodcarving. It was when the boy was ten that the Theriaults inflicted the massive bleak expanse of open cast asbestos mines on him. And he was as miserable as hell in the gloomy, joyless town.

It is probably no coincidence in view of the future, that Theriault senior, a house-painter, was a member of an underground sect calling themselves 'White Berets'. They were very right wing, very Roman Catholic and very fond of wearing ceremonial robes.

So depressing was life for Roch, that he would wander away from the town and hike into the woods. He would return with tales so strange that his poor mother must at times have feared for his sanity. One recurring fantasy was Roch meeting a female bear who adopted him and brought him up with her other cubs. Roch also began to practise a kind of folk medicine centred around the roots and herbs he culled from the woods. Whether or not these nostrums ever cured anybody we do not know; but if he failed to cure his patients, at least he didn't kill them. Not at that stage anyway.

When he was twenty years old, Roch married a local girl, Francine Grenier, and they had two children. Roch even renewed his acquaintance with woodcarving, and made a sort of living out of selling his wares to the few tourists who passed through Thetford-Mines. People say it was about this time he began to exhibit a distinctly odd side to his character. He had, for example, suggested that his in-laws turn their farm into a nudist colony. Being devout Catholics they were rather alarmed and unsurprisingly refused. It was around then, while he was in his middle twenties, that Roch Theriault's interest in herbal remedies developed into an obsession with medicine and surgery. After he had been released from hospital himself he began collecting medical textbooks and reading them late into the night; in fact he became quite a bore on the subject.

In the mid-1970s Theriault became a Roman Catholic, but due to their reluctance to make him leader of the local church, he threw in his lot with the Seventh-Day Adventists, and clearly had his sights set on higher things; he began to affect the robes of a holy man, and made an unsuccessful attempt to take over the congregation. But Roch, they decided, was just a little too weird and his bid was robustly rejected. Theriault found himself without a following and, to complicate matters, without a wife as Francine had returned to live with her parents. Perhaps Francine had seen her own apocalyptic vision of the future and got out while she could.

Undismayed, Theriault took himself to Sainte-Marie-de-Beauce where he realised the first step in his chosen career of medicine; he set himself up as a homeopathic doctor. It proved to be a sound move, because Roch drew around his little business all manner of food faddists and health freaks, people who make good disciples. Which was just as well; in 1978 Roch Theriault was given his message from God, a vision of the end of the world, and it was up to him to save the faithful. Responding enthusiastically to the call, Theriault gathered such sheep as he

113

could into a makeshift flock and led them into the wilderness – the wilderness around the Gaspe Peninsula. And there they settled in a few rented log cabins, Theriault as God's emissary, nine women to act as 'wives', four children and four other men. In the best cult tradition Theriault abandoned his given name and adopted Moses as his new title; the other members of the commune were also expected to change their names to something Biblical. He told the commune that the path to heaven would involve suffering; he was right about that at least.

Work was long and hard, just in order to survive. The little band were working thirteen-hour days often in conditions of crippling cold. Except Moses, of course. He began to hit the bottle increasingly frequently. He sat on his rustic wooden throne dressed in scarlet robes and wearing a gold-painted crown on his head, getting drunker and drunker, squabbling with his disciples, beating up the children, beating up the women, beating up anyone who crossed his path. But there was worse to come on the road to paradise; much worse.

In the meantime, Roch had been flirting with aspects of fundamental Mormonism. That polygamy was his main interest is not to be wondered at. He paid visits of homage to the Mormon polygamist Alex Joseph in America, and was rewarded by being given a new and even more ludicrous name. Joseph anointed him 'King of the Israelites'.

In 1981 the cult took on a new member, a twenty-three-year-old mental patient named Guy Veer, who had discharged himself from Quebec City psychiatric hospital. He learned quickly, and in no time at all had picked up the rudiments of the Master's method of dealing with noisy children. One evening in March, while it was Veer's turn to mind the community's offspring he beat one two-year-old so savagely for crying that the child became unable to urinate. Enter 'Dr' Moses and his medical library. That night Theriault carried out an operation on little Samuel's genito-urinary system; next morning the boy was dead.

In common with most self-proclaimed Messiahs, Roch Theriault was never wrong – there was always somebody else to blame. The death of his patient was blamed on the hapless Guy Veer. Veer was 'arrested' and tried before a court of which the King of the Israelites was judge and jury; the defendant was not unsurprisingly found guilty of murder and sentenced to be castrated. Theriault carried out the necessary surgery.

Child-killing and DIY castration cannot long go unnoticed, and in 1982 a team of police officers from Quebec raided the commune and took seven of its members into custody, including their leader. Theriault was convicted of criminal negligence and spent the next two years in Orsainville Prison.

When he was released in June 1984, Roch Theriault regrouped his cult and led them out of Quebec, where the court had forbidden them to congregate, to a piece of rugged land up in Burnt River, Ontario. Here the faithful began to operate some sort of hill-billy business venture selling handicrafts under the name Ant Hill Kids – which was ironic really, because soon there weren't going to be any kids.

In January 1985 the commune had just got itself up and running when another child died. The coroner's verdict was that the death was due to sudden infant death syndrome – 'cot death'. But the incident had alerted the welfare authorities to the wider question of the safety of other children of God up at the commune. On 6 December 1985 police accompanied staff from the Kawartha-Haliburton Children's Aid Society and they removed all fourteen children, whose ages ranged between six months and sixteen years, and took them into care. Undefeated, Abraham (as Theriault was now insisting on being called) set about a new regeneration programme and over the following two years collaborated with his wives in the production of another nine infants – all of whom were systematically removed and also put in care. This shouldn't have come as too much of a shock, since the first batch of children had already begun to complain that Abraham forced them into sexual acts.

As for the rest of the Ant Hill gang, day-to-day activities were pretty much dictated by Roch Theriault's sexual appetite and the degree to which he had been drinking. In other words, he either spent all day in bed with a clutch of wives, or he roamed drunkenly around the compound picking fights with his followers. On one occasion, a disciple named Oulette was singled out to suffer the extraordinary punishment of having a tight elastic band snapped around his scrotum, which during the day swelled to the size of an orange and became so badly infected that Theriault had to get the man drunk and surgically remove one of his testicles.

It is quite clear that at this point Roch Theriault was desperately ill in his head; what was worse, some of his followers were beginning to realise it. On 28 September 1988 he decided to perform an operation on thirty-two-year-old Solange Boilard, who had made the mistake of mentioning some trivial stomach complaint. Before she knew it, the unlucky woman had been strapped to a wooden table where a paralytically drunk Roch Theriault was giving her a crude enema of oil and molasses via a piece of old piping forced into her rectum. Then he slashed open her abdomen, took out her intestines and ripped off a length with his bare hands. Doc Theriault then delegated another disciple to stitch the gaping incision with a needle and thread. Solange Boilard suffered the most unimaginable agony for almost twelve hours before she died. Even then her corpse was to find no rest. She was buried and exhumed twice over the succeeding weeks. The first time Theriault removed the top of her skull in order to masturbate into Solange's brain; this, he assured his bewildered disciples, would bring her back to life. Of course it did no such thing. On the second occasion Theriault removed from the decomposing body a rib which he took to wearing around his neck in a leather pouch. Finally, poor Solange Boilard's remains were cremated. But the madness did not end there.

The following month Gabrielle Lavallee was 'cured' of toothache by the simple expedient of Theriault tearing eight teeth out of her mouth with a pair of pliers. On 26 July 1989, the same woman foolishly mentioned that she had a bit of a stiff finger. Drunk as always, and as always ready with an *ad hoc* surgical remedy, Theriault transfixed Gabrielle Lavallee's hand to the table with a hunting knife. It failed to have the desired curative effect, but it did cause gangrene to set in to the arm. There was only one thing for it; Theriault hacked off the arm between the shoulder and elbow with a couple of swings from a blunt cleaver. When after a few days it looked as though infection was setting in to the untreated stump, Theriault cauterised it with a red-hot bar of iron.

And that was the beginning of the end for the Ant Hill Kids commune. Terrified out of her wits and suffering indescribable pain, Gabrielle Lavallee fled the compound in search of the police and medical treatment. Like rats leaving a sinking ship all but two of Roch Theriault's disciples also decamped, leaving Abraham and the pitiful remnants of his harem to make themselves scarce before the law arrived. It was some credit to their ingenuity that the fugitives remained at liberty in the wilderness for six weeks before a combination of land patrols, tracker dogs and helicopters ran them to ground.

Less than a week after his capture, on 10 October 1989, Roch Theriault pleaded guilty to three charges of aggravated assault and one of causing grievous bodily harm to Gabrielle Lavallee, for which he was imprisoned for twelve years. But by now the once-faithful had begun to talk about Solange Boilard, and when the police had recovered and identified her charred remains at the Burnt River compound, Roch Theriault – looking now rather less like an Old Testament prophet without his straggling hair and two-foot-long beard – appeared before Mr Justice Claude Paris to be committed for trial on a charge of second-degree murder.

It was not until 18 January 1993 that Roch Theriault stood before a jury at Kingston, Ontario, and when he did he pleaded guilty as charged. Before sentencing him to life, the judge gave Theriault the opportunity to address the court, and he made use of the occasion to try to gain sympathy with a rambling, whining account of his own 'odious' character. Speaking in his native French he told the court: 'I had unknowingly combined love, hate, religion, alcohol and violence in my body's helpless state; I fed my spirit on illusions of grandeur . . . I will carry the mental scars for the rest of my life.'

117

As for his hapless band of disciples, they too will carry scars, both mental and physical, for the rest of their lives. The children, the Ant Hill Kids, fared better: of the twenty-two taken into care by the authorities nearly all were found secure foster homes where they are growing up like normal children.

Roch Theriault is allowed conjugal visits at Milhaven Institution, and for this purpose Francine moved close to the prison. Two other 'wives' have joined her and they have opened a bakery. Theriault (Moses, King of the Israelites, Abraham, call him what you will) will be eligible for unsupervised day parole in October 1996.

ORDER OF THE SOLAR TEMPLE

The Crusader and the Antichrist

The most inexplicable aspect of the Solar Temple was its followers. Not latter-day hippies or drop-outs, not wild-eyed fanatics, but well-heeled men and women, well educated, mainly middle-class and many middle-aged. Unlike many cults they did not live communally; indeed they kept their membership secret even from close friends.

This 'normality' is the more astonishing because what the cult members were being asked to believe was one of the most preposterous pieces of humbug ever laid before a congregation by its leader. In this case the leader was Luc Jouret. To start with Jouret claimed that in a former life he had been a Crusader, a member of the Knights Templar, and that the sword which the flock were required to venerate had been given to him 1,000 years ago. Jouret also believed in sun worship of the kind practised by the Druids. Add a sprinkling of the imminent Age of Aquarius and a quasi-Christian expectation of Armageddon and things are becoming complicated. Throw in champagne and free sex and it becomes *very* complicated. But that was not the end of it. Luc Jouret had convinced his disciples that on the Day of Judgement they would all be transported to the star Sirius, where eternal happiness beckoned.

So what of Luc Jouret? Records tell that he was born in Kikwit in the Belgian Congo (now Zaire) on 18 October 1947. The family fled to Belgium fearing reprisals following decolonisation. Luc attended the University of Brussels and graduated in medicine in

119

1974, to begin a distinguished career in homeopathy. He was also enthusiastic about the possibilities of spiritual healing, and made several trips to the Philippines, Peru and India. From Brussels Jouret moved to Luxembourg and then to the town of Annemasse on the border of France and Switzerland. Here he practised as a homeopathic doctor. At around this time Luc Jouret became obsessed with the Knights Templar and joined the Renewed Order of the Temple. When its leader Julien Origas died in 1984, Jouret briefly succeeded him – until he became tiresome and was ejected both from his position of power and from the movement. Smarting under this humiliation Jouret moved over the border into Geneva, Switzerland, where he established the International Organisation of Chivalric Solar Tradition, appointing himself New Grand Master.

In 1986, the Grand Master emigrated to Canada's Quebec province where he purchased a large semi-detached house in Morin Heights, fifty miles north of Montreal. Here, in June 1987, Jouret founded the Order of the Solar Temple. Living next door was Joseph Di Mambro. Seventy-year-old Di Mambro, who became the financial 'brains' of the Solar Temple, had already been convicted of fraud by a Provence court and jailed. On his release he had established a sect calling itself the Centre for the Preparation of the New Age. Perhaps not surprisingly, Jouret and Di Mambro teamed up to set about milking their gullible followers of their money. A brash, bullying man, di Mambro had soon earned himself the nicknames 'Napoleon' and 'Little Hitler'.

Before long the Solar Temple was stockpiling weapons and building a nuclear fallout shelter in preparation for the apocalypse. In 1993 Jouret was arrested by the Sûreté du Québec, charged with possession of a restricted weapon (a gun with a silencer) and fined £500. Charges brought early in 1994 accused Luc Jouret and two others of making telephone death threats to Quebec's former Public Security Minister, Claude Ryan. However, the case collapsed and the three were released.

The Swiss branches of the Temple were located in a couple of chalets and a farmhouse in the tiny village of Cheiry, north of Geneva, and in Salvan a hundred miles away to the west of Switzerland. Neighbours never had the need to complain of strange goings-on; in fact the faithful of the Solar Temple seem to have been the sort of folk one would give a right arm to live next door to. In one report a neighbour mentioned occasionally hearing the quiet strains of classical music, but that mainly the cultists 'were very discreet, arriving in small, ordinary cars at around eight o'clock in the evening . . .' To anybody who has had the privilege of living among these polite and gentle people they would have seemed 'typical' Swiss.

Until they started killing each other. Until they decided to create their own Armageddon. That was in October 1994. More precisely, on the fifth day of that month.

Concerned that twenty-three people seemed to have disappeared from the area, police officers paid a visit to the Solar Temple headquarters in Cheiry. By the time they arrived the farmhouse had burned down leaving only the basement chapels. If they had not witnessed such tragedy the two rooms might be described as looking like something lifted from a fun-fair. A panelled passage led down from the ground floor of the house to the chapel, where walls had been painted in a hotch-potch of red, blue and purple interspersed with mirrors in the shape of church windows. In a further inner sanctum was a collection of ceremonial robes and various knick-knacks, such as chalices clearly to be used in rituals. Dominating the room was a picture of a Christ-like figure (uncannily resembling Luc Jouret) with a large red rose hovering over its head. The rose, it appears, was the Solar Temple's symbol of earthly perfection. One journalist writing from Cheiry summed the scene up as 'a teenager's idea of what is magical and mysterious'.

But it was not only the paraphernalia of a hocus-pocus cult that police discovered. They found part of the cult itself. Arranged in a circle with their feet towards the centre were twenty-two robed corpses, their lifeless eyes looking up at the painting of Christ/ Jouet. Most had suffered gunshot wounds to the skull, ten had plastic bags tied over their heads and others were manacled at the wrists. Incongruously the floor of the prayer room was littered with champagne bottles. The farmer who rented the buildings to the cult was found shot dead on his bed. The plastic bags were a big puzzle until one former member explained that plastic bags were part of ritual dress 'to demonstrate how far man had become estranged from his natural state'.

Given the nature of apocalyptic cults and the apparently organised 'exit' of the victims, the first suggestion was of mass suicide. An audio cassette taped to the farmhouse door helped give support to the notion. But as the victims had been shot, where were the guns? A number of firearms were recovered from the property, but ballistic tests proved them innocent of the Solar Temple deaths. Murder? Mass murder?

While detectives were puzzling over this question another fire was blazing, this time in the Alpine village of Granges-sur-Salvan. Three adjoining chalets were ablaze, one of them owned by Luc Jouret. In the charred remains were twenty-five bodies – members of the Solar Temple and their children. The Swiss police did not know it at the time, but in Canada their counterparts were investigating the deaths of five people in a fire at Joseph Di Mambro's Morin Heights home. Two were wearing insignia with the initials 'TS' for Temple Solaire. The remaining three, including a three-month-old baby, had been stabbed to death.

The odd thing was that it was beginning to look as though all three incidents were a combination of murder and suicide. A Swiss authority on cults, Jean-François Mayer, had earlier received several letters from members of the Solar Temple indicating their intention to take their own lives. One read: 'We are leaving this earth to rediscover, lucidly and freely, a dimension of truth and absoluteness'. On the other hand, some of the victims had packed suitcases, suggesting that they intended to leave under their own steam. Unless, of course, they were preparing for the trip to Sirius. One thing was certain, all the fires had been set deliberately by the use of sophisticated remote-control devices. In one, petrol cans had been wired up to a telephone which, if it rang, caused an electrical charge to ignite the fuel.

A breakthrough in the suicide/murder dilemma arrived with the report of the pathologists. They had examined the victims of Cheiry and found that they had been injected with an unknown 'powerful substance' before they died. It was also discovered that while some cultists may well have killed themselves, others certainly had not. One person, for example, had three bullet wounds in the head, but only one hole in the bag which covered it; another had two bullet wounds but no hole in the bag. One of the slain had been shot eight times.

Whether or not it played any significant part in the killing, money had been a contentious subject within the group for some time. Members were being asked to pay ever-increasing fees, and in addition Jouret and Di Mambro were commandeering their possessions. One of the curiosities of the Solar Temple hierarchy was the sliding scale of 'donations' that accompanied each step up the ladder. Further weight was conferred on this theory when it was at first thought that Jouret and Di Mambro had escaped and gone into hiding.

On 10 October the press carried reports that Joseph Di Mambro's charred body had been identified by his family among the dead of Salvan. Although the immediate police response was that the identification was 'unreliable', it was confirmed three days later. What was more, the investigating judge, Jean-Pascal Jaquemet, announced that the cult's leader Luc Jouret had also died alongside his disciples at Salvan. He had been identified from dental records.

At the same time, police in Geneva arrested Patrick Vuarnet, a close friend of Jouret. He had confessed to posting a suicide letter to the press on the cult's behalf – but claimed he had been ordered to do so by Jouret. It reads, in part, 'Because of police intimidation and the victimisation of our members, we have decided to leave this world, for a dimension of truth and perfection.'

Now other Solar Temple followers were beginning to talk and

the mystery of the Morin Heights murders was solved. The three stabbed victims were identified as Nicky Dutoit, a British woman, her Swiss husband Antonio and their son Christopher. Mr Dutoit had been Joseph Di Mambro's chauffeur and Mrs Dutoit had been nanny to his daughter. Although Di Mambro told the couple they must wait for his say-so to have a baby, they went ahead anyway. This so enraged the awful Di Mambro that he declared the child the Antichrist and had the whole family executed. It has been suggested that the execution was carried out by cultist Joel Eggar who died at Salvan.

Appendix: The Knights Templar

The Knights of the Temple (better known as Knights Templar) were established in 1115 when Hughes de Payens, Godfrey de Saint Adhemar and seven other French knights began to patrol the road from Jaffa to Jerusalem protecting pilgrims. They took monastic vows to wear only clothes given to them and to own nothing but their weapons. Their first name was Poor Knights. When King Baldwin donated rooms in his castle which was supposed to have been built on the site of the Temple of Solomon, they became Knights Templar.

In 1128, the Knights were made the official military wing of the Cistercians with the encouragement of the Pope. They wore a white hooded mantle similar to those of the monks, except on active duty when it was replaced by a white cloak, later with a red cross on the left breast. As the donations from Europe's royalty increased, so temples were built in countries as far apart as Britain and Sicily. Each temple was under the command of a Master, and they were responsible to a Grand Master in Jerusalem. At the peak of their power the Templars owned more than 9,000 establishments throughout Europe.

The main reasons for the downfall of the Knights were their fondness for secret initiations and meetings, which aroused suspicion of occult doings, and their meddling in European politics. The Templars lost the last of their bases in the Holy Land, the fort of Sidon, in 1291. It is thought that around 20,000 knights died fighting the Muslims. The Knights Templar had also made the error of lending large sums of money to King Philip 'The Fair' of France. It was unwise because Philip was both needy and greedy. Having glimpsed the size of the Templars' wealth, he hatched a plot to get his hands on the whole of the fabled Templars' treasure. The only way this could be achieved was to accuse the Knights of heresy – which was done simply by rounding them all up, torturing them until they confessed to devil worship, or alchemy or some such nonsense, then seizing their assets. It was so successful that most of Europe's rulers joined in. On 18 March 1314 the last Templar was burned at the stake.

Small pockets of Knights Templar reappeared over the next few centuries, but effectively the Order had been broken up. There is still an international Ancient and Noble Order of the Knights Templar which describes itself as a non-profit Fellowship Society. As in days of old much of the Order's income is given to charity.

GREAT WHITE BROTHERHOOD

Visions, prophecies of bloodshed, and a Russian John the Baptist

Although it is one of the most interesting of the modern cults, detailed information on the Great White Brotherhood is tantalisingly scant.

The sect was founded by a Ukrainian physicist and dissident, Yuri Krivonogov (also called 'John the Baptist'), and his second wife, Marina Tsvygun, who describes herself as 'the incarnation of Christ and the Virgin Mary'. She also uses the name Maria Devi Khristos. From its origins in the Ukraine, the Brotherhood spread rapidly to Russia, Belorussia and Moldovia, attracting a following of hundreds of thousands.

Unlike smarter cults, the Great White Brotherhood confidently predicted that the world would end, accompanied by mass suicide, on 24 November 1993; it was later brought forward to the 14th. Of course the world did no such thing, but that did not stop riots in the streets of Kiev in the run-up to Armageddon. So worried were they at the prospect of 150,000 faithful brothers and sisters hitting town that the city authorities called in Interpol. Alarmed at the prospect of not being able to commit suicide with her disciples, 'the living God on earth' had gone into hiding to avoid arrest. About 500 followers were already being held in prisons and hospitals where many were refusing to eat or drink. Professor Anatoliy Gabriel, head of Kiev's quaintly named 'curative hunger centre', claimed that many of those in detention exhibited signs of brainwashing and the use of mind-altering drugs. At this point the Interior Ministry revealed that a few years earlier Yuri Krivonogov had worked for the Cybernetics Institute on developing psychological trance weapons.

Although the leader herself was still safely out of harm's way, hardly a surface in the city was free from the Brotherhood's poster – Ms Tsvygun, looking demure if a little spooky in her white robes. A leaflet was distributed warning the faithful not to speak to journalists, who 'are in the paid service of the Beast'.

On 11 November, as Doomsday approached, the streets of Kiev were being patrolled by 20,000 police and security officers. Fifty cultists clashed with riot squads in the city's eleventh-century Saint Sophia's cathedral. They had got past security by posing as tourists.

Although she was not yet around, Marina Tsvygun was still confidently expected to be killed by the police and then to rise from the dead just in time to see the world ending. But wait a minute. The face above that lace collar and colourful jumper looks familiar. Unremarkable out of her nun-like costume, the spiritual leader of the Great White Brotherhood had been rampaging around the cathedral unnoticed by the police. So had her husband. In fact it was only when officers spotted their fanatical devotees kissing the couple's feet that they were recognised, and immediately clapped into jail. Not that this kept Marina Tsvygun quiet. She told police: 'My name is God. You will never forget me. The angry God will come – nobody knows when. Because you have insulted God's name you will fall into the Second Circle of Hell.' As for Yuri Krivonogov, he was saying nothing except that his name was Johann Swami.

And so the Great Day came and went with Yuri (or Johann) and Marina languishing in their cells. Without leaders the thousands of dispirited followers simply drifted off to where they had come from. As Armageddon apparently requires the death of Marina Tsvygun, the Kiev authorities uttered a sigh of relief as it was postponed. No heavens to open, no earthquakes, no rivers of blood. And no mass suicide.

EASTERN AND
ASIAN CULTS

HARE KRISHNA (INTERNATIONAL SOCIETY FOR KRISHNA CONSCIOUSNESS)

The young adherents of the Hare Krishna movement, more properly called the International Society for Krishna Consciousness (ISKCON), are familiar sights in most of the world's major cities. With their heads shaven but for a single pigtail at the back, their saffron robes and faces marked with ash, they sway to the sound of drums and finger cymbals as they make their way through the crowded streets. As they go they chant the best-known mantra in the world: 'Hare Krishna, Hare Krishna, Krishna, Krishna, Hare Hare, Hare Rama, Hare Rama, Rama Rama' ('Hare' means Lord and Krishna is the most senior of the Hindu gods). There are over seventy ISKCON centres throughout the world with more than 15,000 followers. Ironically only a handful of centres exist in the faith's country of origin, India.

The movement relies mainly on voluntary donations for their income, though they have a factory in Los Angeles where members make and sell incense. In America, the Hare Krishna movement has been conspicuously active in reforming drug addicts, and they have received much civic praise for their efforts.

Members of the Krishna cult have doctrinal beliefs which set them apart from Christianity. Indeed, they believe that Christ was not the son of God, but a traveller from a distant planet who came to pay homage to Krishna. Krishna, Lord of Absolute Truth, highest of the Hindu gods, has undergone many incarnations. In fact the belief in reincarnation is fundamental to the ISKCON faith; the way that a person lives will dictate the shape they will have in the next life. One rather alarming piece of dogma states that any act performed in the name of Krishna cannot be bad, as

Krishna is beyond the concept of good and evil. (This is a belief that is encountered time and again in this book, where even an act of violence, if it is done in God's (or a god's) name, is not reprehensible (see particularly the chapters on cult exorcism).) However, the followers of ISKCON have a good reputation as peaceable, gentle individuals.

The founder of the Hare Krishna movement was His Divine Grace A. C. Bhaktivendenta Swami Prabhupada. He was born in Calcutta in 1896, and in later life was the manager of a chemical factory. A devout man, Prabhupada was told by his guru in the 1930s that he was destined to carry the Hindu message to America. This was realised in the year 1965, when the swami was almost seventy years old. Having spent some time living in a yoga centre in New York, he was able to set up his own headquarters when a disciple offered to pay the first few months' rent. Here, Prabhupada began to teach the ways of Krishna and was much revered by the hippies who were beginning to emerge at that time, looking for a belief that would preach their own rejection of the materialistic world they saw around them.

In 1977 Prabhupada died; his last wish being that the movement should be put into the hands of a twelve-member international governing commission. Inevitably this led to considerable in-fighting among the newly elected swamis.

Adherents of the movement live communally in 'temples' and are under the guidance of the temple president. The president in his turn is governed by one of the board of twelve. Life in the temple is very strictly ordered, much time being spent in chanting with prayer beads and studying the sect's holy book, the *Bhagavad Gita*. A large part of the day is occupied on the street raising money. This is often carried out by members in 'civvies', that is to say jeans and sweatshirts or similar. These unidentifiable individuals make free gifts of books or records to passers-by; free, that is, apart from the donation that the recipient is expected to give.

There are several levels in the hierarchy of ISKCON, starting with a trial period during which aspiring members live in at the temple and help out in day-to-day duties. At the same time they are taught the philosophy of the group. This induction usually lasts for about six months, following which the prospective members undergo initiation. This complex fire-based ceremony is presided over by the temple president who gives the initiates a new name in Sanskrit, and a triple row of beads which they are expected to wear around their necks for the whole of their life. In a further six months, the new members are assessed as to loyalty and devotion and if their spirituality is up to a certain level the title Brahmin is bestowed, at which stage the initiates are given a secret mantra which must be chanted silently three times a day. Very rarely will a member reach the exalted stage of Sannyassa, a position reserved for only the most devout. It necessitates a life-long vow of poverty and celibacy. Actually, celibacy might come as something of a relief. Sexual activity is not greatly encouraged among members. It is only permitted once every month, and only between married couples Before sex both parties are required to chant fifty rounds of their prayer beads to purify themselves.

The case of guru Jayatirtha and the disillusioned disciple

James Immel (whose Sanskrit name was Jayatirtha) was one of the most talented and dedicated individuals in the Hare Krishna movement. He joined in London shortly after the cult was established in 1967. Following teaching trips to Krishna temples in India, America and Canada, he returned to England to live with the community at Bahktivendenta Manor, close to London. In addition to being a respected guru, Immel was a womaniser and a committed drug-user – which was, quite literally, to be the death of him.

A young woman disciple who had become quite infatuated with Immel had taken it into her head to follow him around the Manor's grounds as he was at his morning chanting. This was in order to get a snapshot of her hero. That morning she was going to get more than that. After a frolic on the turf, both Immel and his admirer stripped off and got on with what naked couples frequently get on with. Unfortunately for the groping guru, a woman photographer had snapped his every move. And decided to blackmail him for a luxury trip to India.

Immel's other weakness, LSD, was also getting him into trouble at the movement's headquarters in Bombay. He was finally suspended for a year in 1982. Which may have hurt less than the order to stay celibate.

It so happened that on a trip to Nepal James Immel made the acquaintance of a young English follower. His name was Nataipanda (at least, his Krishna name was); and he was not pleased to discover that having made the pilgrimage to Kathmandu, the great guru was an acid-head. Indeed, when Immel flatly refused to pay his fare back to England, Nataipanda, with somewhat uncharacteristically churlish Krishna behaviour, threatened to turn him in to the local police as a drug addict. A danger serious enough for James to genially change his mind, thrust $500 into the young man's hand, and promise to guide him to a traditional lake ceremony early the next morning. It was halfway out on the water that Immel hurled his travelling companion over the side of the boat; then held his head under water till he drowned. The verdict of the police authorities was 'accidental death'. Immel had got away with murder – even though it had cost him $500.

But it was only a matter of time before drugs caught up with him. Back in London, Immel was staying with another Krishna disciple named John Tierney (and called Navaniticera). An incorrigible drug-user himself, Tierney's brain was in a state of disintegration – to the point that he began to *suspect* that Immel was not Immel, but Rasputin. Then he became *convinced*. Then he became convinced that it was his mission to remove the mad monk from the world for ever, which he effected with a knife to the stomach. And for good measure he cut Immel's head off. It is said that he was still cradling it when the police arrived.

BHAGWAN SHREE RAJNEESH

In common with many popular Eastern religious cults, that founded by the Bhagwan (meaning according to one source, 'master of the vagina') Shree Rajneesh owned its spread to the disaffectioned hippie groups of the 1960s and 1970s.

Bhagwan Rajneesh was born in the town of Agra in Uttar Pradesh, on 4 December 1940. He was raised by middle-class grandparents who provided the child with the best of educations, culminating in the study of philosophy at Jabalpur University, where he later taught the same subject. By the year 1974, Rajneesh was confident enough of his principles of sex-led meditation to open an ashram in the city of Poona, to the south of Bombay. This was at a time when every hippie worth his beads and bells was heading for India in search of spiritual enlightenment, and whether it was part of a previously plotted masterplan or not, Bhagwan Rajneesh found himself not only at the centre of attention but also at the hub of a lucrative enterprise. People, he discovered, were eager to give their everything to be nearer the godhead. One of Rajneesh's most famous, and most cynical, quotations is: 'That the materially poor can ever be spiritual is out-and-out absurd.' No surprise, then, that in 1981 he moved to the 'land of plenty' where he established an ashram on a 125-square-mile tract of land in Oregon. Here Bhagwan Rajneesh enjoyed the luxury to which he clearly felt entitled. These little perks included a private plane and a fleet of Rolls-Royce cars, the extent of which nobody seems sure (the figure ranges between a mere dozen and almost a hundred). Meanwhile sex was still being used as bait for the well-heeled disciples who were beginning to flock to his door.

So many, in fact, that a lot more doors needed to be opened. At the height of its popularity the cult had around 600 centres around the globe.

By then the Bhagwan had taken on a new title: 'Osho'. Thus did the movement also then rejoice in the name Osho – and continues to do so, though these days it is the more businesslike Osho International Foundation (once somewhat scurrilously called 'Club Meditation').

The Bhagwan died in India in 1990 (where he had fled to avoid charges of immigration fraud). The suggestion that death was as the result of Aids has never been established. Osho, and its huge existing and potential earning power, seems to have been taken over by a top 'religious' executive called Swami Prem Jayesh. In fact the swami is the former Michael William O'Byrne, a Canadian real-estate investor with an eye to the future well-being of the Bhagwan's legacy – and we are talking millions of dollars, multi-million dollars. Osho International Foundation has so many fingers in so many pies that it is difficult to count the hands. How Osho's Rollers were distributed is anybody's guess.

All in all it seemed the kind of story that would interest nobody who was not financially or spiritually involved with the Oshi. Another cult, another swami or two, let them get on with it. Then, surprise, surprise, the cult of Oshi hit the British courts.

Sally-Anne Croft, Susan Hagan and a rusty .357

Two British women, senior officials in the late Bhagwan's empire, were being made the subjects of extradition orders to the United States to face trial for plotting murder. Murder? Plotting murder!?

It was in 1993 that the British Home Office was requested by the American Government to extradite forty-two-year-old Sally-Anne Croft, a chartered accountant, and Susan Hagan, aged forty-six, an aromatherapist. The women had been members of the Bhagwan's so-called Rasneeshpurin headquarters in Antelope, Oregon, in the early years of the 1980s. They were being extradited to face charges connected with an alleged conspiracy to murder Mr Charles Turner, Federal Attorney for Oregon, who was investigating possible immigration offences by members of the Bhagwan Shree Rajneesh cult. At the time, Sally Croft (cult name Ma Prem Savita) was a senior financial adviser to the commune and stood accused of authorising the purchase of guns to be used in the assassination. Mrs Hagan (cult name Ma Anand Su) was said to have been present when the manner and means of Turner's death were discussed in 1985. Which was the same year that the two accused women left the cult after becoming disillusioned with the extravagant lifestyle of the Bhagwan.

It was not until the end of April 1993 that Kenneth Clarke, the then British Home Secretary, ordered the Croft/Hagan extradition. It was suggested at the time that the incentive might have been the reciprocal extradition from America of IRA suspects. Mr Clarke said: 'I am satisfied that a clear *prima facie* case has been found against both women. The charge is a serious one. The strength of the evidence and the guilt or innocence of the accused should be determined by a court of law and not by me.'

There was, inevitably, fear expressed that Mrs Hagan and Ms Croft would suffer from US prejudices against the cult. This, Mr Clarke countered with: 'Any prejudice, if it existed, would also apply to the prosecution witnesses, and I find myself unable to believe that a jury in Oregon would be bound to be prejudiced as claimed. I reject that assumption.'

And Mr Clarke's assumption was in turn rejected by Hagan and Croft, their defence team and their supporters, including legal heavyweights Lords Scarman and Longford. Sally Croft told a press conference: 'I simply cannot take stock of what is happening. We have received so much support in this country that the Home Secretary's decision is totally unexpected. We know that we have no hope of a free trial if we are sent back. There is an attempt to demonise us by the US authorities who want to prove our guilt long before we get to an American court . . . We are facing a situation which is made even worse by the prejudice that has been heightened by events in Waco where so many people died a short time ago.'

As well as the allegedly corrupt activities of the British pair, the world was learning about other sinister misdeeds claimed to have been committed by the Bhagwan's faithful. Such as a mass poisoning campaign in Antelope restaurants. More by luck than good judgement there were no fatalities, though upwards of 750 people suffered greater or lesser symptoms of salmonella poisoning. It was as a result of charges brought against some of the members after the cult disbanded that the accusations against Ms Croft and Mrs Hagan were made. Not, it must be added, as an act of altruism, but as part of a plea-bargain sought by those already in custody.

The following year, 1994, the two women were still awaiting the outcome of the political wrangling that was holding up proceedings, lumbering from one delay to the next. The case had even seen the replacement of Kenneth Clarke by Michael Howard as Home Secretary. As for the press, they seemed to be alleviating the boredom by recording any number of different addresses for Ms Sally Croft. At first she had resided in Blackheath; then a little further down the hill in Greenwich. At the time of her appeal, Sally Croft was on the same day reported living at Totnes, Devon, and Mayfair in central London. On 27 July 1994, both women were on their way by plane to an entirely new address, to Muttnomah County Detention Center, Portland, Oregon. Four years after the warrant for their extradition had been issued at Bow Street magistrates' court, London, and just two hours after two High Court judges refused a writ of habeas corpus, and described the women's fourth application for a judicial review as 'an abuse of the process of the court'.

Meanwhile former law lord, Lord Scarman, was voicing his unease: 'I am dismayed by the extradition, but we mustn't let dismay and a certain amount of anger take over from good judgement.'

On 30 July Sally-Anne Croft and Susan Hagan appeared for the first time in an American court. Before Judge Donald

Ashmankas, the two women were remanded to stand trial on 7 September 1994, and released on condition that they were electronically 'tagged' so that their whereabouts could be monitored. In a curious back-swipe, US Attorney Baron Sheldhal commented that he was surprised by the fuss being made in England over the Hagan/Croft affair. He was especially puzzled by Lord Scarman's outburst, but confessed it did not mean much to him. 'We don't have lords here,' he added.

From the residents of Antelope, where Hagan and Croft worshipped at the feet of Rajneesh, the message was stronger: 'You can tell the people of England that if they had been through what we did, they would have a very different perspective on this. What we had was damned near a war.'

Local people were telling just what it *was* like having their own resident mystic on the doorstep preaching free love and cosmic orgasms. At first the colonisation of the old Muddy Ranch by a couple of hundred orange-robed *sannyassin* was greeted with good humour and tolerance – not least because the cult seemed to have a fair amount of money to spend; the ranch alone had cost $6 million. Then the newcomers became greedy and started to expand. They certainly made no friends in the county court when they demanded the farm be classified as a city in order to circumvent planning regulations. Thwarted in this direction, the Rajneeshis began to buy up whole chunks of Antelope – the local café became Zorba the Buddha, serving only vegan food. Vastly outnumbering the indigenous population in the polling booths, the cultists took control of the council in the 1982 elections, and immediately voted themselves the right to a police force; heavily armed, of course.

Now the 2,000-strong Rajneeshis began openly to harass and abuse members of the local community. Came the time of the county elections and the cult bused in thousands of homeless people in an attempt to rig the voting. When this failed, people began to fall sick with food poisoning after eating and drinking in the Rajneeshi salad bars. It was shortly after this that the Bhagwan's chief lieutenant, Ma Anand Sheela (real name Sheela

Silverman) hatched a plan to murder the cult's enemies, including US Attorney Charles Turner. Enter Sally-Anne Croft and Susan Hagan.

Ms Croft herself had been accused of participating in a sham marriage in order to remain in America. It was this activity which was being investigated by the Immigration and Naturalisation Service with the help of Mr Turner. Alma Peralta, already serving two years for plotting murder, claimed: 'Savita [Croft] and I and other commune members saw the investigation threatening our continued existence. Rajneesh and hundreds of members would face prosecution, imprisonment and, in the case of foreign nationals, deportation. Between May 26 1985 and August 1985 Savita and I attended meetings where we planned and discussed the way we would carry out the murder of US Attorney Charles Turner.' Another convicted member of the conspiracy, Phyllis Caldwell, testified that she was given 'thousands of dollars' to go to New Mexico to buy guns.

The trial finally opened in Portland at the beginning of July 1995. Both Sally Croft and Susan Hagan pleaded not guilty and, with little hope of sympathy from an Oregon jury, seemed resigned to listen to the litany of accusations levelled against them by the very people who were once their friends. Lovers, even. Sally Croft's one-time partner, David Knapp (renamed Krishna Dava), had struck a bargain with the FBI whereby, in exchange for immunity from prosecution on charges including attempted murder, arson and conspiracy to murder, he would testify that, ten years previously he, Croft, Hagan and others attended meetings at which they plotted to kill Charles Turner. Knapp also explained the sham marriage system operated by the cult. He himself had gone through just such a ceremony in order to provide an Indian woman with American citizenship. He concluded: 'If the immigration authorities had deported every foreign national who had gone through a sham marriage the ranch would have collapsed.'

A quite separate piece of bizarre information revealed that Sheela Silverman had ordered a cult member to assassinate the

Bhagwan's doctor by stabbing him in the buttocks with a poisoned syringe. The attempt failed.

By the end of July it was all over. Whether it was justice or not will be hotly debated for a long time to come. Mrs Hagan's legal representative, Colleen Scissors, said: 'Forgive me if I'm blunt, but the fact is Charles Turner is alive and well.' Countered by prosecutor Scott Glick, brandishing the rusty .357-calibre revolver recovered from a lake: 'We don't have to wait for the shot to be fired. The intent here was to shoot Charles Turner.'

And Mr Turner himself? He welcomed the five-year prison sentences handed down to each of the defendants in December 1995. Now retired from office as state attorney, he added his final comment on the case: 'Reporters changed their minds when they realised there was a great deal more evidence than they might have been led to believe.' On the criticisms of using informants as witnesses, Mr Turner pointed out that all countries which operated a jury system did so. Finally, the former attorney spoke of his beliefs as a devout Christian: 'I defy anyone to find any case from my thirty-one years as a law enforcement officer in which being a Christian has interfered with any legal decision I have made. I am very upset – it is a convenient mechanism to use Christianity against someone by saying they cannot be fair.'

Sally-Anne Croft and Susan Hagan serve their sentences at the minimum-security Geiger Corrections Center, Spokane.

'KING' OF THE BLACK THAI

Bogus mass suicide in Vietnam

What seemed an amazing tale of cult mass suicide when the story first made, albeit minor, news in October 1993, would in the following months prove to be far more sinister.

The original report centred around events among the Black Thai villagers living in a small hamlet called Ta He in Son La Province, about 200 miles north-west of Hanoi. Ca Van Liem, a local man, so the newspaper account ran, had duped the villagers into believing that, blind as he was, he was an unrecognised king who, for a consideration, would ensure that following a mass suicide they would all find themselves in heaven. On 2 October 1993 fifty-three inhabitants of this remote hill tribe village died of wounds caused by flintlock pistols and other even more primitive weapons.

It was only one month later that the November issue of *Vietnam Insight* reported that, on the night of 2 October, government soldiers annihilated around sixty people of the Thai Den minority in the province of Son La, the number including nineteen children. The first that Reuters and the United Nations knew of the incident was a government report that 'a few local thugs' had been up to mischief. Subsequently, the official line was that 'King' Ca Van Liem had instigated a mass suicide.

According to those drafted into the area to clean up the mess, most of the dead had been shot; others had been clubbed with rifle butts. Some appeared to have been fleeing the area, wounded, when they were cut down.

It was more than six months before the real truth began to emerge. On 14 June 1994, the State Radio in Hanoi broadcast a speech by General Do Trong Lich, commander of the Second Military Region and a member of the Party Central Committee. He described the incident at Son La as a perfect example of how to quell a 'peaceful evolution' rebellion. The General continued: 'The conspiracy of peaceful changes had happened in the jurisdiction of our military region, with sophisticated tactics and ruthless, fanatical behaviour. The situation in Son La province was the evidence . . . Outside reactionary groups have conspired with local bad elements to carry out "peaceful evolution", luring people into forming a reactionary organisation, expanding its forces, spreading its propaganda and influence, controlling and neutralising the local government. Therefore the fight against peaceful evolution is the central, number one task of our Military Region's armed forces in the present situation.'

It is needless to say that the Vietnamese Government obstructed the efforts of the UN Human Rights Delegation to look into the occurrences at Son La. The moral may be that if there is something worse than a sinister cult, it must be a corrupt military government.

SATANISM

In order to gain control of their minds and wills, young children are constantly (not just during the rituals) subjected to a ghastly gauntlet of cruelties that include, briefly: beatings, starvation, needles and electric shock; smearing with and ingestion of urine, feces, blood and flesh; long isolation in dark, fearful places; drugs; forced sexual revels with other children, animals, adults, or the dead; forced murder of specially bred or adopted babies; rebirth to, or marriage with, Satan, etc.

(Ron Stanley, Order of Preachers)

The most difficult aspect of any debate on Satanism is not whether it is a good thing or not, but *what it is*. You will appreciate from the brief word-sketches below that there are as many different approaches to Satanism as there are Satanist groups. In fact there are almost as many approaches as there are individuals within a group – and few if any fit the description above. It helps, I suppose, if you are fond of Satan and share his aspirations. But beyond that the cult member is free. Unlike cults employing coercive or bullying tactics to impose power or levy money, the words most frequently heard in Satanist philosophy are self-awareness, individuality, self-fulfilment . . . A spokeswoman for the Church of Satan describes it as 'user-driven'. She continues: 'Members are involved and advanced exactly as their own desires, abilities and accomplishments dictate.' Anton Long, Grand Master of the Order of Nine Angles, echoes it: 'Genuine Satanism – like all genuine magick – is a path, way or method of

147

self-development. Rituals may be and often are part of this, but these rituals all conform to certain patterns: they are always intended to aid and explicate self-understanding and development.'

It is necessary to emphasise this positive approach because Satanists have had a very bad, and for the most part unfair, press. In an article headed 'Anti-Satanist Hysteria Spreading', K. Bolton fills us in on the way New Zealand is following the United States. Mr Bolton is the editor of *The Watcher*, the New Zealand Voice of the Left Hand Path (renamed Ordo Sinistra Vivendi):

> NZ newspapers have recently carried a few items on Satanism which give us an inkling as to the nature of the hysteria that has been whipped up in the USA by Christian preachers and their dupes in the media and police depts. The latter-day witch-hunt began in the USA with all manner of stories of Satanic child abuse, ritual murder of animals and babies, 'infiltration' of day-care centres, etc. These wild and weird allegations were quickly picked up by sensationalist-mongering journalists and talk-hosts who gave instant and credible platform for all manner of neurotics to parade before TV audiences with their tales of how they had been molested by Satanists as children. Despite the publicity that has been given to such allegations, and the fervent Christian policemen who have made a personal crusade out of combating the devil's disciples, an FBI study has concluded that the claims are baseless.

Satanists do *not* systematically sacrifice babies in dark underground caverns, any more than Mormons do. But both have black sheep in their pens. They are the subject of this book.

Let us look at Satan himself before we start on his more errant disciples. Most early civilisations had 'chief' devils: the Egyptians had Set, the malevolent dog-headed god; for the Greeks it was the snake-headed giant, Typhus; and the Assyro-Babylonians acknowledged Tiamat, a dragon-goddess who represented chaos and evil.

In Hebrew 'Satan' means adversary or enemy. He makes an early appearance in the first book of the Old Testament as the serpent:

Now the serpent was more subtil than any beast of the field which the Lord God had made. And he said unto the woman, Yea, hath God said, Ye shall not eat out of the garden? (Genesis iii, 1)

The early Church taught that the fall of the angel Satan (sometimes called Lucifer) preceded the creation of man:

How art thou fallen from Heaven, O Lucifer, son of morning! how art thou cut down to the ground, which didst weaken the nations! For thou hast said in thine heart, I will ascend into heaven, I will exalt my throne above the stars of God: I will sit also upon the mount of the congregation, in the sides of the north. I will ascend above the heights of the clouds; I will be like the most High. (Isaiah xv,12ff)

Satan then goes on to be a popular adversary in the New Testament, where he is probably best known for tempting Christ in the wilderness and turning up at the Last Judgement. This is vital to remember, because it is a common mistake to think that if there had been no Christ there would have been no Satan. In fact Lucifer predated the Saviour by about 2,000 years.

However, since the spread of Christianity it is probable that Satanism has roughly paralleled it with the Gnostics forming some of the earliest cults in the first few centuries AD. Despite their suppression in AD 392, the beliefs of the Gnostics spread throughout Europe and Asia Minor carried by such sects as the Messalians, the Paulicians and the Bogomils. During the fourteenth and fifteenth centuries the Roman Catholic church battled tirelessly against supposed witchcraft and devil-worship during the reign of terror of the Inquisition. The Knights Templar were condemned for worshipping Baphomet and their Grand

Master was burned in Paris in 1314. The Satanic cult Brethren of the Cross was wiped out in Thuringia in 1453. The purges continued throughout the following four centuries when Satanist rituals, black masses and human sacrifice were regularly exposed. In our present 'enlightened' century, Satanists are generally disapproved of but largely tolerated as a 'lunatic fringe'.

At the base of much Satanic activity is the concept of blood sacrifice. True, in most instances the blood is that of a few luckless chickens, but there is ample evidence of much more sinister goings-on at a higher level in some of the more organised cults. Indeed, the growing threat of black-magick-inspired killings has so alarmed some police forces that officers are receiving special instruction in order to 'respond to the growing incidence nationwide [USA] of cult-related crimes and rituals'. One of the major influences on modern Satanists is Anton LaVey's *Satanic Bible*, and his organisation, the Church of Satan.

It is all but impossible to keep up with the number of devil-worship groups which spring up and disappear around the world; the following are just a sample.

CHURCH OF SATAN

Anton Szandor LaVey's Church of Satan is the largest and best-known Satanist organisation in the world. It is also one of the oldest. LaVey himself was born on 11 April 1930 and, so he claims, had become entranced with the occult by the tender age of seven. When he was fifteen, Anton dropped out of school and, according to his official biographer, Blanche Barton, started 'hanging around pool halls in the company of gamblers, pimps, prostitutes, hustlers and pool sharks'.

Then LaVey ran away to join Clyde Beatty's circus where he became first a cage boy to the big cats, followed by a spell as an assistant lion tamer. In 1947 LaVey was working in an amusement park in Long Beach, California, where he picked up all manner of stage conjuring skills which would be so vital to his ritual activities later on; because Anton LaVey had also been gradually increasing his knowledge and understanding of occult practices.

LaVey married in 1950, and in keeping with his new-found responsibilities exchanged the fairground for San Francisco City College, from which he emerged with a major in criminology. His degree led Anton LaVey to the San Francisco Police Department, where he spent three years as a crime scenes photographer. This was often a very unpleasant, gruesome activity, which led LaVey not only to quit the police, but become finally convinced that there could be no good God.

The next – and most ambitious – stage of his life was when LaVey sank all his savings into an old house, painted it entirely black and opened it up for lectures and discussions on witchcraft and black magick. Those who became regular participants he called his 'Magick Circle'.

On 30 April 1966 – Walpurgisnacht – Anton Szandor LaVey shaved his head, donned a long black robe and announced that the Age of Satan had just begun and he was the Black Pope. Ambitious. The Magick Circle became the core of LaVey's disciples, though the movement would soon spread across the United States and Canada.

Early on in the development of his cult LaVey laid down the 'Basic Teachings and Beliefs' of the Church of Satan:

> The Church of Satan worships Satan, most clearly symbolised by the Roman God Lucifer, the bearer of light, the spirit of the air, and the personification of enlightenment. Satan is not visualised as an anthropomorphic being, rather he represents the forces of nature. To the Satanist, the self is the highest embodiment of human life and is sacred. The Church of Satan is essentially a human potential movement, and its members are encouraged to develop whatever capabilities they can by which they can excel. They are, however, cautioned to recognise their limitations – an important factor in this philosophy of rational self-interest. Satanists practise magick, the art of changing situations or events in accordance with one's will, which would, using normally accepted methods, be impossible.

He also decreed what he called 'Nine Satanic Statements':

> 1. Satan represents indulgence, instead of abstinence!
> 2. Satan represents vital existence, instead of spiritual pipe dreams!
> 3. Satan represents undefiled wisdom, instead of hypocritical self-deceit!
> 4. Satan represents kindness to those who deserve it, instead of love wasted on ingrates!

5. Satan represents vengeance, instead of turning the other cheek!
6. Satan represents responsibility for the responsible, instead of concern for psychic vampires!
7. Satan represents a man as just another animal, sometimes better more often worse than those that walk on all fours!
8. Satan represents all of the so-called sins, as they lead to physical, mental, or emotional gratification!
9. Satan has been the best friend that the church has ever had, as he has kept it in business all of these years.

Although it is in the nature of such cults as the Church of Satan to suffer schisms whereby breakaway groups are set up by disaffected followers, LaVey was to some extent to blame for the frequent splits in his own Church. It was after all he who encouraged disciples to set up their own branches across the country. For a fee, of course.

However, perhaps Anton LaVey's greatest contribution to the spread of Satanism is his *Satanic Bible* (1969), a sort of do-it-yourself book for black magicians. It has been a notable item in the possession of psychopathic killers – though this is hardly LaVey's fault. *Satanic Bible* was followed by *The Compleat Witch* (1971) and *Satanic Rituals* (1972).

'Evil, evil . . .', the case of the Night Stalker

The Night Stalker was a serious disciple of the devil. Police knew that even before they knew his name. They knew because he scrawled pentacles on his victims' bodies and walls after he killed them.

Between June 1984 and August 1985 the unknown sadist terrorised the middle-class suburbs of east Los Angeles. The first victim was seventy-nine-year-old Jennie Vincow, whose throat was slit in her home in Glassell Park on the night of 28 June 1984.

Dayle Okazaki, thirty-four, was next, shot through the forehead on 17 March 1985 in her Richmond condominium. For good measure the attacker shot and wounded her flatmate on the way out. Her description was the first clue the police had. Thirty-year-old Tsai Lian Yu was dragged from her car and shot the very same night.

The most brutal murders were those of sixty-four-year-old Vincent Zazzara and his wife Maxine. Zazzara had retired as an investment adviser to pursue his dream of opening a restaurant; his wife was a successful lawyer. On the night of 26 March 1985, Mr and Mrs Zazzara were at home in their luxury ranch-house by the San Gabriel River, when an intruder broke in and shot them both. Then in an orgy of sadism he hacked at Maxine Zazzara's body with a knife, carving ragged wounds in her chest, neck, face, abdomen and groin. Worse still, the killer had gouged out both her eyes and taken them with him. The bodies were not found until two days later.

Although he went on to kill again in the middle-class suburban areas around the city, it was not until June 1985 that the Los Angeles police officially announced that they had a serial killer on the loose; the press christened him the 'Night Stalker'. What they could not possibly have known was that the killer already called himself the 'Night Prowler'. It was the title of one of the songs by his favourite heavy-metal band, AC/DC.

Two months after the Zazzara murders, William Doi was killed at his home in Monterey Park and his wife was raped and battered. This was followed by attacks on eighty-four-year-old Mabel Bell and her sister Florence Long on 29 May. Mrs Long survived the battering, but Mabel died in hospital on 15 July. Meanwhile, on 27 June, Patty Elaine Higgins and Mary Louise Cannon fell victim to the Stalker – both had their throats cut open. Joyce Lucille Nelson died on 2 July, and on 20 July the Night Stalker claimed no fewer than three victims: an elderly couple, Maxson and Lela Kneiding, shot dead, Chainarong Khovananth shot dead and his wife raped after being forced to promise Satan she would not scream. Elyas Abowath was shot dead on 8 August and his wife was raped and beaten. On the 17th of the same month Peter Pan and his wife Barbara were shot, and before he left their home the Stalker scrawled his familiar inverted pentagram on the wall in Barbara Pan's pink lipstick, with the words 'Jack the Knife' written underneath. The final victim was twenty-nine-year-old William Carns, shot dead on 24 August; his fiancée was forced to recite the words 'I love Satan' as she was sexually violated. The killer made off in their car. He had made his first mistake.

Desperation and a belief that the Stalker was invincible were reducing the community to panic, when FBI officers at Quantico, checking out the abandoned getaway car, discovered the smudged fingerprint of a petty crook named Ramirez, a drifter from El Paso, Texas. Photographs were circulated to the media, and at nine o'clock on a Saturday morning in August 1985, a well-heeled LA suburb, as usual busy with its weekend shoppers, became the scene of a drama that ended the fear.

A man had been observed unsuccessfully trying the doors of parked cars. When he attempted to pull a woman out of her car, he was attacked by her husband. Then everybody recognised the man whose face had been staring at them from the front page of the morning papers. Richard Ramirez had come shopping for another victim and found himself the victim of the mob. Bruised and bloody, the Night Stalker was rescued by the police just in time to save him from being lynched. So badly had he been mauled that Ramirez needed treatment at the county hospital.

While under arrest, Richard Ramirez claimed that it was the devil who made him commit the crimes. According to one account Ramirez told police: 'I love to kill people. I love to watch them die. I would shoot them in the head and they would wriggle and squirm all over the place, and then just stop. Or I would cut them with a knife and watch their faces turn white.' He boasted that he had met and spoken with Anton LaVey at the Church of Satan. LaVey seems to have remembered the occasion, and ironically described his guest as 'one of the nicest, most polite young men I ever met'.

Throughout his trial, Richard Ramirez was by turns sullen and explosive; at one moment flashing the devil's pentagram scrawled on his hand to the eager press photographers, saying 'Hi Satan', then falling silent for hours before placing his fingers to the sides of his head like a demon's horns and intoning, 'Evil, evil . . .'

It almost seemed at one point as if his invocation of demonic help might be bearing fruit as two juries in succession had to be dismissed – the first because one of its members, who was clearly unimpressed by the honour of sitting in judgement on the devil's disciple, fell into a deep sleep, the other because one of the jurors was murdered in a quite unconnected incident.

As he was convicted of twelve first-degree murders, one second-degree murder and thirty other major offences of rape and burglary, Ramirez was sentenced to death. Summing up for himself, he observed: 'You maggots make me sick. I am beyond good and evil. Legions of the night. Night breed. Repeat not the errors of the Night Prowler and show no mercy. I will be avenged. Lucifer dwells within all of us!' It was quite a performance. But Richard Ramirez had not quite finished yet. As he was taken from the court through a small knot of journalists, everybody wanted to know what he thought of the sentence. Ramirez leered back at the expectant hacks: 'Big deal. Death comes with the territory. See you in Disneyland.'

Richard Ramirez dwells on Death Row; and as California carries out the death penalty very sparingly (only twice since reintroduction in 1975) he is likely to dwell there for some years to come.

The case of Bunny Dixon and the *Satanic Bible*

This was a robbery plan hatched by a ouija board which ended in murder. It began on a warm Florida afternoon. On 20 July 1987 Daniel Paul Bowen and his girlfriend, seventeen-year-old Elizabeth Trowne, met their friends Tony Hill and Bunny Dixon. They climbed into a car, which just happened to be stolen, and loaded in a small arsenal of firearms and knives. When the little gang – who had been having great fun playing with the guns – reached a secluded part of the countryside, Tony stopped the car. He got out, walked round to the trunk, dragged out the body of a man and let him drop to the ground. He looked oriental and was, in fact, twenty-five-year-old Ngoc Van Dang. He didn't tell them that, he couldn't, his mouth was heavily taped, as were his wrists and ankles. Tony Hall relieved the unlucky man of what he had of value, then he and Bunny Dixon took it in turn to shoot bullets into him. In a final gesture of abandon, Bunny took a knife and carved a Satanic cross on his body. Then she jumped into the car beside Tony and they sped off leaving their none-too-happy companions on the side of the road with a corpse. In fact they were so angry that the word 'police' came to mind.

Even so it was not until the following day, the 21st, that Daniel Bowen and Elizabeth Trowne walked into the police station at Weldon, North Carolina. The story they had to tell was this: They had been minding their own business down in Tampa, Florida, when they had been forced at gunpoint to witness a murder. It was a great mercy, Bowen said, that they had lived to tell the tale.

The pair were packed off home while local officers got on to the telephone to their counterparts in Tampa where, surprise surprise, there was no sign of the murder so eloquently described by Bowen and Trowne. Perhaps we should go over it with them again, detectives thought. And since officers had been provident enough to take down and verify addresses, David Bowen and Elizabeth Trowne were going over it again. This time it was slightly nearer the truth, and they led police officers to where the body of Ngoc Van Dang still lay. Realising, perhaps, that they were up to their ears in it and might as well do themselves some good, twenty-three-year-old Bowen confided that the other man was none other than his old cell-mate Tony Hall. As for the fourth member of the team, she turned out to be Bunny Nicole Dixon, an old friend of Elizabeth's from detention-centre days.

The final truth. The real truth. Was even more bizarre. As the result of her regular perusal of the *Satanic Bible*, Bunny Dixon had become a committed Satanist. In gratitude she offered to bear

Satan's child – the Antichrist. Along the way she had learned to use a ouija board and it was when she used it the day before the killing that it had suggested they kidnap somebody and steal their car. It had said nothing about murder; they just got carried away, she said.

Indeed they were. To Florida in 1989 to stand their trials. Tony Hall was sentenced to death; David Bowen to life imprisonment; Bunny Dixon collected fifty years and Elizabeth Trowne seventeen.

'On the choice of a human sacrifice', the case of Phillip Gamble

Particularly in the United States, much 'Satanism' results from adolescent preoccupation with sex, drugs and heavy-metal music. A bit of harmless dressing-up just adds to the fun. Those who have studied the subject of Satanic cults have identified a number of categories, usually according to seriousness of intent. The lowest is:

> *The Dabblers*: They adopt Satanic trappings for a brief period of time, usually for entertainment rather than any serious purposes. Many modern youths fall into this category.

Phillip Gamble's little coven at Airport High School in Monroe County, Michigan did fall into this category. Unfortunately Gamble took it seriously. Far too seriously.

During the night of 2 February 1986, the Gamble household was awoken by the crash of shotgun blasts. The recipient of these two murderous shots was Phillip's seventeen-year-old brother, Lloyd, a senior at Carleton, Michigan. As there were only three people to suspect, and it was unlikely that two of them would assassinate their son in the middle of the night, it was no time at all before Phillip Gamble was sitting in the police station telling his story to the increasing disbelief of his listeners.

He was, he said, a practising Satanist and had offered his elder brother to his Master as a sacrifice. Besides, he added, he was also doing Lloyd a favour by sending him, albeit prematurely, 'to a higher plane of consciousness'. He had chosen that particular night of 2 February because it was Candlemas. To Christians, Candlemas represents the feast of the Purification of the Virgin Mary, and the presentation of the infant Christ in the Temple. To witches, though, it has a different meaning and is celebrated on February Eve. It even has a different name (or, rather, names): Imbolc, Oimelc or Brigid. According to one source, Imbolc is from Old Irish (possibly meaning 'in the belly'), Oimelc means 'ewe's milk' (it is the lambing season) and Brigid is the Celtic fire goddess, who rules healing, smithcraft, poetry and inspiration. Brigid's fire represents healing, visions and tempering, while *februum* is Latin for purification, thus the month of cleansing. Quite what it means to amateur Satanists, such as Phillip Gamble, to make it a time for killing is a mystery. Unless it be simply an act against Christianity, in which case any festival, saint's day or Sunday would do just as well.

When a team of police searchers arrived to look over Phillip's room at home they found the predictable gimcracks associated with the amateur magician: robes, a sword and dagger, the obligatory heavy-metal discs. And something else. A copy of Anton LaVey's *Satanic Bible* which had become ragged with use.

A partial explanation for Phillip Gamble's act of madness might be found within the covers of this popular volume. Chapter 9 is headed 'On the choice of a human sacrifice'. The first paragraph proposes that:

> The supposed purpose in performing the ritual of sacrifice is to throw the energy provided by the blood of the freshly slaughtered victim into the atmosphere of the magical working, thereby intensifying the magician's chances of success.

Aha! Phillip Gamble might have thought. Human sacrifice. Satan would like that. Then he read the list of options, probably not realising that they are all states of mind potentially inflicted by the sacrificee:

> The 'ideal sacrifice' may be emotionally insecure, but nonetheless can, in the machinations of his insecurity, cause severe damage to *your* tranquility or sound reputation. 'Mental illness', 'nervous breakdown', 'maladjustment', 'anxiety neuroses', 'broken homes', 'sibling rivalry', etc.

Sibling rivalry! Is that why he blew his brother's head away? Maybe it was because Phillip was only fifteen years old and misunderstood. Or perhaps he had read his *Satanic Bible* too carelessly. Because if he had been more attentive, he would have known that his hero Anton LaVey was speaking most forcefully *against* blood sacrifice:

> The fact of the matter is that if the 'magician' is worthy of his name, he will be uninhibited enough to release the necessary force *from his own body*, instead of from an unwilling and undeserving victim.

Not blood. Semen. LaVey has frequently advocated masturbation on such occasions.

The thrill killings of Scott Waterhouse

There is nothing more frightening than fear. That unidentifiable dread. The same unidentifiable dread that, during 1983, invaded the small New England town of Sandford, Maine. Then the faceless apprehensions took on a form. Not a solid form, an ethereal one. It was an ancient fear. A universal fear. The fear of the devil. The good folk of Sandford became convinced that a group of Satanists were meeting at night in an old mill close to

160

the town. The police investigated, of course, but found nothing. It did little to dispel the unease that was spreading through the town.

It was leading up to Hallowe'en, an ancient festival more associated now with pumpkin heads and 'trick or treat'. But not for Sandford; they had a new terror. A number of young girls, and adults too, began to receive death threats signed by 'The Cult'. At last the police had something tangible to investigate, and as the result of their inquiry, a dozen or so youths were arrested on charges of issuing death threats and criminal mischief. And that seemed, officially at least, to be the end of the matter – there was no predatory Satanist cult, just a gang of thoughtless kids feeding off local fears. Hallowe'en came and went without incident. That year's autumn passed uneventfully through to the next year's spring.

Then the strangled body of twelve-year-old Gycelle Cote was found floating in the Mousam river at the point where it meanders through town. It was 30 April 1984, and Gycelle had been reported missing the previous evening when she failed to turn up for supper after going to meet friends. She had left her home in Jackson Street late in the previous afternoon to keep her regular Sunday rendezvous with friends in the wooded area around Pike's Hill; when they arrived she couldn't be found.

It is always distressing when a young innocent child is robbed so prematurely of its life, but for the residents of Sandford it seemed like confirmation of another fear – that Satan was robbing them of their children.

Perhaps it was the sheer horror of it that kick-started people's memories, but within hours of their pleas for help from the community the police received reports of four sightings of the same person near Pike's Hill on the afternoon of Sunday 29 April. One witness recalled seeing the youth wearing a combat jacket with his hand on the shoulder of a girl fitting Gycelle's description walking close to the river. The youth was Scott Waterhouse, eighteen years old, a high school junior with a record of abetting theft.

On the afternoon of 3 May, Waterhouse was pulled in for questioning at the station in Alfred while a team of officers exercised a warrant to search his home. What they found would vindicate the fears of the past twelve months. In Waterhouse's room at home and his locker at school, detectives discovered items proving the youth's deep psychological involvement with Satanism: a notepad listing what he called 'The Satanic Rules', another containing 'Questions about Satan', a bizarre letter purporting to be written to Waterhouse by Jesus Christ and a manuscript sheet of 'Notes about Satanic/Christian Beliefs'. A glimpse into the background of Scott Waterhouse revealed that he had first become attracted to devil-worship after reading a copy of Anton Szandor LaVey's classic, *Satanic Bible*; though he was clearly so emotionally disturbed that almost anything could have pushed him over the edge, particularly as he had begun to use LSD and marijuana. As he became more obsessed with the ritual of black magick, so Waterhouse began to develop an active streak of malevolence – in particular he enjoyed threatening teenage girls with death. 'Make the most of your every waking moment because your days are numbered' was a favourite.

Scott Waterhouse pleaded not guilty to the charge of murder when his trial opened in November. The jury did not agree and convicted him as charged. On 20 December 1984, in sentencing him, Judge Broderick told Waterhouse: 'The evidence indicates that you enjoyed killing. And there is every reason to believe you would do it again given the chance. Thrill killing deserves the maximum penalty of life imprisonment.' Perhaps the community of Sandford rests a little easier now, because in Maine life for first-degree murder means *life*.

TWENTY-TWO DISCIPLES
OF HELL

The case of David Berkowitz, the 'Son of Sam'

It was only when they found the letter addressed to the New York Police Department that detectives realised that they were dealing with worse than an ordinarily weird killer. Up to that point he was just another serial slayer leading the NYPD a merry dance and putting the city into a state of terror. The letter read, in part:

> I am deeply hurt by your calling me a wemon [woman]-hater. I am not. But I am a monster ... I love to hunt. Prowling the street looking for fair game – tasty meat. The wemon of Queens are prettyist [prettiest] of all ... I live for the hunt – my life. Blood for Papa ... I say goodbye and goodnight. Police: Let me haunt you with these words: I'll be back! I'll be back! To be interpreted as – Bang Bang Bang Bang Bang – Ugh!! Yours in murder,
>
> Mr Monster

There were also rambling references to blood-drinking and cannibalism; and the writer referred to himself variously as 'Beelzebub' and the 'Chubby Behemoth'. The hand-scribbled letter had been left in an envelope at the scene of Mr Monster's sixth attack, the fatal shooting of Valentina Suriani and Alexander Esau – killed as they sat in their car in the Bronx. The pattern was becoming dreadfully familiar.

The terror had begun at one o'clock on the morning of 29 July 1976, as Donna Lauria, a young medical technician, and her friend, Jody Valente, a student nurse, were sitting in their car outside Donna's home in the Bronx. As they were talking a man walked calmly out of the darkness, took a gun from a brown paper bag and started shooting; he left Donna dead and Jody with a thigh wound. On 23 October of the same year, Carl Denaro and Rosemary Keenan were shot at and wounded as they sat in their car outside a bar in Queens and then, at midnight on 27 November, Donna DeMasi and Joanne Lomino were shot and wounded while sitting on the steps outside Joanne's home in the same district.

By now ballistics experts were working on bullet-mark comparisons, and the result of their tests established that all three attacks had been carried out with the same .44 Bulldog – giving the murderer the provisional name 'The .44 Killer'. Then on 30 January 1977, another couple, John Diel and Christine Freund, were fired on in their car in Queens – the bullets killed Christine but left her companion unharmed. Further senseless, random attacks were made on 8 March when nineteen-year-old student Virginia Voskerichian was shot dead in the street, and on 14 April when Valentina Suriani and Alexander Esau were killed. And now the 'Chubby Behemoth' was taunting them.

Aside from the letter found by members of the 'Operation Omega' team formed to investigate the series of killings, he also wrote a letter to New York *Daily News* columnist Jimmy Breslin on 1 June. He concluded his letter: '. . . Not knowing what the future holds I shall say farewell and I will see you at the next job? Or should I say you will see my handiwork at the next job? Remember Ms Lauria. In their blood and from the gutter, "Sam's Creation" .44.'

'Sam's Creation'? Now the *Daily News* had a new name for the killer, 'Son of Sam'. Through his column, Breslin replied to the letter, goading the killer into making another move; it was a dangerous game, and there were still more attacks and one death to come. The first, on 26 June, was in Queens, where Salvatore Lupo and Judith Placido were wounded while they sat in a car. Then on 31 July Stacy Moskowitz and Robert Violante became

Son of Sam's last victims; shot in their car, twenty-year-old Stacy died in hospital, Robert Violante was blinded.

But like many before him, the mystery killer known as Son of Sam had made his one big mistake. While he was at the last shooting he left his yellow Ford Galaxie blocking a fire hydrant, and was given a traffic violation ticket. When he returned from the car he took the ticket off the window and threw it in the gutter – a gesture of defiance which was seen by a passing motorist. She might have thought no more of it had she not seen the young man later while she was out walking her dog; this time he was carrying something up his sleeve that looked as though it might be a gun. When the police were informed, they ran a check on the car that the ticket had been issued to and came up with the name David Berkowitz, resident in the suburb of Yonkers. When police found his car there was a loaded .44 pistol on the seat, so they settled down to wait until Berkowitz came out of his apartment to claim it. Now confronted by armed officers, Berkowitz was taken from the car and asked, 'Who are you?' 'I'm Sam,' he replied. David Berkowitz went quietly to the police station where he made a full confession. It was all very much of an anti-climax, with the pudgy twenty-four-year-old cutting a most unlikely figure as a dangerous multicide.

David Berkowitz had been born in June 1953, and had suffered the kind of deprivation, rejection and insecurity shared by many multiple killers. As his paranoia grew over the years he began to entertain the notion that women despised him and thought him ugly. In 1974, so he later claimed, Berkowitz became aware of 'the voices' as he lay in the darkness of his squalid apartment; the voices were telling him to kill. When police searched the Yonkers flat after his arrest, they found the walls covered with scribbled messages such as 'Kill for My Master' – a sinister clue to Berkowitz's involvement in Satanism.

The origin of the name 'Sam's Creation' seems to have been Berkowitz's neighbour Sam Carr, whose black labrador, Harvey, kept Berkowitz awake at night with its barking. Worse still, so Berkowitz later claimed, the dog was possessed by demons, which the creature sent into his head ordering him to kill. He began sending a series of hate letters to Carr, and in April 1977 Berkowitz shot and wounded the dog; it had been his intention to kill Harvey, but apparently the demons spoiled his aim.

An obvious paranoid schizophrenic, Berkowitz was thought sane enough to stand trial, though that process was pre-empted by his pleading guilty. On 23 August 1977, he was sentenced to 365 years, which he serves at the Attica correctional facility. On 10 July 1979, Berkowitz was attacked in prison and his throat slashed with a razor. Although the wound required fifty-six stitches he refused to name his assailant, but hinted that it was connected with an occult group with which he had once had dealings, and whose members were trying to silence him.

Then, from his prison cell, David Berkowitz began to send out letters elaborating on his membership of a killer cult which was responsible for some of the Son of Sam murders (probably the Twenty-two Disciples of Hell). One, dated October 1979 reads, in part:

I don't really know how to begin this letter, but at one time I was a member of an occult group. Being sworn to secrecy or face death I cannot reveal the name of the group, nor do I wish to. This group contained a mixture of satanic practices which included the teachings of Aleister Crowley and Eliphas Levi. It was (still is) totally blood oriented and I am certain you know just what I mean. The Coven's doctrines are a blend of Druidism, the teachings of the Secret Order of the Golden Dawn, Black Magick and a host of other unlawful and obnoxious practices

As I have said, I have no interest in revealing the Coven, especially because I have almost met sudden death on several occasions (once by half an inch) and several others have already perished under mysterious circumstances. These people will stop at nothing, including murder. They have no fear of man-made laws or the Ten Commandments.

Ironically, two of Sam Carr's sons, John and Michael, were members of the same group. There is some evidence to support the theory that the Son of Sam killings were the work of more than one person when one looks at the witness statements describing a tall, thin man with long fair hair – almost the exact opposite of the black-haired 'Chubby Behemoth'. In fact the former description fits John 'Wheaties' Carr almost perfectly.

One person who noticed these inconsistencies very early in the case was New York journalist Maury Terry, for whom the pursuit of the occult involvement in the Son of Sam killings became little short of obsessional. Terry's extensive study, *The Ultimate Evil* (Doubleday, New York, 1987), is too complex to précis here, but there is little doubt that the series of murders for which David Berkowitz has been held solely responsible is far wider-reaching in its occult implications than the official version credits. In particular, Maury Terry warns that the so-called 'Twenty-two Disciples of Hell' of which Berkowitz and the two Carr brothers (both now dead in mysterious circumstances) were members, still exists. Terry concludes his book with a list of recent cases which seem to indicate that they are still actively killing.

THE HARDY BOYS

The Hardy Boys and their 'Sacrifice to Satan'

Most campus Satanic cults are very mild affairs indeed. Usually an opportunity for drink, drugs and sex, and for those who like dressing up, black robes. This group was something entirely different – given to heavy drug-dealing, unnecessary violence *and* Satanism. The cult centred on Jim Hardy, as many things did at Carl Junction High, Joplin, Missouri, His closest henchmen were Theron Roland and Ron Clements and they liked to be known as 'The Hardy Boys'. It was Clements who turned the others on to Satanism after a read of LaVey's *Satanic Bible*. The other two were more hands-on devil-worshippers, vying to outdo each other in the cruelty of their animal sacrifices to Satan. Soon things were going to change.

Nineteen-year-old Steven Newberry was not one of God's most attractive youths. He was, in short, fat and smelly. But he was enthusiastic about the cult and free with his money. He was also going to be the Hardys' first and only human sacrifice.

The Boys had been discussing the matter for months, and during the summer of 1987 Steve Newberry had been suggested as a candidate and then rejected. Principally because of the looseness of his purse-strings when it came to buying people drugs. By October Steve's name was being mentioned again.

The date of Hallowe'en – ideal for such devilry as blood sacrifice – was thwarted when the Newberry family went on a short holiday. On Thanksgiving evening – a time when the sacrifice of turkeys is more appropriate than that of schoolboys –

Steven was delighted to be invited to join the in-crowd in the woods to catch some live 'offerings'. In the end everybody's nerve failed, and all they achieved was arousing Steve Newberry's suspicions.

Even so, on 6 December Steve was back in the woods with the gang beating a sacrificial cat to death. Then the Hardy Boys turned to beating the sacrificial student to death. 'Why me?' asked a shocked and bewildered Steve Newberry. 'Just for fun!' Clements answered. As he lay into Newberry with a baseball bat, Jim Hardy was chanting rhythmically, over and over: 'Sacrifice to Satan! Sacrifice to Satan!' Finally the deed had been done and the bloody remains of Steven Newberry hidden.

But it was never going to be as easy as that. Like many immature criminals, the Hardys could not resist boasting about killing 'the fat boy'. The bragging was heard and the police informed. All three were arrested and the following year tried, convicted and given life sentences.

While they were in custody, Hardy, Roland and Clements admitted being linked to other Satanist groups in the state, including the notorious Crowd, based in Joplin, Missouri. That group's main activity was drug-running, though one member was thought to be associated with the Hardy Boys if not with the murder.

PROCESS CHURCH
OF FINAL JUDGEMENT

Arguably the most sinister of the modern killer cults, the Process Church of Final Judgement was founded in 1963 by Robert and Mary Anne DeGrimston. Full name Robert DeGrimston Moore, he was born in 1935, inappropriately the grandson of a vicar. DeGrimston came to cults via Scientology, where he met Mary Anne MacLean. The couple eventually separated from the Hubbard Institute and formed their own group, initially called 'The Process'.

From the outset it was clear that followers of the DeGrimstons needed to be servile to survive (Robert and Mary Anne preferred to be known as, respectively, 'God' and 'Goddess', though Mrs DeGrimston was not averse to being addressed as Josef Goebbels). As with many similar organisations The Process placed great emphasis on financial rewards – for the DeGrimstons, that is – and having tired of the sumptuous headquarters in London's Mayfair, they flew to the Bahamas and thence to Mexico. When the Mexican authorities became too inquisitive, it was back to London again, this time under the name 'Omega'. Following a whistle-stop tour of Europe, Omega came to rest in New Orleans, now operating as the Process Church of Final Judgement.

Success built on success, and soon there was a San Francisco chapter, where Process met hippiedom and the biker gangs. Some indication of the dangerously unbalanced state of Robert DeGrimston's mind (he was now alternatively calling himself 'Christ' and 'Satan') can be found in one of his more popular treatises: 'My prophecy on this wasted earth, and upon the corrupt creation that squats upon its ruined surface is *Thou Shalt Kill.'*

It was clearly a philosophy that, sinister as it was, attracted no small amount of support. Except from the US Immigration Service, who had finally caught on to the fact that the God and Goddess and their English coterie were living on very outdated visitors' permits. It was back to London for the DeGrimstons, though they left behind healthy Process chapters in many major American cities. Probably the most publicly notorious aspect of Process was its association with Charles Manson, who even called his 'Family' the 'Final Church' at one stage. By now Process had splintered into such sub-groups as the Companions of Life and the murderous Four P Movement whose name was taken from the symbol of Process.

In the early 1970s the Process Church of Final Judgement eventually dissolved. As did the relationship between Robert and Mary Anne DeGrimston. Mary Anne briefly flirted with a new Foundation Church of the Millennium, then disappeared from sight; Robert simply disappeared from sight.

Their legacy, though, is reported to be alive and well and still causing mischief. According to journalist Maury Terry, the murders of Robert and Mary Hirschmann in New York were connected with the Process. And 'Son of Sam' David Berkowitz has claimed an association.

Two birthdays, an anniversary and the death of Arlis Perry

California is no stranger to killings, but the ritual 'annihilation' of Arlis Perry at Stanford was particularly grotesque. Nineteen-year-old Arlis and her newly married husband Bruce were both deeply committed Christians and a rather serious couple. He was about to enter Stanford medical school.

On the night of 12 October 1974, Arlis Perry decided to pop down to the post-box to send some mail. Bruce went too, and on the way back in the car there was a disagreement about a flat tyre, and Bruce got out to walk the half mile to their Hall of Residence. Meanwhile Arlis also got out of the car and paid a night visit to the nearby Stanford Memorial Church. At midnight the security staff cleared and locked the building.

When his wife had not arrived home by 12.15 a.m., Bruce Perry walked back to where their car was parked outside the church. Finding both locked, and being in no better mood than after the earlier row, Perry went home to wait. At three o'clock he reported Arlis missing. When the Memorial Church's security guard made his regular stop-off inspection at some time after 5.15, he was alarmed to find a side door forced open; from the inside. He was even more alarmed when he discovered the semi-naked body of Arlis Perry.

It was clear to most people professionally obliged to visit the scene that this was a ritual murder. An altar candle had been wedged between the victim's breasts and held in place by her crossed arms; another candle had been pushed into her vagina. A pair of jeans had been arranged over her spread legs to form a diamond shape. Although she had also been badly beaten, the cause of Arlis Perry's death was the ice-pick driven into the back of her head.

With their prime suspect, Bruce Perry, cleared from the investigation, detectives were beginning to get the whisper that Arlis may have been seeing somebody other than her husband. Was it possible that she had arranged a meeting with a man in the church? Why had she gone out to post letters that night when there was no Saturday collection? Had she picked a fight with Bruce at that spot deliberately because he was in the way? A lot of questions; with not many answers.

Then an isolated incident happened in Bismarck that could have indicated an occult connection. Somebody had very carefully, very neatly stolen one gravemarker from the cemetery. Arlis Perry's. For use in a ritual? To prove a point? More questions. All that was known locally was that Arlis had contacted the Satanists in the forlorn hope that she could save their souls.

For the time being the trail was at an end.

The case was reopened in a curious way. David Berkowitz, who had been jailed for the 'Son of Sam' killings, sent a package from his New York prison cell four years after the murder of Arlis Perry. It was addressed to a police lieutenant and contained a book on witchcraft. Beside the underlined passages in a chapter on the Process Church of Final Judgement, a note had been written in the margin: 'Arliss Perry. [In all his letters David Berkowitz spells Mrs Perry's name Arliss – it seems unnecessary to perpetuate this particular mistake.] Hunted, Stalked and Slain. Followed to California. Stanford Uni.'

At the same time, in Santa Clara, police officers were examining an anonymous letter posted in New Orleans. It contained press cuttings about Berkowitz and some about the death of John Carr, whose name regularly cropped up in connection with the speculation over the Son of Sam killings. Maury Terry was the only one to notice that Carr's birthday was the same day Arlis Perry died. Which was also Aleister Crowley's birthday; and the fifth anniversary of Charles Manson's imprisonment.

Two days later, on 25 October 1978, Berkowitz sent off another missive:

Look there are people out there who are animals . . . They *Hate* God. I'm not talking about common criminals. You know who I'm talking about . . . They will even kill in a church. Do you think I am joking? Do you think I'm just bending your ear? Well, do this – do this quickly, I'm serious: call the Santa Clara Sheriff's office (California). This is by Santa Clara University and close to Stanford University. Please ask one of the sheriffs who have been there since late '74 what happened to *Arlis Perry*. Remember this name: Arlis Perry! Please don't let them give you the 'Psychopathic Homicidal Maniac' line or something similar. They know *how* she was murdered. They cannot tell you who did it or why. It was *no* sex crime, *no* random murder. Ask them *where* she was killed. Ask them how. Ask

173

them how often she wandered into the building of gold, purple and scarlet. Please ask them for the autopsy report. Let the police provide you with everything – every little detail. Make them tell you what she went through. Don't let them skip one single perverted atrocity that was committed on her tiny, slender little body. Let the Santa Clara police tell you all. Oh, yeah, lastly (and this is important), make sure you ask them where she lived – I mean where she came from. Doing this will solve the whole case . . .

Followed by another:

. . . cults as you know flourish around college campuses. They also flourish around military bases. Drugs flow all over these two places. Young servicemen and young college students are involved in sexual relations. So mix the two of them up. Put them near each other and what do you have? You've got a pretty wild, dedicated and nasty bunch of young, zealous, anti-establishment devil-worshippers. And what a deadly mixture it is. My, my. Didn't Miss Perry wander around the Stanford Campus frequently? [With hindsight we know that she did.] Well, start adding, kid. What have we got here?

To journalist Maury Terry, Berkowitz claimed that a Satanist contract killer (later identified as William Mentzer) had been showing round photographs of Arlis at a meeting of the cult. Despite this and other information turned up by Terry, the case remains unsolved.

POSTSCRIPT:

Last Judgement?

In 1983 Los Angeles police named 'Satanist hit-man'

William Mentzer as a suspect in the murder of millionaire Roy Radin. The following year he was linked to the shootings of James Pierce and June Mincher, and was caught on tape boasting about the murder of Roy Radin. On 22 July 1991 Mentzer and his accomplices were convicted of murder. Mentzer was sentenced to death.

'Helter Skelter', the Hole and 'Mad Charlie' Manson

He has been called the most dangerous man in America; and Charles Milles Manson is not going to disagree with that. One of his more memorable quotes runs like this: 'From the world of darkness I did loose demons and devils in the power of scorpions to torment.' Not entirely unexpected from a man who believes he is Satan as well as Jesus Christ. The problem was that other people believed him too. They also believed in his version of Armageddon. This event Manson called 'Helter Skelter' (after one of the Beatles' songs). The time was almost nigh, he prophesied, when blacks would rise up and slaughter the whites – except Manson and his followers, of course, who would survive to inherit the earth. The trick was to be this. The so-called 'Family' would hide away in the Hole until the battle was over. In his usual muddle-headed way, Charlie had adopted a legend of the Hopi Indians who believed that their nation had emerged from 'The Hole'. This became fused in his mind with the bottomless pit described in the Book of Revelation. When the Manson Family emerged from the Hole, Charlie would be recognised as the incarnation of Christ and they would take over.

After a singularly unpromising early life Charles Manson, born the son of a teenaged prostitute, arrived via several spells in institutions and prisons, in San Francisco. It was at the height of the hippie phenomenon, and the streets were crowded with young men and women searching for a new age of spiritual enlightenment. And Manson was there to provide it. No matter his

175

upbringing and retarded educational development, Charlie's charisma attracted a following of utterly devoted disciples: his Family. Soon they would be expected to demonstrate that devotion by killing for him.

It is impossible to calculate how many murders there were. Vincent Bugliosi, prosecutor at Manson's trial, does not dismiss Charlie's own estimate of thirty-five. However, the most notorious became known as the Tate/LaBianca killings, and took place in the summer of 1969. At the time the Family were occupying a disused movie-set ranch owned by George Spahn. While at the ranch, Manson organised the 'Land Armada', a fleet of armoured (stolen) dune buggies that would protect the homestead during 'Helter Skelter'.

Shortly after midnight on Saturday 9 August 1969, four shadowy figures could have been found skulking in the grounds of the secluded mansion at 10050 Cielo Drive in Beverly Hills. 'Tex' Watson, Patricia 'Katie' Krenwinkel, 'Sadie' Atkins and Linda Kasabian had arrived to cause a spot of mayhem. 10050 Cielo was occupied that night by actress Sharon Tate (her husband, the film director Roman Polanski, was away on business), who was heavily pregnant, and four friends. In an orgy of overkill, the Family left all five victims horribly butchered. Voytec Frykowski alone was stabbed more than fifty times, slashed, shot and so savagely bludgeoned with the butt of a gun that the weapon shattered. On the front door to the house the word 'Pig' was painted in blood; not one of the murderous gang had had the slightest idea whom they had killed – they were just random victims. On 11 August, just two days after the Tate murders, after motivating themselves with drugs, a group consisting of 'Tex' Watson, Susan Atkins, Katie Krenwinkel, Linda Kasabian, Clem Grogan and Leslie van Houten went on a second murder spree. A little after 1.00 a.m. the Family invaded the Silver Lake home of businessman Leno LaBianca and his wife Rosemary; like the Cielo Drive victims, the choice appeared to be random. After stabbing and slashing the LaBiancas to death, Manson's disciples inscribed the mottoes 'Death to the Pigs',

'Rise' and 'Healter [sic] Skelter' in blood on the walls; as a final act of gratuitous violence, the word 'War' was carved into Leno LaBianca's abdomen.

Then they went to ground, and might for all we know have remained in the Hole for a lot longer had Susan Atkins not been picked up for a prostitution offence. And had she not admitted the Tate murders to a fellow prisoner. On 1 December 1969, the Family were rounded up and charges of murder were laid against the principal members. Manson, Krenwinkel, Atkins and van Houten were tried together and, on 19 April 1971, after one of the most extraordinary trials in California's history, they were convicted and sentenced to death for the Tate/LaBianca murders. In view of the state of California's suspension of capital punishment, the death sentences were subsequently reduced to life imprisonment.

Manson appears to have dominated his equally degenerate disciples with a mish-mash of corrupted Biblical philosophy combined with his magnetic sexual attraction for the female members of his Family. There is also evidence that Manson was heavily involved with various occult and Satanic cults, such as the Kirke Order of Dog Blood, which underpinned the Family's killings. Notably, it has been suggested that Mad Charlie was a member of the notorious Four P Movement.

FOUR P MOVEMENT

Because most cults are relatively benign with just a few rogue elements, it is difficult to credit the evidence of groups which are totally malevolent – even, some might say, bordering on evil. If published information is to be believed, then the Four P Movement (an offshoot of the sinister Process Church of Final Judgement) is just such a group.

Most of the reliable evidence derives from research carried out by Ed Sanders in preparation for his book on the Charles Manson case (*The Family*). The Four P originated in California around 1967, and recruited mainly from the college campuses. The leader of the group is thought to have been a wealthy middle-aged businessman who called himself the 'Head Devil', or 'Grand Chingon'. The cult's rites were performed in accordance with star movements and initially embraced the sacrifice of dogs – invariably Alsatians and Dobermanns. The singular aspect of these ritual sacrifices was the manner in which the animals were painstakingly skinned and completely drained of blood. It is possible that the celebrants drank the blood as part of the ceremony.

Worse still were the human sacrifices. It is claimed that victims were fastened to an altar and stabbed to death with a dagger fitted with six blades of different lengths, allowing the stomach to be pierced before a shorter blade dug through into the heart. The heart, according to some alleged witnesses, was then removed and shared around the congregation as a tasty tit-bit.

Being one of the more satanic of the Satanist cults, it is not surprising that Four P attracted more than its share of notorious killers – not least Charlie Manson. Ed Sanders recalls that several of the 'Family' even referred to Manson as 'Grand Chingon'. Another member claimed that dogs had been sacrificed, and it is true that large quantities of animal bones were found at one of the Family homesteads. As Michael Newton points out: 'A peculiar form of refuse for a group reputedly composed of vegetarians.' David Berkowitz, alias 'Son of Sam', claimed membership of Four P and also implicated mass killer Fred Cowan. Stanley Baker claimed that his series of murders resulted from the direct orders of the Grand Chingon.

Although law enforcement agencies claim knowledge of the Four P Movement's involvement in drugs, pornography and white slavery (as well as murder), they have yet to make a legal case against the group. Partly, they say, because different sections of the Movement meet and act under different names, unknown even to other sections. Thus making informing against the whole of Four P impossible.

Stanley Baker, hit-man for the 'Grand Chingon'

On 13 July 1970 California Highway Patrol officers picked up a radio report that there had been a hit-and-run smash between two cars around the Big Sur area; three people in one of the cars had been hurt. The two men who sped away from the scene of the accident were described as 'long-haired hippy-types'. A couple of hours later two suspects matching the description were picked off the street and taken in for questioning. Stanley Dean Baker was twenty-two years old, his buddy Harry Allen Stroup just twenty; both freely admitted being involved in the hit-and-run. So far a routine traffic violation, one of a countless number of such humdrum incidents that waste valuable police time. But 13 July 1970 was about to become very different.

A routine search of Stan Baker's pockets turned up a well-thumbed copy of Anton LaVey's *Satanic Bible* and a human finger bone. This latter was explained by Baker with the disarmingly straightforward statement: 'Yeah, I'm a cannibal.' The devil-worshippers' handbook was also simple to explain. When he had been at college in Wyoming, Baker had joined a Satanic cult called the Four P Movement – and he had the tattoos to prove it.

Four P is one of the more notorious groups originally founded in California, but later spreading across the western states via college-campus recruitment. It is alleged that cultists graduated from the sacrifice of animals to the sacrifice of human beings, the blood from which was ritually drunk by participants in the ceremony. Among the better known multiple killers said to have been involved with the Four P are Charles Manson and various members of his 'Family', David Berkowitz, the 'Son of Sam' killer, and Fred Cowan, the Nazi sympathiser whose shooting spree in New York left four fellow employees, a policeman and himself dead.

And Stanley Dean Baker, of course, who was now claiming to have sacrificed numerous lives at the request of Four P's leader, the 'Grand Chingon'. One he remembered particularly well; it had taken place the previous 20 April, when forty-year-old lighting designer Robert Salem was butchered in his San Francisco apartment. He had been stabbed twenty-seven times, and his head was almost severed from his body. Baker obligingly left his fingerprints on the walls in the victim's blood. And what of that other grisly relic found in Stanley's pocket – the finger bone? That, apparently, had been harvested from a more recent sacrifice in Montana. Showing no evidence of remorse for his evil ways, Baker considerately gave detectives detailed directions to the isolated spot on the Yellowstone River where James Schlosser's body could be found – or most of it anyway. The unfortunate Schlosser's heart and several more fingers had been removed to provide Stanley and his chum Harry with a light snack.

On 20 July 1971, Stanley Baker and Harry Stroup were convicted by a Montana jury of first-degree murder and ordered to be confined in the state prison. Stroup behaved himself inside and was released in 1979. Baker continued his affair with Satan, and formed a devil-worshipping coven in prison. It was at this time he suffered the humiliation of having LaVey's Church of Satan turn down his application for membership. His behaviour became so disruptive that he was eventually removed to a high-security institution in Illinois. Crouching in the corner of his cell baying at the full moon might have helped get him there.

Stan Baker earned parole in 1985 and faded into obscurity until he was found by a journalist six years later living in Minneapolis.

'A member in good standing', 'Nazi' Fred Cowan and the Four P

Fred Cowan was a bigot and a bully and, as it transpired, a very dangerous one. Not for nothing was he called 'Nazi' Fred Cowan, and 'Second Hitler'; the Nazi insignia tattooed on his massive body-builder's arms gave it away. So did his irrational hatred of Jews and blacks. He always claimed he hated black people because one refused to come to his assistance during the Vietnam War. The only problem with that excuse is that Cowan never fought in Vietnam. It is true he had been in the army, but he had been unceremoniously kicked out following two courts-martial.

When he returned to New York after his spectacularly unsuccessful military career, Cowan got himself a job at the Neptune Worldwide Moving Company. He also began to take a profoundly unhealthy interest in decorating his apartment with Nazi swastika flags, photographs of his heroes – Hitler, Himmler, Eichman ... and guns. He also joined the fanatical National States Rights Party.

Despite Fred Cowan's racist threats – such as to blow up a synagogue – he might have been able to keep a lid on his anger for a while longer. Had it not been that his boss at Worldwide Moving, Norman Bing, was Jewish; and had it not been that Bing suspended his reluctant employee for some trifling misdemeanour. Having spent the two weeks of his suspension nursing his hatred, Cowan returned to work on 14 February 1977, Valentine's Day. He was armed with a veritable arsenal of firearms. Inside the building he shot dead four employees. When the squad car arrived Cowan opened fire on it and killed a policeman.

By now the building was surrounded by SWAT teams; marksmen just waiting for a glimpse of their target. The stand-off lasted more than seven hours. At 2.40 p.m. a single shot rang out from inside the Neptune building; Fred Cowan, like so many mass killers, had taken his own life. Whether he was really a nice man in a brutish man's body, as some claimed, we will never know. But before he put a gun to his own head, Fred Cowan sent a telephone message to the mayor: 'I'm sorry to be causing the city so much trouble.'

As the result of a prison interview with 'Son of Sam' killer David Berkowitz, there is some reason to believe that Fred Cowan was in some way associated with the Four P Movement. This is not as surprising as it might seem, as quite a number of Satanist cults have links with extreme right-wing and Nazi organisations. The portion of the interview that suggests Cowan's association follows. (The questions are put to Berkowitz by lawyer Felix Gilroy, the date is October 1978.)

Gilroy: Do the words 'witches' coven' mean anything to you?
Berkowitz: I have heard it before.
Were some of these people involved in the witches' coven?
I believe they were. Yes.
Were you in the same coven?
Yes.
Did you meet regularly?
Well, I can't really say. I don't want to say.
Was Mr Cowan involved in that?
I don't want to talk about it.
. . .

182

'Night Stalker' Richard Ramirez in court. (*Topham*)

Inverted pentacle of
the Satanists
incorporating the
Goat of Mendes.

Indian guru Bhagwan
Shree Rajneesh.
(*Popperfoto*)

Followers of Rajneesh
at Rancho Rajneesh in
Rajneeshpuram,
Oregon. (*Topham*)

Shoko Asahara, leader of the Aum Shinri Kyo. (*Popperfoto*

Aftermath of the Tokyo subway gas attack, 20 March 1995. (*Associated Press/Topham*)

THE OATH OF A FREEMAN.

I·AB· being (by Gods providence) an Inhabitant, and Freeman, within the iurifdictiō of this Common-wealth, doe freely acknowledge my felfe to bee fubject to the governement thereof; and therefore doe heere fweare, by the great & dreadfull name of the Everliving-God, that I will be true & faithfull to the fame, & will accordingly yield affiftance & fupport therunto, with my perfon & eftate, as in equity I am bound: and will alfo truely indeavour to maintaine and preferve all the libertyes & privilidges thereof, fubmitting my felfe to the wholefome lawes, & ordres made & ftablifhed by the fame; and further, that I will not plot, nor practice any evill againft it, nor confent to any that fhall foe do, butt will timely difcover, & reveall the fame to lawefull authoritee nowe here ftablifhed, for the fpeedie preventing thereof. Moreover, I doe folemnly binde my felfe, in the fight of God, that when I fhalbe called, to give my voyce touching any fuch matter of this ftate, (in which freemen are to deale) I will give my vote & fuffrage as I fhall judge in myne owne confcience may beft conduce & tend to the publick weale of the body, without refpect of perfonnes, or favour of any man. Soe help mee God in the Lord Iefus Chrift.

Mark Hofmann's forgery of 'The Oath of a Freeman' which led to two brutal murders.

Gordon W. Kahl of the Posse Comitatus. (*AP/World Wide*)

Adolfo de Jesus Constanzo, known as 'El Padrino'. (*Associated Press*)

The palo mayombe *nganga* found at Constanzo's ranch. (*UPI/Bettmann*)

The burning cross of a Ku Klux Klan rally in Maine in 1987. (*Topham*)

Double lynching.

Byron de la Beckwith is arrested in connection with the assassination of civil rights leader Medgar Evers (*below*), who was ambushed outside his home in Jackson, Mississippi, on 12 June 1963. (*Topham*)

A National Guard helicopter flies past the burning Waco compound, 19 April 1993. (*Popperfoto*)

Vernon Howell, aka David Koresh, self-styled messiah of the Branch Davidians. (*Popperfoto*)

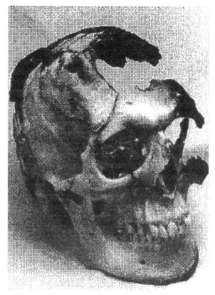

Koresh's skull, retrieved from the ashes of Waco. A bullet hole can be seen in the centre of the forehead.

Was Fred Cowan a real person when you knew him?
Yes.

KNIGHTS OF THE
BLACK CIRCLE

'Tell Satan you love him', the case of Ricky Kasso

Ricky Kasso was born in March 1967 and despite – or perhaps because of – his secure affluent background, he soon went to the bad, and before he had entered teenage was experimenting with drugs. By the time he reached high school, Kasso (which he delighted in telling people rhymed with 'asshole') was described by counsellors at his school as 'socially and emotionally handicapped'. At age seventeen, Ricky liked to be known on the streets around Northport, Long Island, as the 'Acid King'; a title he had bestowed on himself. It was after reading LaVey's *Satanic Bible*, his only book, that he became obsessed with Satanism and black magic to the point where reality and fantasy overlapped dangerously.

Although never a formal member, Ricky Kasso hung round on the periphery of the Northport High School Knights of the Black Circle, a student drug 'n' orgy cult. In his spare time – of which he had a lot – he was fond of initiating his own circle of substance-abusing hangers-on into his own brand of immature worship of Satan, whom he described as 'my main man'. Ricky's closest friend at this time was James Troiano (called 'Dracula' because of his teeth), less dominant, but Kasso's equal in almost every other brand of unpleasantness. One of Ricky's biggest fans was seventeen-year-old Gary Lauwers, who followed the Acid King rather as a dog follows its master.

In 1984, Ricky Kasso led his merry men on a pilgrimage to the notorious house at Amityville where Ronald 'Butch' DeFeo had massacred his family ten years earlier. It was 30 April, the witches' feast of Walpurgisnacht, so Ricky knocked together an altar and they all shouted a few praises to Satan. It had been the intention to sacrifice Gary Lauwers to the 'main man' during this *ad hoc* celebration. The idea seems to have fizzled out, and Gary lived to tell the tale – for a few more weeks anyway.

A month or so later, at the start of June, Kasso found he was missing several twists of 'angel dust' (PCP), and repeatedly accused Gary Lauwers of having stolen them. On 16 June Kasso, Troiano, Lauwers and a youth named Albert Quinones hid themselves away in Newport's Aztakea Woods to partake of some mescaline at one of their 'hell parties'. During the course of subsequent reveries they renewed the dispute over the allegedly pilfered drugs. The result was a vicious attack by the dope-crazed Kasso. The disciple, in trying to escape, was felled by Troiano and held down while Ricky repeatedly drove a hunting knife into his body, shouting at the wretched boy: 'Tell Satan you love him!' Lauwers' disinclination to embrace the church of Satan at the moment of his death resulted in Kasso gouging out his eyes. Ricky and 'Drac' covered the body with leaves, though poor terrified Albert had long since taken to his heels.

Despite the fact that Ricky Kasso was openly boasting of his human sacrifice, it was not until 5 July that anybody had the courage to tell the police. That day Kasso and Troiano were arrested and held at Rivershead jail. Two days later the Acid King hanged himself in a cell with his bed sheet. Albert Quinones turned State's evidence, but having been out of his head on drugs at the time of the 'sacrifice', proved a very unreliable witness against James Troiano at his trial in April 1985. This, combined with some irregularity in Dracula's confession, led to his eventual acquittal on the charge of murder, though he was incarcerated on a charge of burglary. He is reported to have become a 'born-again' Christian.

One of the noticeable features of this trial was the way in which the prosecution avoided mention of devil-worship. This is not uncommon in such cases, and the reason is that while an

185

average jury can accept and analyse evidence of homicide, many have no background that will assist them to understand the mumbo-jumbo activities of fringe cults. It is also a tactic of defence attorneys – no jury, they figure, ever let a killer off because he worshipped Satan as well.

A MISCELLANY

Outside the United States of America Satanism is far less well organised, and groups, where they exist, rarely have evocative names or jealously guarded hierarchies. These groups tend not to be involved in organised crime and so are less inclined to homicide. This does not mean that such activity does not exist. The following are selected notes on Satanic killings.

'Satan's laughing hit-man', the case of Rodney Dale

The press nicknamed him 'Satan's Laughing Hit-man'. And it is true that he did have the mark of the Beast, 666, cut on the palms of his hands. It is also true that as he ran amok in the Burleigh Heads district of Australia's Gold Coast he was laughing; he 'hit' eight people in a thirty-minute reign of terror, one of whom died.

On the afternoon of Saturday 7 April 1990, police officers were alerted to the fact that a lone gunman was firing shots with a .223-calibre rifle and a pump-action shotgun from the balcony of a flat in Tweed Street into the crowded thoroughfare below. Within minutes police cars had been dispatched to the scene of the incident, though by the time they arrived, the man had moved to a position outside the CES [social security] office, leaving behind him his first victim. As the gunman continued firing wildly, five ambulances and further police units were arriving.

One of the things that moved into his line of fire was a trio of cars taking a bride and her family to her wedding. As Robyn Porter and her father sat in their chauffeur-driven limousine

187

behind the two cars carrying the bridesmaids, the mad sniper opened fire with his automatic rifle, showering the vehicles in a hail of bullets. The driver of the limousine was hit in the left arm and shoulder and the right hand, but bravely drove on until he was out of firing range. The wedding did go ahead, and after the ceremony, with courageous understatement, the new Mrs Robyn Kelly said: 'The wedding went well, but the shooting put a damper on it.'

Meanwhile, the first of the ambulances, with a heavy police escort, was ferrying victims to the hospital, and the gunman was still shooting randomly at a nearby hotel complex. At this point a hero enters in the person of thirty-eight-year-old Sergeant Robert Baker. Armed with a Magnum revolver, Baker walked straight across the highway towards the gunman. What followed was more like a Wild West shoot-out than a scene in the sunshine strip of Australia's popular holiday resort.

As Sergeant Baker approached his target he called to the man to drop his firearm; instantly the gunman's weapon was trained on him, loosing off a spatter of bullets which, miraculously, failed to hit the officer who had also opened fire. The afternoon's bloodshed ended as the gunman dropped his weapon after receiving a shot to the arm.

By the following morning the newspapers named the maniac gunman as twenty-six-year-old Rodney John Dale. Neighbours spoke of him as being 'a very nice, friendly guy . . . he was always pleasant and always very happy'. He was also, according to other sources, involved with a Satanic cult – which may explain why he had carved the number 666 into the palm of each hand before he left home.

Quite how significant Rodney Dale's peripheral involvement with the 'black arts' was in relation to his shooting spree only psychiatrists will be able to elucidate. However, there was no shortage of word space given to the opinions of the 'opposition'. Mrs Jan Groenveld, director of the organisation Freedom in Christ and somebody who has dealt extensively with dabblers in the occult, claimed that people who were already psychologically disturbed were liable to be strongly influenced by occult activity: 'A person who was fascinated by Satan worship and listened to [heavy metal] music groups like AC/DC, Black Sabbath and Metallica could be pushed into violent behaviour.' She added, quite correctly, that in the United States there were people waiting on Death Row because of occult-influenced crimes.

That Rodney Dale is 'psychologically disturbed' is denied by nobody. Indeed, his own defence lawyer, Mr Bill Potts, suggested that his client might be suffering from some form of psychosis and urged that he be psychiatrically examined in prison and, if necessary, treated. It was so ordered by the Southport magistrates.

Death of a 'kinky knix council chief', the case of Colin Henry

It was a story made for the more flamboyant of the tabloid press – 'Why I Killed Kinky Knix Council Chief' roared one. The 'I' of the story which followed this banner headline was Colin Henry; the 'Kinky Knix' referred to a black PVC basque, which was being worn by 'Council Chief' Christopher Rogers when he was stabbed to death in what the papers referred to as a 'bizarre row over witchcraft'.

The reason the public was being given this glimpse of a world many didn't even know exists was because thirty-seven-year-old joiner Colin Henry was standing his trial at Nottingham Crown Court for the murder of Councillor Rogers, the forty-year-old deputy chairman of Manchester City Council's education committee.

Mr Peter Joyce QC, opening for the Crown, on 7 February 1994, said the killing had taken place the previous February, when Christopher Rogers visited the house at Catton, Nottingham, where Colin Henry lived with his homosexual lover who was also a friend of Rogers. Chris Rogers and the friend went out together for a meal and then returned to Henry's home and the three of them settled down to an evening's entertainment – which in their case was the watching of pornographic sado-masochist videos and dressing up in women's underwear. And some might say, why not? The problem arose when the consumption of alcohol caused tempers to fray, and an argument – really about nothing – ended in murder.

It emerged in evidence that while Christopher Rogers was an enthusiastic supporter of Satanism, Colin Henry's preference was for witchcraft. The pair began to squabble over the relative merits of their different passions, the result of which was that Councillor Rogers made the mistake of calling Henry 'stupid', a suggestion which Colin Henry resented and which would cost Rogers his life. A little later that night, Henry, still smarting from the insult, stabbed his guest twice in the chest with a six-inch-bladed sheath knife, shouting: 'You'll never call me stupid again.' About that he was absolutely right, though he denied committing murder. In his own testimony, Colin Henry said that he could remember little of the argument, save that Christopher Rogers was trying to convert him from witchcraft (of which he was apparently a bonded high priest) to the worship of Satan.

However, juicy meat for the tabloids as this was, it had nothing on the revelations contained in the expert testimony of pathologist Professor Stephen Jones. Professor Jones told the court that he had found many small injuries to the victim's body indicating that he was at least as enthusiastic a masochist as he was a Satanist. There were descriptions of floral design scratch marks around Rogers' nipples and arms, and other scratches and scars on the buttocks.

In Colin Henry's defence, psychiatrist Dr David Gill said that Henry genuinely believed the boasts he claimed Rogers made of being involved in the kidnapping, torture and death of as many as five young men. The psychiatrist said that Henry was convinced that his victim 'had mental powers to manipulate him'. None of which swayed the jury, who convicted Colin Henry of murder, and he was sentenced to life imprisonment.

Female Satanist cult rape, mutilate and murder man

The tabloids were in with a bang. 'Satan Girls' Bloodlust' shrieked the *Sun*! That was in October 1989, when the news from Brisbane, Australia reached the world. It appeared from this report that 'A gang of Satan-worshipping women drank pints of blood after hacking a man to death in their evil lust for thrills.' The man, it turned out, was forty-seven-year-old father-of-five, Edward Baldock. Baldock (silly man!) was picked up by a woman one night after he had been drinking heavily. Thinking he was on to a sure thing he went willingly to a deserted yacht club in Brisbane. Even more eagerly, Ed Baldock shucked off his clothes in readiness for passion promised. It must have given the naked man quite a shock to find himself surrounded by four knife-wielding Satanists.

When the case came before a Brisbane court in February 1991, it had already been dubbed the 'Lesbian Vampire Trial'. In the dock to begin with was Tracey Wigginton, the leader of the group. She had pleaded guilty to the murder of Edward Baldock – though it would have been difficult not to as her bank card was found in one of the victim's shoes. Wigginton did not testify in her own defence, but two psychiatrists who had examined her thoroughly said she claimed to have been regularly sexually assaulted by her grandfather between the ages of eight and eleven. According to the medical evidence, Tracey Wigginton demonstrated no fewer than four quite distinct personalities. After her trial she was sentenced to life imprisonment.

Her lesbian lover, Lisa Ptaschinski, had told the jury that Wigginton was a vampire who lived on human blood, or if that was in short supply, animal blood from the butcher. She also claimed to be able to disappear, except for a pair of disembodied 'cat's eyes'. Describing the murder of Edward Baldock, Ptaschinski said her lover went into what she described as a 'feeding frenzy' after their victim had been stabbed fifteen times and his head all but severed from his body. For her part in this horrific crime Lisa Ptaschinski also collected a life sentence.

The two other women, twenty-four-year-old Kim Jervis and her lover Tracey Waugh, also twenty-four, gave additional evidence against Tracey Wigginton, while pleading not guilty to their own charges. Waugh accused Wigginton of possessing mind power – 'You can't stop yourself from doing what she tells you to do.' She added that she had not actually seen Tracey Wigginton drink blood, but 'smelled it on her breath'. Tracey Waugh was acquitted of all charges, while Kim Jervis was sentenced to eight years for manslaughter.

Steven Mignogna, the devil and the man from the Vatican

Most serious occultists and Satanists have never heard of 'Satan's Revels'. Eighteen-year-old college drop-out Steven Mignogna had – and he was as pleased as Punch about them. He wasn't keen on drugs or booze, but it was his chance to have sex with a young virgin. More about the heavy-metal music later.

It was on a Tuesday evening; the date was 2 August (the day of the Satanic Revels) and the year 1988. Mignogna had collected his best friend and together they drove to the long, built-up ribbon strip of US Route 30, where it bisects North Huntingdon in Westmoreland County. Steve knew they could pick up a couple of young girls at the shopping mall, and it was in the video arcade that they scored. Thirteen-year-old Penny Ansell and twelve-year-old Melissa Baker. The girls had been dropped off by Penny's mother who agreed to pick them up again at ten o'clock. Why two well-bred, intelligent youngsters, barely into adolescence, would leave a busy, friendly environment to go off with a couple of strangers is a puzzle. Tragically, they did not have long to regret it.

As soon as the girls had settled themselves into Steve Mignogna's red truck, off he sped to his parents' house in nearby Trafford. Here, he pulled Melissa Baker into a bedroom and, half persuading half raping, he had intercourse with her. Then he threw Melissa into the bath and repeatedly slashed at her throat

192

and chest with a knife until, with a jab to the heart, he killed her. There was blood everywhere – and he still had one to go! Whether Mignogna was appalled by the mess, or whether he was incapable of two in an evening, Penny Ansell was not sexually assaulted. But she was stabbed to death.

It had all been too grotesque for Steve's buddy. After reluctantly helping to dispose of the plastic-wrapped bodies in a remote spot, he went straight home and told his parents what had happened. They told the police. The police recovered the corpses and took Mignogna into custody. Once he was in a cell the part-time Satanist made it clear that he was explaining nothing. Not that it mattered. With his victims' blood on everything he touched, and his pal's eye-witness testimony, it did not look as though Steven Mignogna stood much of a chance. But that was to reckon without divine intervention.

The trial was set for March 1989, and the state's case was advanced by Assistant District Attorney John Peck. To add a touch of the burlesque to an often harrowing process, Mignogna was being defended, in part at least, by Father Orlando Prosperi, Catholic priest and attorney to the Vatican. Father Orlando had returned to his home county as a result of ill-health, and presumably thought he might as well do something useful. So he offered to represent the defendant free of charge.

It was certainly a novel defence for such a serious case, and one that did not meet entirely with the court's approval. In short, it was not Steven Mignogna who had committed those sordid crimes of rape and murder – it was Satan, pornography and heavy-metal music.

When his time came, Assistant DA Peck announced that he would be seeking convictions for first-degree murder and the death penalty, not against Iron Maiden or the devil, but against Mignogna.

It took a week to select a jury, and the trial opened on 14 March before Judge Joseph Huddock. Steven Mignogna arrived resplendent with a death's head tattoo on his arm.

Barely able to hold back his tears, the only living witness to

193

the savagery, Mignogna's friend and reluctant companion on that August night, became the prosecution's star turn. The jury had to wait until defence lawyer Debra Pezze addressed the court for any of the promised insight into Satanism. Ms Pezze quoted the section from a state police bulletin 'Satanism and the Law Enforcement Response'. It dealt with the Satanic Rituals: 'Many rituals have violent sexual overtones and violent criminal acts have come to the attention of investigators as a result of these Satanic coven rituals.'

Attorney Pezze then described the design of a skull, the words Black Sabbath and the number 666 emblazoned across her client's T-shirt. 'On the night of the crime,' she continued, 'they listened over and over again to this Guns 'n' Roses stuff' (apparently the song called 'Appetite for Destruction'). For his part, Father Orlando managed to antagonise the court in general, and in particular the judge, who rebuked his behaviour regularly.

The expert psychiatric witnesses were little better. One who had never spoken with Steven Mignogna claimed that he had been influenced by messages of violence on heavy-metal music records. Another insisted that recordings and videotapes of such groups as Judas Priest and Mötley Crüe contained subliminal messages that glamorise violence and the abuse of women.

Despite another spirited and colourful (and lengthy) speech from Father Orlando in which he told the court that the real villain was Steven's friend, and it had been him who committed the murders, it was not a closing speech which won the hearts and minds of the jury. Just two and a half hours were all they needed to return two guilty verdicts of first-degree murder and statutory rape.

At the sentencing hearing the same jury recommended against the death penalty in favour of life imprisonment. Perhaps they were, after all, moved by Father Orlando's final dramatic gesture when, with arms outstretched, he quoted Christ: 'Forgive them for they know not what they do. Look at Steve Mignogna. For he did not know what he was doing.' To give the attorney credit, it was Holy Thursday!

Judge Huddock handed down two consecutive life sentences,

pointing out as he did so that he would do everything within his power to ensure that Mignogna will never be released.

The 'private world' of Christopher Farrage

Chris Farrage, a paranoid schizophrenic, battered and knifed his mother because 'she intruded into his private world'. It seems that her 'intrusion' was to clean the lounge of their Tunbridge Wells home while her son was sitting there.

Eighteen-year-old Farrage, like many teenagers at that stage in their life, had been depressed by his performance in A-level examinations. This led to an almost obsessive interest in so-called death-metal music and Satanism. He was convinced that the devil was encouraging him to harm people, that this future was already mapped out for him. However, Farrage's confidence took another knock when, despite an elaborate ritual, Satan failed to materialise for him.

On 30 January 1995, forty-eight-year-old Margaret Farrage returned from the local shops and began to dust around her son who was slumped in a chair in the lounge. This filled him with what he described as 'an enormous rage'. He picked up a barbell and began to beat his mother mercilessly about the head and shoulders; then Christopher fetched a knife. When Mrs Farrage was examined in hospital – her son, realising what he had done had called an ambulance – she had severe stab wounds to the neck, chest and stomach, in addition to twenty-six bruises to her head and body. She died later in hospital.

At Maidstone Crown Court in September 1995, Christopher Farrage pleaded guilty to manslaughter due to diminished responsibility. He is at present detained in a hospital psychiatric unit.

Teenage Satanists kill classmate

In Germany, three teenage devil-worshippers strangled a fifteen-year-old fellow-student because he wanted to join in their Satanic activities. The three received prison sentences of between six and eight years.

Conscripts murder two women

In December 1993 two Greek military conscripts and another member of their twenty-strong Satanic coven were charged in Athens with the kidnap, rape and murder of two women during Satanic rituals. By the time they came to trial eighteen months later, a further count of the abduction, torture and murder of a fifteen-year-old girl had been added to the charge sheet.

POLITICAL AND
SOCIAL CULTS

KU KLUX KLAN

It was a time of turmoil. The almost unbelievable tragedy of a civil war in which brother fought brother, father fought son, neighbour fought neighbour. As with most wars, the original grievances were forgotten in the struggle for territory and survival. The rules which had governed the American Civil War were quickly forgotten. For those who care about history, this is the way it began.

In 1861 the Southern, or Confederate, States (South Carolina, Mississippi, Florida, Alabama, Georgia, Louisiana and Texas, later joined by Virginia, Tennessee, North Carolina and Arkansas) insisted on maintaining what they called their individual 'state rights'; not least the right to own black slaves. Their first move was to secede from the national 'Union' of states. The northern states then went to war to preserve the Union. For the next five years the Confederate army, under the overall command of General Robert E. Lee, and the army of the Union, under General Ulysses S. Grant, fought a series of bloody battles which would leave 359,528 of Grant's men dead and 258,000 of Lee's.

On 1 January 1863 President Abraham Lincoln issued a proclamation emancipating slaves. Two years later he was assassinated by John Wilkes Booth as an act of revenge for the Confederate cause. Following their decisive victory at the Battle of Gettysburg in 1863, the Union troops overran most of the Confederate states. On 9 April 1865 General Lee surrendered at the Appomatox Court House, and the last remnants of the Confederate army turned themselves in on 26 May.

At least that is the official date. But for some time after the official surrender disaffected soldiers roamed the Southern states in vigilante bands. Angry and humiliated by defeat they were outraged to return and find large areas of land in the hands of former slaves (who also now had the vote) and renegade ex-Union troops (the original 'carpetbaggers') looting their homes.

Enter General Nathan Bedford Forrest who, with half a dozen Confederate veterans, founded the Invisible Empire of the Knights of the Ku Klux Klan in Pulaski, Tennessee. It was their idea – initially successful, if ludicrous – to have their members dress in white robes and hoods (their horses were shrouded too) to persuade the educationally disadvantaged blacks that they were the ghosts of dead Confederate soldiers out for revenge. As for the name, it has been suggested, perhaps a little frivolously, that it derived from 'cycles' (a circle). Then 'cycles' became 'Ku Klux' (if you have a strong imagination). Then they added 'clan' – sorry, 'Klan'.

The first gatherings were fairly modest affairs confined to the state of Utah (then called Utah Territory). Although the primary targets were the recently freed slaves, many of whom were lynched in the most frightful manner, the Klan also took pride in intimidating Mormon missionaries who had openly opposed what they called 'secret societies'. It is likely that this essentially local band of bullies would have faded away naturally with the approach of the twentieth century. But that was to reckon without the huge success of one of Hollywood's pioneering movies and the cinema's first true 'epic'. In 1915 D. W. Griffiths' pro-Klan film, 'The Birth of a Nation' (originally titled 'The Clansman'), was released to a tumult of flag-waving xenophobia. In the forefront was a 'new' Ku Klux Klan. Based now in Atlanta, Georgia, the Klan actively projected a national image. There were branches in every state, and by 1925 the Knights were claiming a membership exceeding two million. One of the great ironies of 'The Birth of a Nation' is that the 'villainous' Negroes were played by white actors in cork-blacking make-up.

Although the 'new' Klan retained their early hate targets, the Knights of the 1920s added extreme nationalism and anti-

Catholicism to their repertoire. The mainly Freemason/anti-Mormon 'Klavern' (group) founded in Salt Lake City in 1921 had disbanded, though 1925 saw a huge expansion of activity following a recruitment drive by national organisers, for no obvious reason calling themselves 'Kleagles'. A revitalised Salt Lake City branch even established the Women of the Ku Klux Klan, and played host to the regional assembly (or 'Klonklave'). Even so, the downfall of the Utah Klan was again nigh – helped on by the commissioners of many of the state's cities banning the wearing of masks in public places. Another part of the problem in Utah was the lack of inflammatory issues, such as a high rate of ethnicity, bad law and order, or sinking public morality. Indeed, in this fiercely Mormon state, quite the reverse was the case.

There was a further revival feeding off opposition to the civil rights movement in the 1970s, but the Klan's Utah days were over. They hanged a few effigies and burned a few crosses, but by the following decade most of the extremists had either transferred their 'Klankraft' to states where they were still 'needed', or had joined one of the newer white supremacist groups, such as the Aryan Nations or the Christian Patriots. One organisation keeping a close watch on the activities of the Knights claims to have identified around 350 such groups across the nation.

However, if the Klan's showpiece state had proved ungrateful, there would always be a home somewhere. Illinois, where the ghostly white figures still hold marches and nocturnal rallies. Or Alabama, where the Knights are led by Grand Wizard Thom Robb, and where into the nineties cross-burning is still a popular pastime. But this piece of relatively harmless tomfoolery masks a sinister rise in the number of hate crimes alleged to be Klan inspired.

In 1991 there were more than 1,000 reported crimes against Jews and blacks in New York alone. More terrible perhaps, was the news that as late as 1987 the scourge of lynching had still not been eradicated in the South. In February of that year an all-white Alabama jury awarded $7 million to the mother of Michael Donald, a nineteen-year-old black who had been beaten and strangled to death by members of the local chapter of the Ku Klux Klan and his body left hanging from a tree. In what may have been an over-optimistic assessment of the verdict, State Senator Mr Michael Figures was reported as saying: 'This is a landmark ruling which will make sure the Donald death was the last Klan lynching.' Just three years later, in October 1990, an award was made for $2.5 million against a former Ku Klux Klan chief for allegedly inciting the killing of a black man in Portland, Oregon. Mr Bill Tuttle, a historian at the University of Kansas, is of the firm belief that the Klan is more blatantly racist now than in its 120-year history.

But there is more. Not only did Klan groups recently increase from sixty-nine to seventy-five over one year, but leaders are now beginning to seek political legitimacy. The aforementioned Grand Wizard Robb, Pastor of the Christian Identity Church, has got his eye on the state legislature in Arkansas. Lynching parties are being replaced by political parties, and the Klan is in there with the best and the worst of them.

In their electioneering promotional material, the modern Klan describes itself as 'the oldest, largest, and most professional Whites Rights group in the world . . . committed to upholding and defending Western Christian civilisation'. However benign – even laudable – this may sound, other aims on the 'Klan Political Agenda' still ring with the chilling echoes of the past:

1. *Americans First.* Not those in Mexico, Vietnam, Somalia, Haiti, or some other third world country.
2. *Drug testing for welfare recipients.* If they are drug users their welfare check, food stamps and public housing should be cut.
3. *America should be owned by Americans* – not Japanese, Arabs or Jews.
4. *Close our borders.* The flood of illegal aliens coming across our borders needs to be stopped.
5. *Outlaw homosexuality and inter-racial marriages.* Both these abominations against God and nature must be stopped.

One former Imperial Wizard who put down the hood to take up the cloth said in 1994: 'You are not going to see white sheets and burning crosses any more, but in its new guise the Klan is even more dangerous.'

There is no doubt that this new-look Klan is evangelical. Senior ambassadors have journeyed from the United States to Germany, Russia and Britain, where the Klan is reported to have several hundred members. They are especially interested in collaboration with extreme right-wing political parties, such as John Tyndall's British National Party.

POSTSCRIPT:

'Hi Hitler'

However undesirable the Klan may be, it is not entirely without its humorous moments. In 1994, at Fort Lauderdale, Florida, a self-confessed white supremacist stood his trial for the murder of a prostitute in 1985. Thirty-eight-year-old Donald Leroy Evans asked the court for permission to wear the robes of the Ku Klux Klan. He also wanted his name on all court documents to be changed to 'the honourable and respected name of Hi Hitler'. Evans believed that Hitler's followers were saying not 'Heil Hitler', but greeting him with 'Hi Hitler'.

Appendix: Lynching

Despite the notional triumph of justice and equality resulting from the success of the Union forces during the American Civil War, Reconstruction brought with it a heavy backlash, particularly from the Southern states, where white supremacy began to be upheld by the increasingly desperate means of *ad hoc* illegal executions, or lynchings. Between 1882, when the earliest records were kept, and 1927, 4,951 people were lynched. Although the majority of these summary executions – particularly those that took place in the North and West of the Union – were by simple hanging or shooting many of those in the Southern states were characterised by a quite appalling level of sadism and gratuitous cruelty. In 1893, for example, a mob of upwards of 10,000 spectators gathered at Paris, Texas, many travelling from miles around to witness the lynching of a mentally retarded black man accused of killing a small child. First red-hot pokers were pushed into his body; then his eyes were burned out, and flaming brands forced down his throat. After almost an hour of this torture, the unfortunate man was burned alive. Although the increasing urbanisation of the South and the greater effectiveness of the National Guard in controlling the savage mobs led to a gradual decrease in unlawful executions in the first years of the twentieth century, there are still sufficient records to show that there were isolated pockets of the community where lynch law continued to govern the relationships between whites and blacks. In 1918, in a five-day orgy of mob violence in Georgia, eight blacks were murdered, one of them a pregnant woman who was slowly roasted alive and her baby cut from her womb and trampled by the crowd; two others were burned to death for no greater crime than allegedly 'talking back' to whites.

Lynching at Memphis
The following is an eye-witness account of a lynching that took place on 22 July 1893. It was written by Ida Wells-Barnett, who was editor of a black Memphis newspaper until she was herself driven out by the mob in 1892, and became a life-long public campaigner against lynching:

Memphis is one of the queen cities of the south, with a population of about seventy thousand souls – easily one of the twenty largest, most progressive and wealthiest cities of the United States. And yet in its streets there occurred a scene of such shocking savagery which would have disgraced the Congo. No woman was harmed, no serious indignity suffered. Two women driving to town in a wagon were suddenly accosted by Lee Walker. He claimed that he demanded something to eat. The women claimed that he attempted to assault them. They gave such an alarm that he ran away. At once the dispatches spread over the entire county that a big, burly Negro had brutally assaulted two women. Crowds began to search for the alleged fiend. While hunting him they shot another Negro dead in his tracks for refusing to stop when ordered to do so. After a few days Lee Walker was found and put in jail in Memphis until the mob was ready for him.

The *Memphis Commercial* of Sunday 23 July contains a full account of the tragedy from which the following extracts are made:

At 12 o'clock last night, Lee Walker, who attempted to outrage Miss Mollie McCadden last Tuesday morning, was taken from the county jail and hanged to a telegraph pole just north of the prison. All day rumours were afloat that with nightfall an attack would be made upon the jail, and as everybody anticipated that a vigorous resistance would be made, a conflict between the mob and the authorities was feared.

At 10 o'clock Captain O'Haver, Sergeant Horan and several patrolmen were on hand, but they could do nothing with the crowd. An attack by the mob was made on the door in the south wall and it yielded. Sheriff McLendon and several of his men threw themselves into the breach, but two or three of the storming party shoved by. They were seized by the police but not subdued, the officers refraining from using their clubs. The entire mob might at first have been dispersed by ten policemen who would use their clubs, but the sheriff insisted that no violence be done.

The mob got an iron rail and used it as a battering ram against the lobby doors. Sheriff McLendon tried to stop them, and one of the mob knocked him down with a chair. Still he counselled moderation and would not order his deputies or the police to disperse the crowd by force. The pacific policy of the sheriff impressed the mob with the idea that the officers were afraid, or at least would do them no harm, and they redoubled their efforts, urged on by a big switchman. At 12 o'clock the door of the prison was broken in with the rail.

Walker made a desperate resistance. Two men entered his cell first and ordered him to come forth. He refused, and they failing to drag him out, others entered. He scratched and bit his assailants, wounding several of them severely with his teeth. The mob retaliated by striking and cutting him with fists and knives. When he reached the steps leading down to the door he made another stand and was stabbed again and again. By the time he reached the lobby his power to resist was gone, and he was shoved along through the mob of yelling, cursing men and boys, who beat, spat upon and slashed the wretch-like demon.

The mob proceeded north on Front Street with the victim, stopping at Sycamore Street to get a rope from the grocery. 'Take him to the iron bridge in Main Street,' yelled several men. The men who had hold of the Negro were in a hurry to finish the job, however, and when they reached the telephone pole at the corner of Front Street and the first alley north of Sycamore they stopped. A hastily improvised noose was slipped over the Negro's head, and several young men mounted a pike of lumber near the pole and threw a rope over one of the stepping pins. The Negro was lifted up until his feet were three feet above the ground, the rope was made taut, and a corpse dangled in mid-air. A big fellow who helped lead the mob pulled the Negro's legs until his neck cracked. The wretch's clothes had been torn off, and as he swung, the man who pulled his legs mutilated the corpse. One or two knife cuts more or less did not make much difference in the appearance of the dead rapist, however, for before the rope was around his neck his skin was cut almost to ribbons. One pistol shot was fired while the corpse was hanging. A dozen voices protested against the use of fire-arms, and there was no more shooting. The body was permitted to hang for half an hour, then it was cut down . . . The body fell in a ghastly heap, and the crowd laughed at the sound and crowded round the prostrate body, a few kicking the inanimate carcass . . . Then someone raised the cry of 'Burn him!' It was quickly taken up and soon resounded from a hundred throats. Detective Richardson, for a long time single-handed, stood the crowd off. He talked and begged the men not to bring disgrace on the city by burning the body, arguing that all the vengeance possible had been wrought.

While this was going on a small crowd was busy starting a fire in the middle of the street. The material was handy. Some bundles of staves were taken from a nearby lumber yard for kindling. Heavier wood was obtained from the same source, and coal oil from a neighboring grocery. Then the cries of 'Burn him! Burn him!' were redoubled.

Half a dozen men seized the naked body. The crowd cheered. They marched to the fire and, giving the body a swing, it was landed in the middle of the flames. There was a cry for more wood as the fire had begun to die owing to the long delay. Willing hands procured the wood, and it was piled up on the Negro, almost for a time obscuring him from view. The head was in plain view, as also were the limbs, and one arm which stood out high above the body, the elbow crooked – held in that position by a stick of wood. In a few moments the hands began to swell, then came great blisters all over the exposed parts of the body; then in places the flesh was burned away and the bones began to show through. It was a horrible sight, one which perhaps no one there had ever witnessed before. It proved too much for a large part of the crowd, and the majority of the mob left very shortly before the burning began.

But a large number stayed, and were not a bit set back by the sight of a human body being burned to ashes. Two or three white women, accompanied by their escorts, pushed to the front to obtain an unobstructed view, and looked on with astonishing coolness and nonchalance. One man and woman brought a little girl, not over twelve years old, apparently their daughter, to view a scene which was calculated to drive sleep from the child's eyes for many nights, if not produce a permanent injury to her nervous system. The comments of the crowd were varied. Some remarked on the efficacy of this style of cure for rapists, others rejoiced that men's wives and daughters were now safe from the wretch. Some laughed as the flesh cracked and blistered, and while a large number pronounced the burning of a dead body as a useless episode, not in all that throng was a word of sympathy for the wretch himself.

The rope that was used to hang the Negro, and also that which was used to lead him from the jail, were eagerly sought by relic hunters. They almost fought for a chance to cut off a piece of rope, and in an incredibly short time both ropes had disappeared and were scattered into the pockets of the crowd in sections of from one inch to six inches long. Others of the relic hunters remained until the ashes cooled sufficiently to obtain such ghastly relics as the teeth, nails and bits of charred skin of the immolated victim of his own lust. After burning the body the mob tied a rope around the charred trunk and dragged it down Main Street to the court house, where it was hanged to a center pole. The rope broke and the corpse dropped with a thud, but it was again hoisted, the charred legs barely touching the ground. The teeth were knocked out and the finger nails cut off as souvenirs. The crowd made so much noise that the police interfered. Undertaker Walsh was telephoned for, who took charge of the body and carried it to his establishment, where it was prepared for burial in the potter's field today.

Byron de la Beckwith and the death of Medgar Evers

Although the racist assassination of Medgar Evers was a fundamental landmark in the overall struggle against segregation in the Deep South of America, it should be seen in the wider political perspective. On 9 November 1960 John F. Kennedy was elected President of the United States by a narrow margin over Richard Nixon, and early indications were that he intended to implement a sweeping range of reforms aimed at giving the South's long-oppressed black population a measure of equality of opportunity. By May of the following year black activists had already begun to exercise their own strength when the so-called 'freedom riders', white and black, deliberately challenged the segregation laws relating to state and interstate buses in Montgomery, Alabama. Crowds of angry whites, many of them members of the Ku Klux Klan, attacked the freedom riders with fists and clubs, and Governor John Patterson was obliged to impose martial law in an attempt to halt the rioting. Meanwhile, the leader of the mainly peaceful black demonstrators, the Reverend Dr Martin Luther King Jr, had to be protected from a white mob as he held a church service. By 1962 Dr King was the undisputed leader of the 'integration movement', and in July he was arrested for leading an illegal march in Georgia, and the following month for holding a prayer meeting on the steps of Albany's city hall; arrested with him was the Reverend Ralph Abernathy, another leading anti-segregationalist. On 30 September James Meredith became the first black student to attempt to enrol at the University of Mississippi, provoking an angry white backlash that led to rioting in which three people were killed and more than fifty injured, despite a force of 750 federal marshals led by the Deputy District Attorney. By the spring of 1963 dissent was spreading across the South, and in Alabama Governor George Wallace threatened to defy federal authorities by refusing to implement desegregation. When the civil rights leader Medgar Evers was ambushed and shot dead on 12 June it sparked off riots across the southern states.

The following account of the murder of Medgar Evers and the thirty-year battle to convict Byron de la Beckwith of the crime is told through contemporary news-media accounts, supplemented (in square brackets) by additional new information.

NAACP Leader Slain in Jackson: Protests Mount
Jackson, Mississippi, 12 June 1963

The victim of the shooting was thirty-seven-year-old Medgar W. Evers, field secretary of the National Association for the Advancement of Coloured People. Mr Evers, a native of Decatur, Mississippi, and an army veteran of the Second World War, had been one of the key leaders in the Negroes' drive here to win a promise from the city to hire some Negro policemen and to appoint a bi-racial committee.

He left a mass meeting at a church last night, stopped at the residence of a Negro lawyer and then drove to his home on the city's northern edge. He arrived at his neat green-panelled and buff-brick ranch-style home on Guynes Street at 1.14 a.m. He parked his 1962 light-blue sedan in the driveway, and as he turned to walk into the side entrance opening into a carport, a sniper's bullet struck him just below the right shoulder blade. The slug crashed through the front window of the house, penetrated an interior wall, ricocheted off a refrigerator and struck a coffee pot. The battered bullet was found beneath a watermelon on a kitchen cabinet. Mr Evers staggered to the doorway, his keys in his hand, and collapsed near the steps. His wife Myrlie and three children rushed to the door. The screaming of the children awoke the neighbours. One said he had looked out of his bedroom window and saw Mr Evers' crumpled body in the carport. He had rushed out and crouched behind a clump of shrubbery, fired a shot in the air to scare off the gunman and shouted for help. Police who arrived a short time later helped place the still-living victim into a neighbour's station wagon. As the vehicle sped towards

University Hospital, those who accompanied the dying man said he had murmured weakly: 'Sit me up', and 'Turn me loose'.

When news spread through town of Medgar Evers' death, a spontaneous demonstration collected in the late morning, when approximately 200 Negro teenagers marched from the Masonic Building on Lynch Street, where Mr Evers had his office. About a hundred city policemen and deputies armed with riot guns and automatic rifles stopped them a block away. A total of 145 demonstrators, including seventy-four aged seventeen and under were arrested. One girl was struck in the face with a club, and deputies wrestled a middle-aged woman to the sidewalk.

Evers knew that his position with the NAACP was a dangerous one, but since an early age he had been confronting racist violence. Only shortly before his death he had recounted how, when he was just fourteen years old, a friend of his father's was lynched for allegedly insulting a white woman – he had never forgotten the sight of the murdered man. Ten days before he was shot, Mr Evers said in an interview: 'If I die it will be in a good cause. I've been fighting for America just as much as the soldiers in Vietnam.'

As early as 4.00 a.m. President Kennedy was informed of the murder, and was reported to be 'appalled by the barbarity of the act', while his brother, Attorney General Robert F. Kennedy, said he was 'saddened and shocked by the crime'. However, many southern senators, including their leader Richard B. Russell of Georgia, made it clear that the untimely death of Medgar Evers would in no way affect their implacable opposition to civil rights legislation. One somewhat eccentric reaction to the tragedy was the offer made by Ghana for an 'African Peace Corps' to be sent to the United States on what was described as a 'civilising mission'. Meanwhile, the NAACP had announced a reward of $10,000 for the arrest and conviction of Medgar Evers' killer; this supplemented the $5,000 reward already offered by the mayor and City Commissioners of Jackson.

In its editorial comment, the *New York Times* invoked President Kennedy's plea for a 'vast moral awakening': 'But beyond the bulwarks Congress writes into law is the necessity for the reassessment of individual attitudes and behaviour, for which the President called so eloquently. The justification for fuller implementation of constitutional guarantees does not rest primarily in the damage discrimination does to our world image, or the danger that it will touch off mass disorders, or the vast waste it entails in our economic and social resources. Important as all these are, real as all of them are, they are less costly than the hurt we do ourselves by the systematic humiliation of one-tenth of our people solely on the basis of colour. Every family, every home, every community is in the front lines of the crusade for decency to which Mr Kennedy has summoned America. We can all be bucket-carriers, helping to quench "the fires of frustration and discord" that rage in every city, North and South.'

Jackson Negroes Clubbed As Police Quell Marchers
Jackson, Mississippi, 13 June 1963
Police attacked adults and teenagers as they congregated chanting: 'We want freedom', and battered them into submission. Six demonstrators were struck or choked by police nightsticks drawn across their throats, others were snatched or pushed from a Negro home; a white sociology professor, John Salter, was felled by a blow to the head before being arrested and put in custody. This was the second major confrontation with the city police since the murder of Medgar Evers the previous night.

Evers Lying in State
Jackson, Mississippi, 14 June 1963
Despite a tense atmosphere among the city's Negro population, not helped by the sweltering 101-degree temperature, officials issued permits for a march following funeral services offered as a final tribute to slain integration leader Medgar Evers. This could, of course, be seen as a simple exercise in damage limitation on the part of the city council, as widespread sentiment had been expressed for a mass march whether officials granted a permit or not, and without sanction it could more easily have

degenerated into a violent confrontation.

By now considerable solidarity was being shown by other high-profile Negro individuals and groups. Dr Martin Luther King Jr had sent messages of support from his Atlanta-based Southern Christian Leadership Conference; and James H. Meredith, who became the first of his race to enrol in a white educational establishment – the University of Mississippi – and whose cause Medgar Evers had championed, called for an end to mass protest marches and the implementation of a general strike of Negro workers.

All this time Medgar Evers lay in state dressed in a modest dark grey suit and white shirt, his blue-trimmed Masonic apron around his waist and an Elk emblem hanging round his neck. Hundreds of mourners had filed past his grey metal casket at the Collins Funeral Home.

Washington, 17 June 1963
Hundreds of Negroes turned out to honour the memory of Medgar Evers; about 500 marched behind the hearse carrying his body from Union Station to the funeral parlour. Leaflets bearing a picture of Mr Evers and the slogan: 'He sacrificed his life for you' were handed to members of the huge crowd lining the streets. As a war veteran, Medgar Evers was provided with a plot in the military section of Arlington cemetery in recognition of his three years' service with the Allied armies in Northern France during 1943–6.

Evers Interred at Arlington
Washington, 19 June 1963
Medgar Evers was buried with full military honours under the tall oaks at Arlington National Cemetery while soldiers held a United States flag over the coffin and fellow civil rights workers sang what has become the movement's anthem – 'We Shall Overcome'. As smoke from a volley of rifle fire hovered in the air, Bishop Stephen Gill Spottswood of Washington, chairman of the NAACP, reminded mourners that: 'He is not dead, the soldier

213

fallen here. His spirit walks through the world today . . . I hope Medgar Evers will be the last black American to give his life in the struggle to make the Constitution come alive. He laid down his life for Negroes that they might be free from segregation and discrimination, that we might share in the full fruits of democracy. Now, he rests from his labours.'

Mississippi Man Seized by FBI in Evers Slaying
Washington, 23 June 1963

The FBI announced the arrest of forty-two-year-old Byron de la Beckwith in connection with the murder of Medgar Evers. Beckwith was taken into custody at 11.00 p.m. yesterday and was being detained on a holding charge of violating the 1957 Civil Rights Act; in precise terms the complaint charged Beckwith 'and others unknown' with conspiring to injure, oppress and intimidate Medgar Evers in the free exercise and enjoyment of rights and privileges secured to him by the constitution of the United States. The FBI undertook to provide all the information they had gathered against Beckwith to the authorities in Jackson pursuing the killing of the civil rights leader. Meanwhile in Jackson, Hinds County District Attorney William L. Waller said he would be bringing a murder charge against Beckwith.

J. Edgar Hoover, director of the FBI, announced that his agents had linked Beckwith to the Evers case through a fingerprint found on a telescopic sight on the gun abandoned not far from where the victim was shot. A bureau expert explained that the Gold Hawk 'scope' had been traced by a process of elimination, first asking the manufacturer to list the serial numbers of all items sent to their local distributors, and then tracing each number to its individual purchaser. The sight that agents were interested in was sold to none other than Byron de la Beckwith. But there was an added bonus – a fingerprint had been deposited on the sight which, when compared with Beckwith's service record, proved a perfect match.

Byron de la Beckwith was described as a chronic letter-writer on the racial issue. He is said to be a lifelong resident of Leflore

County and a member of a prominent local family. He is a gun collector and a Marine veteran of the Second World War. It was later revealed that when he became aware of being under surveillance by FBI agents Beckwith communicated with his lawyer, Mr Hardy Lott, and arranged to turn himself in to the police.

[*Some time later we were to learn much more of the eccentric life of Byron de la Beckwith – 'Deelay' to his friends. Beckwith was born in California, though when he was just five his father died and Byron and his mother returned to her home in Greenwood, Mississippi. The family, as might be expected, had adhered to the Confederate cause during the Civil War, and Beckwith's grandfather, Lemuel Yerger, had ridden with General Nathan Bedford Forrest's cavalry. (Forrest later became the first Imperial Wizard of the Ku Klux Klan.) Byron was eleven when his mother died, and his guardianship was taken over by the Yergers – Uncle William to be precise. It is recalled that when he was young, Byron was naturally surrounded by hundreds of black servants and plantation workers, and by some accounts got on well with them. Perhaps he was flattered by the name they called him – 'Little Captain'. Beckwith was sent to the Webb School at Belt Buckle, Tennessee, where he was a poor student, and then attended Mississippi State University, but did not graduate. At the age of twenty he joined the Marines and fought with them in the South Pacific during the Second World War; he was awarded the coveted Purple Heart at the Battle of Tarawa where he was wounded.*

When he returned home to Mississippi, Byron de la Beckwith married the former Mary Louise Williams and took his new bride to live at the almost derelict plantation house where he had spent his childhood, and which was all that was left of the family fortune. Whether it was the pressure of living close to poverty, or whether it was the regular physical abuse which Beckwith was accused of giving his wife, she eventually left him in 1960. That said, whatever Mary Louise may have thought of him, Beckwith was by all accounts the very model of a Southern gentleman, known as a courteous man and well liked around Greenwood. He found his niche as a salesman, first in tobacco products and later in fertilisers. One former employer described Deelay as a friendly man 'with the gift of the gab'. He was also a dyed-in-the-wool racist and segregationist. Beckwith's return to Mississippi from the conflict in Europe had confirmed him in his political views. He became, as one acquaintance put it, 'rabid'. He regularly attended meetings of the Sons of the American Revolution, lectured to the KKK, and joined the White Citizen's Council. It was said that his favourite 'purist' organisation was the Identity Group: 'They live by the Bible' – whatever that may mean. One thing that it meant to Deelay was that he took up position outside church on Sundays, a gun tucked in his pants, to 'see off niggers'. And when he wasn't protecting the church, he was at the bus station making sure the Nigra didn't get uppity and use the white waiting rooms. Depending on your point of view, Deelay was a good ol' boy or an out-and-out Fascist. And possibly a murderer; but it would take Mississippi almost thirty years to prove it.]

Trial of Beckwith Is Opened
Jackson, Mississippi, 31 January 1964
[*Many local residents, of both colours, saw little chance of Deelay being convicted, the defendant himself included. There was a story that District Attorney William Waller, prosecuting, had some difficulty selecting a jury. In order to find a panel of twelve, Waller had to find that number of people who could answer in the affirmative the question: 'Do you believe it's a crime for a white man to kill a nigger in Mississippi?' It took him four days to find his jury.*]

'Our witnesses will show in ten ways that Byron de la Beckwith is guilty of this crime.' That is the way Mr William L. Waller opened the state's case. In the small courtroom packed mainly with Negroes, a Jackson detective, John Chamblee, told the jury how, by standing on the spot where Medgar Evers died and directing his flashlight in a straight line the light picked out a clump of small sweetgum trees and honeysuckle vines in a vacant lot opposite; he found the vines bruised and a branch snapped, as though somebody had been standing and lying there. Another officer then testified that he had found a .30–06 Enfield rifle hidden in the honeysuckle not far from the trees.

Vital evidence was presented by Mr I. T. McIntyre, a farmer from Greenwood, who testified that he had sold a .30–06 Enfield rifle which he had bought through a Canadian mail-order outfit, to Mr Beckwith in January 1960. The manufacturer of the rifle and the date on which it was made were the same as the murder weapon.

Rifle Is Linked to Beckwith

Jackson, Mississippi, 1 February 1964

Agents from the Federal Bureau of Investigation presented the court with evidence that the telescopic sight on the murder weapon had been sold to Mr Byron de la Beckwith, and furthermore a fingerprint on the scope no more than twelve hours old matched his.

Jackson, Mississippi, 3 February 1964

Two white taxi-cab drivers testified that Beckwith was in Jackson four days before the shooting inquiring for the address of Medgar Evers: 'He asked me if I knew where the Negro NAACP leader lived. I said I did not.' Beckwith then went back to the station and consulted the telephone directory and returned to the cab driver, Mr Speight, to ask where Livingston Drive was. 'I said that couldn't be it because it was all white.'

If anybody thought such evidence would ruffle Deelay they were wrong. Throughout the trial he seemed to be thoroughly enjoying himself, sharing jokes and handshakes with Governor Ross Barnet, offering cigars to District Attorney Waller, smiling and waving genially to visitors in the court and to the jury. One report says that he is such a popular figure with the court police that he is allowed to keep his gun collection in his cell!

Beckwith's Car Near Scene of Slaying?

Jackson, Mississippi, 4 February 1964

Two witnesses testified today that they saw Byron de la Beckwith's car parked a few hundred feet from Medgar Evers' home on the night of his murder. The parking lot is only 150 feet from the shrubbery from which the assassin's bullet was fired. Three teenage boys also claimed to have seen a white Valiant such as Beckwith drives in the area on the same night.

As DA Waller announced that he was resting his case, Byron de la Beckwith rewarded him with a wide, friendly smile.

Beckwith Takes the Stand

Jackson, Mississippi, 5 February 1964

Although in his testimony today Byron de la Beckwith denied that he was implicated in any way in the murder of Medgar Evers, he was prepared to acknowledge a letter which he had written to the National Rifle Association on 26 January 1963, in which he said: 'For the next fifteen years we here in Mississippi are going to have to do a lot of shooting to protect our wives and children from bad niggers.' As for the evidence of the rifle which killed Mr Evers being his, Deelay's answer was simple: it was stolen the day before the murder. Handed the weapon and asked whether it belonged to him, Beckwith handled it fondly and pulled the bolt, aiming it above the jury's heads, before grumbling: 'There's a little dust in the barrel.'

Before putting his star witness on the stand defence attorney Lott questioned two policemen who swore that on the night in question they had seen Beckwith in Greenwood.

Beckwith Case a Mistrial

Jackson, Mississippi, 7 February 1964

Although the jury were sent to a hotel overnight after failing to reach agreement after a retirement of more than seven hours yesterday, they were still unable to declare a verdict today. The vote taken on the twentieth ballot after eleven hours' deliberation was announced by the bailiff as being split 7–5 for acquittal.

When the jury foreman told the court that it would be impossible for them to reach agreement, Judge Leon F. Hendrick announced a mistrial, and said he would set the date for a second trial.

[*Byron de la Beckwith's second trial opened on 6 April 1964. The courtroom was the same, as was the judge and the attorneys. In fact the final verdict, if not exactly the same, was still a hung jury unable to agree; it was Judge Hendrick who dismissed them after ten hours' retirement, saying: 'I've never been in favour of wearing out a jury'; and then declaring a mistrial. After encountering even more difficulty in assembling a jury than the first time round the judge was obliged to order the court to sit at night in order to try to speed things up. One prospective juror was dismissed when he gave his opinion that the state had made a pretty poor job of presenting its case the first time. And it was much the same evidence at this second trial – there were no new revelations, no new witnesses and nothing new said by any of the former witnesses. The only thing that had changed in the Beckwith camp was the show of force put on by the local Ku Klux Klan who burned ten crosses in the Jackson area on the night before the trial opened, and sent a squad of their toughest and most intimidating members to hang around inside and outside the court. One victim was Mr H. R. Speight, the taxi driver who claimed at the first trial that Beckwith had asked the way to the Evers household; after being allegedly beaten up, he now only thought it might have been somebody who looked like Beckwith. And so on 17 April Byron de la Beckwith walked from court, part conquering hero, part martyr to the cause of white supremacy.*]

No Third Trial for Beckwith
[*Over the following years, the Little Colonel kept a comparatively low profile, earning his living as a fertiliser salesman. In 1967 he did put himself forward as a prospective lieutenant-governor of Mississippi, but without any great hope of success. And then he hit the headlines again. He had been arrested in New Orleans with a bomb in the back of his car and directions how to get to the home of one of the leaders of the Jewish Anti-Defamation*

League. Although he pleaded that he was framed for the job, he
was a long way from the good ol' boys who rallied to his defence
before. After a short trial Byron de la Beckwith was sent down for
five years for possessing explosives.

When he was released, Beckwith returned to Greenwood where
he continued as a salesman and married Thelma Neff, leaving the
ramshackle plantation house for the comforts of her Tennessee
bungalow. By the mid-eighties age was beginning to take its toll
of Deelay's health. In late 1989 it was announced that the district
attorney's office had agreed to open the Beckwith case again with
a view to putting him on trial. The problem was that all the
tangible evidence plus the trial transcripts and other documents
had disappeared or been destroyed. Over the following months
the issue of the trial rested not only on trying to assemble
evidence (for example, the murder rifle was handed over by the
wife of a segregationist judge who, before his death, had just hung
on to it as a souvenir) but also trying to prise Beckwith out of
Tennessee and extradite him to Jackson, where, with the benefit
of three decades' development, there seemed to be a genuine new
need for the city to cleanse itself of the uglier incidents of its past.

On 19 December 1990, Byron de la Beckwith was charged
again with the murder of Medgar Evers. Some idea of what was
involved in getting the new trial under way can be judged from
the newspaper headlines through 1991:]

January 15:	Judge orders Beckwith to return to Mississippi to face trial for first-degree murder
	Beckwith appeals extradition with Tennessee Court of Criminal Appeals
June 4:	Tennessee Appeals Court orders return of Beckwith to Mississippi
June 6:	Beckwith loses extradition fight
June 7:	Original autopsy report on Evers found to be missing
June 8:	Evers' body exhumed from Arlington Cemetery for new autopsy

October 1:   Beckwith loses extradition appeal
October 4:   Beckwith returned to Mississippi
October 30:   Prosecutor seeking to block bail links Beckwith
              with obscure racist group the Phineas Priest-
              hood – called 'God's Executioners'
November 14: Beckwith denied bail; must remain in Jackson jail

[*At last, in the first month of 1994 the long-awaited trial opened.*]

White Supremacist Faces Third Trial for Murder
New York, 17 January 1994
Byron de la Beckwith goes on trial today as Mississippi tries to lay to rest one of the most troublesome ghosts in its troubled racial history. Beckwith, now seventy-three years old, seems to have lost none of his racist views [*Interviewed in jail he was reported as saying 'If you lay down, toss your panties off and let a nigger have intercourse with you, you are going to produce mongrels for ever'*] and in his autobiography maintains the stand he took at the two 1964 trials as far as the evidence against him is concerned – that is, that his rifle was stolen and that he was a hundred miles away in Greenwood at the time of Medgar Evers' murder. However, the new trial was allowed because of subsequent information amounting to 'new evidence'. First, there are fears that the juries at Beckwith's original trials had been screened by a state agency called the Sovereignty Commission set up to maintain segregation in Mississippi. Secondly, Delmar Dennis, a former member of the Ku Klux Klan and an FBI informer, claims that Beckwith admitted to a Klan meeting that he had shot the civil rights leader; he is quoted as telling the meeting: 'Killing that nigger gave me no more discomfort than our wives endure when they give birth to our children.'

The trial will be held in the same courtroom that played host to Beckwith's other appearances, though in order to empanel the least biased jury possible, recruitment will take place in the more liberal northern districts of the state. Nevertheless, in the weeks leading up to the trial, racists have been leafleting the streets reminding prospective jurors that Byron de la Beckwith stands firm as 'A Hero in War; a Hero in Peace'.

Stirring Memories of Hatred
Jackson, Mississippi, 28 January 1994
Once again the people of Jackson have been forced to remember the tragic assassination of Medgar Evers as his wife Myrlie stood in the witness box for the third time and recounted for the court the events of the night she saw her husband die. Bobby De-Laughter, the Hinds County prosecutor, told a jury of eight blacks and four whites: 'What you are going to see from the evidence is a life snuffed out on 12 June 1963, by a bullet that tore through his body, a bullet aimed in prejudice, propelled by hatred and fired by a back-shooting coward . . . The person who pulled the trigger was an absolute, self-proclaimed rabid racist,' continued Mr DeLaughter as he pointed a finger at Beckwith in the dock.

Mississippi Killer Guilty After 31 Years
Jackson, Mississippi, 5 February 1994
It was all over. The new information was tied in with the old and few could have doubted the outcome of this trial any more than previous commentators could doubt the outcome of Byron de la Beckwith's two previous trials. After a deliberation of just over six hours, the jury found Beckwith guilty and he was sentenced to life imprisonment. As he walked from the dock clutching his Bible, his wife Thelma cried out: 'He's not guilty. He's never been guilty and they know.'

But all eyes, ears, and above all hearts, were focused on Myrlie Evers as she spoke the only possible epitaph: 'It's been a long journey, Medgar, I've gone the last mile.'

Willie Edwards, Henry Alexander and the Tyler Goodwin Bridge

He doesn't seem wicked as his face looks out from the page of a newspaper. The smile a little cynical perhaps; eyes a touch narrow. But really not much different from many young American men. What marked Henry Alexander out was that he was a vicious thug and, ultimately, a murderer. Of course that was nearly forty years ago, and Alexander enjoyed freedom from justice until he died from cancer in 1992.

The incident which turned thug into killer took place in January 1957. But the murder of Willie Edwards started long before that, when racial tension and violence began to spread through America like wildfire; especially in the Southern States. It began when Henry Alexander put on the white hood of the Ku Klux Klan. He was not alone, as many individuals who feared the inexorable rise of the civil rights movement took up arms against it.

And of all the civil rights movement's strongholds, Montgomery, Alabama was the strongest. It was the home of its leader, the black minister Dr Martin Luther King Jr. Dr King was himself the victim of an assassin's bullet in 1968. Coincidentally, Henry Alexander was suspected of the bombing of the minister's house in 1956. Twenty-four-year-old Willie Edwards lived in Montgomery too, with his wife and daughters. He had no involvement in black politics, but that didn't prevent the Klan from burning crosses on his front lawn.

In January 1957 things were about to get a whole lot worse. Just before midnight Willie Edwards was returning home from a grocery delivery round when a carload of screaming roughnecks dressed in sheets forced him into the vehicle at gunpoint. Their destination was the Tyler Goodwin Bridge, which spans the Alabama River. Here the Klansmen forced Willie over the parapet, still begging for his life, into the strong, muddy current below. It was only several months later that Willie Edwards' decomposing body was finally recovered.

But Henry's mob was away free. No witnesses to the incident did, or would, make themselves known to the police. And rumours grew that officers knew the people responsible, but as Willie 'was only a "nigger" van driver' it didn't seem to matter much.

And so things remained until Henry Alexander, who had been suffering from cancer for some time, realised that his end was near. Terrified that he might find divine judgement more difficult to evade than earthly justice, he decided to confess to his wife Diana. He apparently also confessed to his brother a number of other gross crimes, one of which was the bombing of a church in Birmingham, Alabama, in which four people died.

With a courage all the more remarkable because of the situation, Diana Alexander contacted Willie's widow Sara Jean and broke the news. Eventually the two women met and became united in their grief. With support from sympathisers and local activists, Diana and Sara Jean have been trying to force the FBI to reopen the case. It is doubtful that they will, and unlikely that anything positive would be forthcoming if they did. Besides, it's too late for Willie Edwards; too late for Henry Alexander. As for their wives, one prays that their new-found comradeship helps them both, for they both need all the comfort they can get.

POSSE COMITATUS

ZOG and the 'martyrdom' of Gordon Kahl

A policy of killing law enforcement officers is not unknown among the more fanatical cults, usually because of a paranoid perception of threat – Waco and Jonestown, for example. In the case of Posse Comitatus it was all but a crusade. And a popular one at that. Indeed, the man who did the shooting, Gordon Weldell Kahl, was described as 'the first American hero of the second American revolution'. Fortunately, it was only those adhering to the principles of the extreme right-wing militia groups who thought he was a hero.

In fact, Kahl had a quite unremarkable upbringing. Born the son of a homesteader in North Dakota in 1920, Gordon left high school and then the farm, drifting through a succession of low-paid manual jobs: fruit-picking, road-building, that kind of thing. During the Second World War he earned a conspicuously honourable service record with the Army Air Corps and was awarded the Purple Heart.

Following his discharge on medical grounds – he had suffered shrapnel wounds – Gordon Kahl married Joan Seil. It is probably significant that his wedding gift to her was a double-barrel shotgun. By this time Kahl was convincing himself that the American Government was gradually being infiltrated by Communists, Jews were taking over the economy and 'niggers' were making a mess of what was left. And in the poverty-stricken areas of the Midwest's 'Farm Belt' Gordon was not alone in his beliefs.

225

Desperate with their circumstances, the Kahls migrated to Los Angeles where, in the socially turbulent years of the 1960s, Gordon found groups marginally further to the political right than even himself – the notorious John Birch Society and more especially Christian Identity. (It was during this period that Gordon Kahl formulated the theory that the assassination of President John Kennedy in 1963 had been ordered by senior members of the Jewish faith. The reason? JFK had discovered their plot to take over the world!) Then there was the Ku Klux Klan, and finally Posse Comitatus. Gordon Weldell Kahl had at last found 'home'. In 1975 he became their Texas coordinator.

Posse Comitatus, a Latin derivative, means 'power of a county', and the cult was founded in 1969 by a member of the American Nazi 'Silver Shirts', Henry L. Beach, a retired dry-cleaner. Their philosophy was described by them as: 'A county government is the highest form of government in our Republic . . . The county sheriff is the only legal law enforcement officer in the United States . . . The sheriff is accountable and responsible only to the citizens who are the inhabitants of his county.' However, should that sheriff fail in his duties, then Posse Comitatus would step in and do his job for him.

It was also a Posse doctrine that the United States, while it was founded as, and wished to remain, a Christian community, had been corrupted by Jews – the 'Synagogue of Satan'. Or, as Gordon Kahl later described it, 'ZOG' – Zionist Occupation Government.

It was a perfect pitch for Gordon. He refused to pay federal taxes. He was imprisoned for refusing to pay federal taxes. He was released on condition he pay them. He refused. And was imprisoned again. And released again.

Among the poor farmworkers, not to pay the taxes being levied seemed like the heaven Gordon predicted when he established his Gospel Doctrine Church of Jesus Christ. He was already a folk hero.

By the early eighties crippling taxes and the escalating rates of interest being charged on loans to barely subsistence farmers, sometimes leading to starvation and suicide, were pushing huge areas of the Farm Belt into the welcoming arms of Posse Comitatus, and Gordon Weldell Kahl, potential saviour.

The Gospel Doctrine Church drew huge crowds on the twin Exploitation/Armageddon pivot. They even recruited a former services 'guerrilla warfare' expert. And they were in the midst of planning their own 'town', a fortified blockade armed against all-corners.

The IRS decided that Gordon Kahl had evaded his taxes for too long. Wisely or unwisely (probably the latter in hindsight) the emissaries of the local sheriff's office went out with a warrant to arrest him. It happened to be the day the township meeting took place, so they lay in wait. Then, around five in the evening the meeting broke up and Gordon Kahl and his 'congregation' left in their cars – followed by the forces of law and order.

A mile or less outside Medina, North Dakota, Kahl's driver, David Broer, became aware of the marshal's convoy following. He stopped, backed into the entrance to a caravan park and was joined by a carload of Gordon's disciples. And by a carload of the marshal's men.

Despite Gordon Kahl's presumably genuine appeal for there to be no shooting, in the escape/chase chase/escape which followed both sides suffered death and injury. Kahl – safely on this side of the grave – is on record as thinking that it was 'worth it'.

All this gung-ho was increasing Gordon's credibility no end. While he was on the run from the police (on accusations of murder) he claimed that the shoot-out was an act of self-defence: '. . . they turned on their red lights, and I knew the attack was under way . . . I was sure then they felt the only thing was to kill us all . . . I want the world to know that I take no pleasure in the death or injury of those people . . . it becomes a matter of survival.' Kahl then added a few words of invective against his 'enemy'. 'We are a conquered and occupied nation; conquered and occupied by the Jews.'

The 'hero' was eventually traced via a sympathiser's ranch in Arkansas to his cottage in the cult's fortified bunker-camp of

227

shacks and mobile homes in the Ozark Mountains. On 2 June the government agencies finally caught up with Gordon Kahl. Officers trying to serve an arrest warrant were met with a barrage of gunfire . . . smoke grenades . . . tear gas . . . an explosion . . .

In that confrontation both Sheriff Gene Matthews and Gordon Kahl lost their lives.

What happened to the spirit of Sheriff Matthews we do not know. As for Mr Kahl, his spirit was carried far and wide, by the Posse and by its associated groups. He became a beacon to light the ambitions of the far right. The splinter-group Aryan Nations took up Kahl's ZOG war cry; another, US One, began awarding points for the murder of Jews and blacks. Gordon Weldell Kahl had, in one sense at least, won.

MOVE

John Africa and the stand-off on Osage Avenue

They were the proverbial odd couple, and a very dangerous odd couple at that. Vincent Leaphart, a black man in middle age, and Donald Glassey, a young white teacher, met in the early 1970s. They shared radical political and social views, which resulted in the formation of the American Christian Movement for Life – abbreviated simply to Move. Fortunately Glassey owned part of a large house in Philadelphia into which the adherents of Move moved. An act celebrated by Leaphart by changing his name to John Africa; he also insisted that everybody except Donald Glassey change their last name to Africa. To begin with there were nine adults, a brood of children, and a couple of dozen scabby cats and dogs.

It was here at the cult's headquarters on North 33rd Street that, in 1973, John Africa began to pen *The Book*, a collection of John's none-too-clear political observations combined with equally unclear suggestions for a back-to-nature life-style – a diet of raw vegetables, for example.

By 1975 the disciples of John Africa had increased to thirty-five people. This enabled him to set up an alternative 'government', doling out posts such as Minister of Information and Minister of Defence. Move was now in direct opposition – soon to be confrontation – with what they called the 'System'; in other words anybody but themselves. As the strength of their numbers, and their confidence, grew, so did Move's presence. They seemed to be everywhere – picketing local education and medical

229

institutions, and yelling political abuse through loudspeakers at ever more frequent rallies. This clearly could not meet with the approval of the System.

At one gathering called to disrupt a meeting of state governors, Move demonstrated what the *Philadelphia Inquirer* described as their most 'baffling' characteristic: 'talking continuously, punctuating each phrase with an obscenity, without ever saying anything comprehensible'.

Before long the houseful of mangy occupants – human and animal – had attracted police attention many times in response to complaints. In 1977 the civic authorities made an order for the eviction of Move from its headquarters. After the cult had barricaded itself behind the doors and windows, Philadelphia mayor Frank Rizzo moved in a police blockade to surround the house. The final showdown came on 8 August 1978, when state troops, firefighters and specially trained marksmen joined the police presence. It was never going to be a simple matter of surrender (John Africa had already declared Move's intention to die for its rights). The cult held its heavily fortified headquarters for much of the day. At about 8.30 p.m., armed police forced an entry into the house. The resulting gunfire wounded four officers, one fatally, and four firefighters.

Following their subsequent trial and conviction, nine members of Move collected life sentences for their part in the incident, and the cult's headquarters was bulldozed to the ground. Peace, it seemed, had once again settled over the neighbourhood.

But there are other neighbourhoods. Soon Move was up to its old tricks again, this time in a house in Osage Avenue, West Philadelphia. In 1981 the first trickle of members arrived, and in no time the neighbours were complaining about the verminous state of the building and its residents. In 1984 cultists built a bunker on the roof – an addition which would prove vital to the second Move stand-off. The Africas promised it would take place on the anniversary of the first: 8 August. On this date in 1984 the scene at Osage Avenue was little different from that at North 33rd, with the Move building confronted by hundreds of police officers. Nothing happened.

It was not until several months had passed that the city council, in consultation with the police bomb squad, hatched a plan for officers to scale the outside of the building and hurl tear-gas canisters through the trap-door of the fortified bunker. Move, meanwhile, had created another bunker in the cellar of the house.

On the night of 12 May 1985, most of the residents of Osage Avenue had been evacuated from their houses to shelter behind police barricades. At the same time armed police units were taking up their positions in front of the barricades. At dawn, Move threw down the gauntlet via its banks of crackly loudspeakers. It was clear the cultists meant to fight to the death of the last member – and take as many of the 'invasion force' as possible with them. Along the rooftop by the bunker, armed cult 'soldiers' had already taken up battle stations.

A fire department water-cannon ineffectively directed thousands of gallons of water at the bunker, while Move retaliated with bullets. While the battle raged, two police officers breached an outside wall of the house and lobbed in tear-gas grenades. And still the cult fought back, while the plan to tear-gas the bunker was launched, and failed.

Having not been successful even in persuading Move to release the children, Police Commissioner Gregory Sambor played his trump card. A bomb containing a gas grenade would be dropped on the roof of the bunker in an attempt to pierce a hole. Just before 5.30 p.m. Lieutenant Powell of the bomb squad flew a helicopter over the bunker and dropped the deadly missile on to the roof of the house. The explosion tore through the fabric, starting fires in the building beneath. Stubbornly, the bunker was still standing. But not for long.

Less than an hour and a half after the bomb was dropped, the Move headquarters was an inferno. And so were six other adjoining houses. Move was still not beaten, and continued to exchange rapid gunfire with police marksmen. It was 11.40 p.m. before the blazing buildings were brought under control – sixty of them, leaving a neighbourhood of charred rubble. From the

Move house only two escaped. John Africa was not one of them.

A successful 'tactical necessity' as Commissioner Sambor defined the operation? Or a 'stupid and tragic' decision as state senator Williams described it? Perhaps somebody should have asked the homeless residents of Osage Avenue.

DEATH ANGELS

The 'Zebra' killings

They were called the 'Zebra' killings because all the victims were white and all the offenders were black, and when the trial opened before Supreme Court Judge Joseph Karesh on 3 March 1975 it was set to become a sensation. Standing in the dock were four ex-convicts named Jesse Cooke, Larry Greene, Manuel Moore and J. C. Simon; a fifth, Anthony Harris, had turned state's evidence and would be dealt with later. The trial would last for one year and six days – one of the longest in California's legal history – and 181 witnesses would pass through the court.

The evidence placed before the jury demonstrated one of the most horrific and senseless examples of black racism that they could ever imagine, a reign of terror that gripped San Francisco for 179 days during 1973–4. In all, the five assassins left a total of fifteen men, women and children dead – all selected at random, their only 'crime' was being white. A further eight victims were seriously wounded.

It had been the ambition of the five killers to join the élite force known as the Death Angels who were committed to black supremacy and the annihilation of what they saw as 'white devils'. In order to qualify for membership of the Angels it was necessary to murder at least nine white men, five white women or four white children. Already the California police were grappling with an alarming number of unsolved homicides – 135 men, seventy-five women and sixty children, most thought to be the result of Death Angel activities.

The aspiring Angels walked the streets in pairs or threesomes, picking people off randomly at bus stops, in telephone kiosks, late-night launderettes, and so on. In response, the police mounted blanket operations in the black areas of the city, pulling thousands of blacks off the streets for interrogation. In the end, though, it was one of 'Zebra's' own members, Anthony Harris, who confessed to his part in the slaughter and implicated his four collaborators. Harris spent a total of twelve days on the witness stand, and his evidence contributed greatly to the unanimous guilty verdicts returned by the jury. All the defendants were given life sentences.

VOODOO CULTS

VOODOO (OR VOUDOUN)

Voodoo is probably the largest, best known and best understood of the religions originating in Africa. Although the basic wisdom existed long before slavery it was this trade in human misery that spread the religions throughout the world. Although voodoo now exists in many countries, its modern form originated in Haiti during the colonisation of Hispaniola. Thus an Afro-Caribbean religion was welded together from tribes taken from all parts of the Dark Continent. The irony of this lies in the fact that the European colonists had sought to isolate the individual tribes.

The French were especially savage opponents of voodoo, finally resorting to a ban on all African religious practices – often on pain of death. It was this widespread persecution that resulted in the political revolution which began in 1791, and led to Haitian independence in 1804.

Voodoo, like most faiths, is dependent upon a belief that powerful spirits exist and that with appropriate prayer and ritual they can be invited to do human, albeit priestly, bidding.

Like followers of other religions, those who tread the path of voodoo have a creation myth to explain the mysteries of the origins of the universe. For them the supreme creator was the serpent Damballah. It is said that the action of his 7,000 coils shaped the hills and valleys, and that he put the galaxies in the sky. When Damballah cast off his skin the waters flowed over the earth, and the sun shone on the water and created a rainbow called Ayida-Wedo, whose beauty the serpent so loved that he married her.

As the great creator is considered far too important to waste time on human affairs, this duty is undertaken by a pantheon of spirits called *loas*. There are hundreds of loas, and many of them have several names. The first loa made itself known to the inhabitants of Ife, a legendary city in West Africa. Ginen, where Ife is located, has been taken by voodoo disciples as the place where the spirit of the departed will be transported to live with those of their ancestors.

The loas fall mainly into one of two categories: Rada loa and Petro loa. The Rada are the gentler, more well meaning of the two, though much less powerful. At their rituals, the faithful wear white and a large fire burns throughout; the iron bar stuck in the flames represents the loa Ogoun. The Petro loas are the other side of the coin, and the ritual procedure resulted from the anger and cruelty that characterised Haiti during slavery. One of the more interesting of the Petro loas is the splendidly named Baron Samedi, Lord of the Graveyard, the loa of the dead. In ceremonies black goats or chickens are sacrificed, and his symbols are coffins and penises.

All the rituals are boisterous affairs with chanting, singing and drumming. The event is presided over by a *houngan*, top in the hierarchy of the priesthood. Two slightly less highly ranked assistants, a man and a woman, are on hand to help the houngan.

The most important part of the rite is to summon the loa of gates and crossroads, Legba. The significance of this is that only this loa can give permission for others to pass to the material plane from the spiritual. This is followed by much sprinkling of water and waving of sacred swords at the cardinal points. The houngan – the only person qualified to summon the loas – uses a white flour to 'draw' a design called a *vever* in the middle of the floor. This is a symbol of the particular loa to be called, and each has a different pattern.

Next the houngan strikes the vever with his *asson*, a sacred rattle, to open the astral connection. The loa cannot refuse or ignore this command, and is obliged to descend to earth. The loa must, of course, be thanked and made to feel at home. This is most commonly done by providing food and drink of its choice, which are laid in the centre of the vever. If a ceremony is important (or for a Petro loa) an animal appropriate to the spirit is sacrificed so that the loa can absorb its life force. A less pleasant custom by far is for the celebrants to drink the blood of the sacrifice.

Harmless enough pranks, or a serious religious ceremony? It depends on your point of view. However, there are some groups using the name voodoo to carry out wholly more sinister activities. At these secret meetings, hooded followers are reputed to practise human sacrifice and to eat human flesh.

Zombies

One of the best-known subjects of voodoo practice is the creation of zombies. The living dead. It is true that popular Hollywood products have done nothing to paint an accurate picture, but it is being claimed that evidence exists for zombification. Not the killing and reanimation by the area sorcerer, but by a method using drugs.

One theory claims that the victim is rendered apparently dead by the use of a powerful poison. After allowing the bereaved a day or two to express their grief, the voodoo magician exhumes the body and administers another concoction to revive it. In the meantime the victim has become a mindless amnesiac, though good material to be used or sold on as a manual labourer.

POSTSCRIPT:

Voodoo justice

Maintenance workers at Dade County courthouse, Florida, have been given the early-morning duty of searching the grounds for gifts left by voodoo followers in the hope that the gods will ensure leniency in their cases. One particular parcel attended by a bomb squad turned out to be a dead chicken. According to a spokesman for the court, the offerings seem not to have had much effect on the due process of the law.

The case of Mirella Beechook and the Lord of the Graveyard

In June 1986, Mirella Beechook appeared at the Central Criminal Court before Sir James Miskin, the Recorder of London. She formally entered a plea of diminished responsibility to the charges of murder which she faced. Although she blamed 'voices' for telling her to kill, the jury found Mrs Beechook guilty not of manslaughter (the diminished responsibility verdict), but of murder. In sentencing her to two life sentences, the judge agreed that although she could not have been acting normally at the time she killed, her mental state did not amount to diminished responsibility.

The court had listened to a chilling tale of two cynical and brutal child murders. It had heard how on the afternoon of Wednesday 18 September 1985, four-year-old Stacey Kavanagh had gone out to play on the housing estate where she lived in Rotherhithe, south-east London. Only her killer ever saw her alive again.

Two hours later Mrs Kavanagh opened her front door in response to an urgent knocking and found a distressed Mirella Beechook holding one of Stacey's red shoes. Lynn Kavanagh knew Mrs Beechook as a neighbour, and her daughter Tina was a friend of Stacey's. Barely able to speak through her anguish, Mrs Beechook said that Stacey had been round and she had taken both the girls to the local shops. When she came out after making some purchases, the children had gone. Thinking that they had gone back home, she returned to the flats in Rotherhithe Street; the children were not there. On the way back to the shops, she said, she had found Stacey's shoe.

Within the hour friends and neighbours were organising

themselves into search parties to comb the immediate area. With increasing desperation the boundaries of the search widened, and the local volunteers were soon joined by specialist teams of police officers equipped with helicopters and tracker dogs. It was just before midnight that one of those dogs confirmed everybody's worst fears. Beneath a thin covering of leaves behind some undergrowth in Southwark Park lay the body of Stacey Kavanagh; she had been strangled. The question now was, what had happened to seven-year-old Tina Beechook?

By dawn Detective Chief Superintendent Roy Gregg, in charge of the inquiry, was saying: 'Every minute that passes makes me more anxious about Tina.' Later the same day, a tearful Mirella Beechook appealed on television to whoever had abducted Tina: 'Leave her somewhere that she can find her way home.'

Less than three days after Stacey Kavanagh's body was found, detectives had compiled a file on Mirella Beechook. She had been born on the island of Mauritius, and had already acquired her family's obsession with the practice of voodoo before she arrived in England in 1974 at the age of fourteen. Mirella still adhered to the off-shoot cult of Gris-Gris while living in London, and her flat was almost a temple to such gods as Baron Samedi, Lord of the Graveyard, Doctor of Death. In 1977 she married Ravi Beechook who, having made her pregnant with Tina, wandered off returning occasionally for 'company'. In 1979, this companionship resulted in Mirella becoming pregnant again; in October Sabrina was born.

Now, it may just have been overactive imagination, but Ravi was convinced that his estranged wife was trying to bewitch him. Perhaps it was finding a photograph of himself with a needle piercing the head; or the effigy stuck with nails and pins that was left on the doorstep. This behaviour, Ravi supposed, was some form of revenge against him for not returning home.

Less than a month after her birth, baby Sabrina was back in hospital with stomach trouble. Following one of Mrs Beechook's visits, nurses became worried about the infant's drowsiness; they became even more worried when they found a sleeping pill under

241

Sabrina's cot. An urgent blood test revealed a dangerously high level of the drug Mogadon.

The result was that Mirella Beechook was examined by a psychiatrist whose advice was that Mirella was not seriously mentally ill (she had insisted that the voodoo curse of the evil eye had caused her to harm her baby) and she was put on probation; Tina and Sabrina, meanwhile, were taken into care. Sabrina was subsequently adopted and in 1980 Tina was allowed back home. Several years later Mirella Beechook was sentenced to three months' imprisonment for shoplifting. Shortly after her release she was again arrested for shoplifting. Less than a week afterwards, while she was still awaiting trial, Stacey Kavanagh was murdered.

Aware of the significance of this information, police officers wisely kept their eye on Mirella Beechook. On 21 September two plainclothes detectives witnessed the arrival of Ravi. They saw him knock on the door, talk briefly with his wife and then accompany her down to the central square of the flats. Then they saw Ravi turn and run back towards the flat; at which point the officers intercepted him. With almost uncontrollable anger and distress, Ravi told them what his wife had just said – that Tina was dead; that she, her own mother, had strangled her . . . Investigating officers entered the flat and found the body of little Tina, tied up in a sack and dumped under the bed. Which is how Mirella Beechook came to be facing two charges of murder at the Old Bailey.

SANTERIA
(PATH OF THE SAINTS)

Like most branches of the voodoo religion, Santeria (or La Regla Lucumi) spread from Africa with the slave trade, reaching such destinations as the Caribbean, Haiti, Cuba and the southern United States.

Cuba's distinctive santeria syncretised the old deities – called *orishas* – of the Yoruba tribe with saints of Roman Catholicism. For example, Ellegua with St Anthony, Orula with St Francis of Assisi and Ochun with Our Lady of Charity. This was a purely pragmatic solution to the slaves' need to mask their native religion, not uncommon when pagan beliefs confronted Christianity. Santeria developed during the eighteenth and early nineteenth centuries, though Miami's practising *santeros* were supplemented by the exodus of political refugees from Fidel Castro's Cuba during the Mariel boatlift in 1980. One leading santeria priest (*babalawo*) has estimated that there are 20,000 such priests in Miami, serving the needs of more than 100,000 santeros.

Santeros believe in a single god called Olorun (or Olodumare) which is the fount of all the universe's spiritual energy (*ashe*). This god communicates to the world through the orishas, which represent all human life and the forces of nature. Followers of the religion in turn communicate with the orishas through prayer, ritual and sacrifice (*ebo*), in order to make their requests for help. However, in order to reach this stage the initiate (*lyawo*) must follow an exacting regime and prove a full knowledge of the songs, rituals and language (*Lucumi*) of santeria. So strict is this rite of passage that the lyawo must dress entirely in white for the

243

first year, must not touch or be touched by anybody, must not look in a mirror or go out at night.

The strong tradition of santeria 'magic' is based on belief in the power and wisdom of the orishas and their ability to influence the destinies of humankind. Santeria shares many similarities with other magical cults in that it concentrates on an individual's personal requirements. Ceremonies are performed to help acquire wealth and power, or even lay curses (sometimes even death) on enemies. One curious example was the santeria altar found in 1990 by troops when they arrested Panama's president (and major drug-dealer) Manuel Noriega. The altar at Noriega's office in Panama City was adorned with curse effigies of the then US President Ronald Reagan and Vice-President George Bush. There were also lists of names to be cursed, including those of American Attorney General Dick Thornborough and William Hoeveler, the federal district court judge who presided over the Noriega case.

Sacrifice is fundamental to the religion of the santeros, and though the offerings are not invariably animal sacrifices, creatures are always sacrificed at important rituals. It is essential that animals used in this way are treated with great respect – they are, after all, the property of the orisha. At the opening of the ceremony it is the general intention to express, in song and action, the belief that all life and all death are sacred, and that one day the celebrants will die as has the animal.

Although most santeros consider their religion harmless and above-board, there is some evidence that along with the essential animal sacrifices some groups have indulged in the blood-sacrifice of human beings.

POSTSCRIPT:

A pig and his family avoid slaughter

One of the most endearing of the santerian fables concerns a pig (his name is not recorded). Now, this porker belonged to a wealthy farmer who devoted his energies to breeding the fattest pigs for slaughter in the district. Every day the animals would be fed the most fattening of swill and afterwards one would be chosen for the market.

A smarter pig than the average noticed that daily one of them went missing. The fattest one. And from that time he determined to eat as little as necessary – a few banana stems and garlic husks perhaps. In this way he managed to maintain his slim figure. The farmer ignored him.

But there was a new plan. Pig decided to save not only himself, but his family. To this end he dug a tunnel. Every day, little by little he made the hole large enough for his needs. Finally, when there was to be a great feast and many pigs slaughtered, he gathered up his kith and kin and they escaped through the hole to freedom.

The legend ends: 'In this way one pig and his family, through patience and the realisation that one can bring death by one's own mouth saved the day.'

The case of Leroy Carter and his missing head

Officers of the San Francisco Police Department are a level-headed bunch in the main, taking the rarely smooth with the generally rough. So when a radio patrol-car report came through that a vagrant had been seen snoozing near the lake in Golden Gate Park, nobody felt too inclined to step on the accelerator. Bums and winos are a dime apiece – leave him to sleep off last night's cheap hooch in the noonday sun. True it was 8 February – 1981 to be precise – and not as warm on the ground as it can be, but most of these derelicts have got a second skin.

It was only when the patrolmen arrived at the sign of 'The Sleeping', and pulled down the top of the night-bag with a night-stick that they knew this was not another routine call-out. The bag contained the body of a black man, minus his head. More puzzling still, in its place were two kernels of corn and a chicken wing. A search of the area around the corpse revealed a cardboard box packed with other pieces of dismembered chicken.

Identifying the victim turned out to be unexpectedly easy. Leroy Carter was a petty crook whose fingerprints and extensive list of crimes were indelibly on file. The reason for his death was more perplexing. The Medical Examiner was convinced that it had been a ritual murder, and the evidence was presented to the coroner of Dade County, Florida, Charles Weltli. Given the huge Cuban immigrant population of Florida, particularly of Miami, it is no surprise that the coroner had become a recognised expert on cases of santeria. This was such a case.

Santeria rituals will almost always involve the sacrifice of some small animal or other – usually a chicken. However, on ceremonies specific to Ellegua, orisha of gates and crossroads (see below) some greater offering may be expected. Charles Weltli was also able to make some confident predictions about the fate of the late Leroy Carter's head. In order to release its magic powers, the head would first have to be buried for twenty-one days, then unearthed and kept for a further twenty-one days until it fulfilled it purpose. The relic would then turn up rather the worse for wear near the scene of the decapitation.

On 22 March, forty-two days after Carter's death, a rotted severed head was found beside Alvard Lake. To date the killing has not been satisfactorily solved.

POSTSCRIPT:

Ellegua

As with most of the orishas, the spelling of this name is fairly vagrant (as also are many other proper names in the Yoruba language). Ellegua will also answer to Elegoa, and is keeper of roads and doors (sometimes, more romantically, 'opportunities'). Ellegua is always the first of the orishas to be honoured in a ceremony because, by standing at the crossroads of the human and the divine, nothing can be accomplished without his approval. Nothing can be done in either world without his permission. In the Lucumi this deity is sometimes called Ashé – 'Spiritual Power of the Universe'.

Ellegua, master healer and magician, is as capable of being cruel as kind, and in the Brazilian Candomble tradition he is associated with the devil. Because he protects the home against danger, most santeros keep Ellegua close to the front entrance, presenting offerings on Mondays and the third day of the month. His favourite gifts, it is said, are sweets, corn, candles, rum and cigars.

Alex Henriquez and his victims' last breath

One of the most disturbing suspected cases of santeria-associated killings took place in New York in 1990. There were initially four suspected victims. All were female, all were presumed to have died from asphyxiation. One, if not all, had their chests crushed – and if the police investigating the murders were correct in their assumptions, this method was used in order that the killer could suck the dying breath out of his victim's mouth. There is a santeria belief that doing so will give the owner of this breath power over the spirit of the deceased; possession, as in the manner of making zombies.

The fourth victim was little Jessica Guzman. She had disappeared from her home in the Bronx on 10 October 1990, and her decomposing body was found on the evening of the 17th along the Bronx River Parkway.

In the hope of identifying a possible serial killer, detectives assigned to the Guzman case reopened files on two similar slayings – those of thirteen-year-old Nilda Cartagena and her fifteen-year-old friend Heriberto Marrero. The two girls had vanished on their way to school on 9 June 1989. Their naked bodies had been found in polythene sacks just off the Hutchinson River Parkway, a mile from where Jessica was discovered.

Although the police subsequently abandoned this line of inquiry, a man named Alejandro 'Alex' Henriquez had been interviewed in connection with the double killing. He was Nilda Cartagena's uncle, a Bronx cab driver. At the time there was some evidence that he had driven the two victims to school on the day of their disappearance, but an alibi more or less stood up. Further suspicion fell on Alex Henriquez when a former girlfriend, a twenty-one-year-old college student named Lisa Rodriguez, was found dead on 19 June 1990. Her body was lying by the Hutchinson River Parkway.

Now, with the murder of Jessica Guzman, the Henriquez connection loomed again. Until the year 1989 he had lived in the apartment just below the Guzman family in the Castle Hills district of the Bronx.

Alex was taken back into custody, and during the course of questioning admitted that he had spoken to Jessica Guzman and two of her friends on 10 October. He was emphatic that Jessica was alive, well and happy when they parted and went their separate ways. While Henriquez was protesting that if the police had anything to charge him with they should, and if not they should release him, reports were coming in from the Medical Examiner's office. Although the bodies had, on the whole, been in too advanced a stage of decomposition for accurate assessments of cause of death, there were no signs of either bullet or stab wounds. In Jessica Guzman's case the most likely cause of death was asphyxiation due to compression of the chest.

Although still convinced that Alex Henriquez was their serial killer, without concrete evidence the police were obliged to release him and allow him to go on holiday to the Caribbean (home of voodoo cults). It may have gone some way to ease their frustration that when Henriquez returned from sunning himself it was to be arrested, charged with both child abuse and an armed robbery (unconnected with the murder investigation), convicted and put away for several years. Despite this, the NYPD homicide squad was still on his case.

And it was a case that looked better by the day. First, a witness was located who testified that he had seen Alex Henriquez and Jessica Guzman in Henriquez's car at 6.30 p.m. on the day she went missing. Henriquez had claimed that he had been at home watching television all evening.

It was at this point that the police looked into another 'unsolved' file: the file marked 'Shamira Bellow'. Her body had been dumped, half naked, from a car that belonged to Alex Henriquez. The car, by then sold on, was traced and, remarkably, yielded to forensic scientists cloth fibres which matched those found on or near the body of fourteen-year-old Shamira.

Meanwhile, routine searches of Henriquez's apartment had rewarded police teams with pieces of clothing belonging to Lisa Rodriguez, the girlfriend who 'has never been to my home'.

The grand jury indicted Alejandro Henriquez with charges of manslaughter and second-degree murder in the deaths of Shamira Bellow, Lisa Rodriguez and Jessica Guzman. The police case was painstakingly thorough and expertly presented. The defendant, who could have expected little less on conviction, was sentenced to three consecutive terms of twenty-five-years-to-life.

ABAQUA

Abaqua is widely recognised as the dark incarnation of Cuban-based santeria, with which it enjoys an uneasy relationship. While santeria can be accused of sacrificing the occasional human being to its orishas (look at the case of poor Leroy Carter above), with abaqua the event is more frequent. Cannibalism is also allegedly practised.

One invariable rule of abaqua ritual is that no black object or animal is sacrificed – though whether this also applies to people I have been unable to discover.

A most remarkable, and grotesque, demonstration of the abaqua cult's desire to remain secret was given in 1978. A Cuban theatre company produced a play in Havana entitled *Abaqua*. The entertainment (*sic*) depicted some very graphic scenes of abaqua rituals – all of which publicity went down very badly with the local cult. In the space of a fortnight following the performance the whole cast had been tracked down and executed. The murders remain unsolved.

PALO MAYOMBE

Adolfo Constanzo and his cloak of invisibility

The cult of palo mayombe – separate from, but similar to, santeria, originated among the Congolese Bantu tribes of West Africa. Like santeria, it was disseminated around the world by the slave trade. Perhaps the most fundamental belief of the *paleros* is that the spirits of the dead (called *nkisi*) have the power to influence the activities of the living.

Most systems of spirit magic require some form of focus – a ritual, perhaps, such as the Roman Catholic Mass, or a sacred object such as the witch's athame, or dagger. For the paleros it is the *nganga*, the cauldron. Into this ghastly pot are collected the relics of death: blood. bones, human and animal body parts, poisonous plants and insects . . . and the sticks. Usually twenty-five sticks protrude from the nganga, and it is this feature which gives the cult its name; *palo* means 'stick' in Spanish. Hence, stick magic.

Adolfo de Jesus Constanzo had a nganga, and among his small band of drug-dealing paleros he was revered as El Padrino, 'The Godfather'. His High Priestess was Sara Maria Aldrete.

Constanzo was born in Miami in 1962, son of an immigrant Cuban mother. Soon after the happy event mother and child relocated to Puerto Rico, but ten years later were back in Miami, in the aptly named district of Little Havana. It was around this time that Aurora Constanzo introduced little Adolfo to the religion of voodoo, and its off-shoot santeria. In 1976, when the boy was fourteen, he was apprenticed to a priest of the palo

251

mayombe cult (who was also sorcerer to the area's main drug-dealers, of which Constanzo learned as much as he did of magic).

Following a few years of drug-related chicanery and exploring his bisexuality, the dashing Adolfo, accompanied by his lovers Martin Quintana and Omar Orea, set out for Mexico City. There he continued to provide the local drug barons with the services of a palo mayombe priest – making animal sacrifices to the orishas to ensure their continued success.

It was around 1985 when Adolfo de Jesus Constanzo, now living at the remote Rancho Santa Elena, outside Matamoros, and having recruited his High Priestess, decided he needed his own nganga. He also determined that rather than merely provide security for drug-runners he would become one himself. And for that he, and his increasing cult following, required a little help from the spirits of the dead.

At first the nganga had been serviced mainly by the inclusion of small animals and the culling of local cemeteries. But big business demanded big sacrifice. Human blood-sacrifice. Now, whenever a major drug deal was about to take place, a live sacrifice was offered and the victim's heart and brains were ripped out to be stirred up along with the other unsavoury ingredients in the nganga. The primary object of the slaughter appears to have been to appease the spirits in return for invisibility and inviolability from police arrest. Not to mention protection from police bullets in the event of a shoot-out.

It was because of this curiously naive faith that Constanzo and his gang were eventually exposed. On 9 April 1989, gang-member Serafin Hernandez, believing that he was invisible, drove through a police roadblock. He wasn't invisible at all, of course, and having been persuaded that he was not invincible to bullets either, he led officers back to the Rancho Santa Elena.

As the search of the Santa Elena progressed, large quantities of marijuana and cocaine were found in a shed, as well as a formidable arsenal of weapons and a dozen brand-new cars fitted with two-way radios. The shed itself was dominated by a makeshift breeze-block altar, and around the building were an alarming number of bloodstains, scraps of human hair and a substance only later identified as human brain pulp. In view of this, the least of the horrors was a prominently displayed severed goat's head. Later, the detainees led officers to the graves of fifteen men and boys. Many of the bodies had been decapitated and all of them had been extensively mutilated.

Needless to say, by this time Constanzo and Aldrete were on the run.

On 5 May 1989, neighbours called the police complaining of a violent quarrel going on in the next-door apartment of a block in Mexico City. When officers arrived on the scene, Constanzo leapt to the window of the apartment and opened fire with a Uzi semi-automatic, provoking a siege which lasted forty-five minutes. During this time Constanzo burned $3,000 in banknotes and threw handfuls more out into the street. Following the ensuing gun battle, Sara Aldrete fled the building screaming: 'He's dead! He's dead!' Police entering the apartment found three of the cult's members alive, but Constanzo and his homosexual bodyguard-cum-lover, Martin Quintana, had been shot dead, locked in a final embrace in a walk-in wardrobe; they had been killed on their own orders, rather than be taken into custody. Sara Aldrete, not surprisingly, denied any involvement in the killings, but was indicted along with the other survivors of the cult on multiple charges including murder and drug offences.

On 8 May 1989 one of the most bizarre press conferences in Mexican police history took place. Before the assembled media representatives cult members under arrest were presented by senior police officers behind a table decorated with lighted candles, swords, black robes, skulls and other voodoo para-phernalia.

Among the 'celebrities' at the conference was Alvaro de Leon Valdez, a professional gangster also known as 'El Dubi'. It was El Dubi who had been ordered by Constanzo to kill him and Quintana. According to his statement, the gunman was not enthusiastic: 'He told me to kill him, but I didn't want to. Then he said I was going to suffer in hell if I didn't. Then he hugged

Martin, and I just stood in front of them and shot them with a machine gun.' De Leon also told horrified reporters that one of the victims, a twenty-one-year-old student, Mark Kilroy, had been kept bound for twelve hours before being killed by a machete blow to the head; then his back had been opened up and his vertebrae pulled out to make a 'magic' necklace.

On a more mundane note, US Customs Agent Oran Neck announced that, behind all the mumbo-jumbo, Constanzo's gang were smuggling as much as 900 kilogrammes of marijuana a week from Mexico into the United States.

In August 1990 Sara Maria Aldrete was acquitted of Constanzo's murder, but sentenced to six years' imprisonment for criminal association. Constanzo's killer, Alvaro de Leon Valdez, was sentenced to thirty years for double murder, and the two other men taken in the Mexico City apartment, Juan Fragosa and Jorge Montes, were tried for the ranch murders and an assortment of drugs and firearms offences and sentenced to thirty-five years each. Omar Orea was convicted of the same crimes but died of Aids before he could be sentenced. Four other cult members were subsequently each given sixty-seven years' imprisonment for the Rancho Santa Elena killings, and in May 1994 High Priestess Sara Aldrete collected sixty-two years for thirteen murders at the ranch.

CULT EXORCISM

The word exorcism derives from the Greek for 'to put out'. In this sense of the term it refers to expelling the real or imaginary (depending upon your point of view) evil spirits, devils and demons which have infested a person or place or have been conjured as the result of some magical ritual. Exorcisms of one kind or another have a classical ancestry, and were certainly practised by the Pagans and the Jews. However, it is customary to associate exorcisms of the 'bell, book and candle' type with the Christian Church, where they have been common practice since the New Testament:

> But if I cast out devils by the Spirit of God, then the kingdom of God is come unto you. (Matthew xii, 28)

It was, and is, usual for the priest or other ordained minister to invoke this power of God's goodness to restrain the malevolence of the spirits.

However, a belief that certain forms of extreme behaviour, notably insanity, are the result of demonic possession is common to a great many of the world's religions. The cure for such manifestations is some form of exorcism; that is, expelling the evil spirits which have taken up residence in the victim's body. Some religions and some sects indulge in quite barbaric physical harassment of the sufferer, believing in the quasi-logic that if the victim's body is made to feel thoroughly wretched, the demons will decamp – treatment which has too often ended with the victim's death.

EXORCISM IN THE CHRISTIAN RELIGION

The practice of exorcism is widely recognised throughout the Christian religion among the major churches and the many offshoots from them. Both the Roman Catholic Church and the Anglican Communion (a family of Protestant churches including the Church of England) currently have among their number a surprisingly large number of experienced exorcists.

One very well known and highly regarded Anglican practitioner is the Reverend J. Christopher Neil Smith, one-time vicar of St Saviours Church, London. He has estimated that he has performed as many as 500 exorcisms a year – almost ten every week. It was early in his priesthood that Reverend Neil Smith began to use his 'spiritual gift'; in fact it followed his own salvation by exorcism after being contaminated by a black magician. It is significant that many magicians, particularly those whose studies are based on the qbalah, themselves have elaborate rituals of protection against possession.

An unusual vehicle for exorcism is used by the Reverend Dr Henry Cooper, the Archbishop of Canterbury's chaplain. At University College London, Dr Cooper maintains a telephone 'clinic' for those troubled by what they believe to be evil spirits. Distressed callers will be asked a sequence of searching questions: whether they believe in God; that He is powerful above all things (such as demons); that the caller believes God will help them; etc. If the troubled soul responds positively to these questions, then Dr Cooper has no hesitation in delivering an exorcism along the following lines: '. . . I bid all that is evil to depart from you, and go to its own place. It will hurt nobody, and remain there, never to return and trouble a child of God. In the name of the Father, and of the Son and of the Holy Spirit. Amen.' Exorcist and patient then recite together the Lord's Prayer, after which Dr Cooper is confident to sign off: 'Now there is nothing to be afraid of.'

The form the exorcism takes in the Roman Catholic Church is laid down in the General Rules for Exorcism. Based on the *Rituale Romanum* of 1614, it has been authorised by the Vatican.

One of the most delightfully simple prayers of protection is called 'St Patrick's Breastplate', a version of which forms part of the final stage of a Roman Catholic exorcism:

Christ be with me
Christ within me
Christ behind me
Christ before me
Christ beside me
Christ to win me
Christ to comfort and restore me
Christ beneath me
Christ above me
Christ in quiet and
Christ in danger
Christ in the hearts of all that love me
Christ in the mouth of friend and stranger.

Despite the formal belief of the main churches that demonic possession is real and requires to be treated with the power of the exorcist (or, rather, the power of God *through* the exorcist), most practitioners are also aware that many manifestations are the result of mental instability. Certainly, if the Reverend Neil Smith does not tangibly 'feel' the presence of evil he is likely to recommend a psychiatrist. The Roman Catholic Church, when it is convinced that there is a case of possession, insists that all the facts are discussed with the local bishop, usually in consultation with a doctor and/or a psychiatrist.

Methodist and Baptist ministers tend to be left to make up their own minds about exorcism, though the Methodists do have formal guidelines for procedure. Other Christian groups, such as the Church of Scotland, believe that 'Exorcism does more harm than good. There is no place for it.' The cases cited below go a long way to support that assertion.

Anneliese Michel and her battle with the devil

Anneliese Michel was born in Klingenberg in 1953. By her middle teens she had already been treated for convulsive fits later diagnosed as epilepsy. Anneliese's older sister, Martha, had died at the age of eight, and this had clearly upset her sibling. However, what may have been more significant in the light of future events was that Martha had been born with three breasts. Among the superstitious local folk this was considered a certain mark of the devil.

In 1973 Anneliese Michel took up study at Wurzburg University, where her behaviour became increasingly eccentric. The walls of her room she covered with images of saints, and she installed an *ad hoc* stoup of holy water. Friends reported finding her kneeling naked on the floor gibbering at unseen presences. Her parents, understandably worried, consulted the local Roman Catholic priest. Between them they decided that Anneliese was suffering an infestation of malevolent spirits; even the girl herself thought so: 'The only conclusion for my suffering . . . the devil is trying to possess my soul.'

Consistent with good practice, the priest alerted Father Adolf Rodewyk, a Jesuit living in Frankfurt. Rodewyk was widely regarded for his study of Satanism and as a leading exorcist. By mutual consent they reported to the regional bishop, and he in turn ordered the exorcism; for this purpose he recommended two men highly experienced in the 'craft': Father Arnold Renz and Father Ernst Alt.

Between September 1975 and her death ten months later,

Anneliese Michel was visited by the priests upwards of seventy times for the purpose of ritual exorcism. According to Renz and Alt the young woman was possessed by the spirits of Cain, Lucifer, Nero, Adolf Hitler, Judas Iscariot and Father Helgar Fleischmann, a priest who had been defrocked for murder.

During these 'cleansing' sessions Anneliese behaved in such a demented manner that she had to be tied to a bed. At the sight of a Bible or crucifix she would be transported into paroxysms of blasphemous cursing. All the while Father Arnold was tape-recording their activities. In one of the more blackly humorous episodes, Judas/Anneliese (speaking in a masculine voice) complained bitterly that thirty pieces of silver for the betrayal of Christ was a miserly sum, and that he was still pursuing a claim for more.

As the months wore on, Anneliese Michel's physical, as well as mental, health deteriorated rapidly. According to her parents and the exorcists, this was because the demons forbade her to eat. On 1 July 1976 Anneliese died; she weighed just over four stone.

It need hardly be said that the doctor summoned to her death-bed absolutely refused to issue a death certificate. Instead he informed the police, and as the result of their report the state prosecutor, Dr Karl Stenger, decided that Anneliese's parents and her exorcists had stood by while she starved to death without making the barest attempt to secure medical help. In other words, homicide by negligence.

Perhaps it lies somewhere in the very nature of such rare cases as this that those convicted of causing suffering and death are treated so apparently leniently. In April 1978 Father Arnold and Father Ernst were each sentenced to six months' imprisonment suspended for three years. The same sentence was passed on Josef and Anna Michel.

A chilling footnote was added to this tragedy when Father Arnold Renz told the court: 'I was convinced then, and I am convinced now that she was possessed by the devil. She died willingly to atone for the sins of others.' In the case studies which follow, this insistence that the death must have been God's will recurs.

Beatrix Rutherford and John the Preacher

Charismatic Christians are, according to one description, typified by a vivid belief in supernatural evil, intense, almost obsessive, religious commitment (to the point of believing themselves utterly infallible), and talking in tongues. This characteristic has its roots in the Acts of the Apostles:

> And there appeared unto them cloven tongues like of fire, and it sat upon each of them. And they were all filled with the Holy Ghost, and began to speak with other tongues, as the Spirit gave them utterance. And there were dwelling at Jerusalem Jews, devout men, out of every nation under heaven. Now when this was noised abroad, the multitude came together, and were confounded, because that every man heard them speak in his own language. (Acts ii, 3–6)

Charismatics also believe in demonic possession and have their own bizarre methods of exorcism. Which was very unlucky for Beatrix Rutherford.

In the late 1970s a former actor turned evangelist, named John Sherwood (but called John the Preacher), walked into a London police station and confessed to killing a woman. This was the unfortunate Miss Rutherford, whom Sherwood had met at a bus stop some weeks earlier. Beatrix was herself almost equally mentally disturbed; indeed, she had made several confessions to murder herself. According to Sherwood's statement: 'I was trying to get the devils out of her . . . I wasn't hitting her, I was hitting the devils . . . I didn't mean to kill her . . . spirits were manifesting themselves and controlling her face. She was groaning, but it was not her voice.'

So John the Preacher and a friend called Anthony Strover decided on an impromptu exorcism. Both were members of what called itself the Invisible Church.

First they dragged the poor woman into a local Pentecostal church, where they prayed over her. When they returned to the flat, Sherwood saw a demon hovering over Beatrix Rutherford. It was his first exorcism, and he was understandably frightened for both himself and Beatrix in the company of this devil. The resulting 'ceremony' began with Sherwood throwing his victim on the bed and holding her down. Then Strover started to beat her savagely. The punching, kicking and stomping went on for about half an hour. Then a spirit which identified itself as Judas Iscariot appeared, and the two men weighed in again with boot and fist. Suddenly Beatrix was very still. Believing that they had expelled the spirits which were tormenting her, Sherwood and Strover spent a few moments in grateful prayer. Then they realised that Beatrix Rutherford was dead. Had been beaten to death.

But if the exorcism had not been a runaway success, perhaps a resurrection would make up for it. Sherwood read from Elijah, then prayed, then tried artificial respiration. Probably to the end of his days he would retain the belief that, as he claimed, death was caused 'by the great force of devils leaving her'.

It is typical of the arrogant sense of self-righteousness entertained by many fundamentalists (especially the charismatics) that at no time did John Sherwood and Anthony Strover doubt that they were doing God's will. Strover claimed: 'I was conscious that what we were doing could hurt her but, as we were dealing with the supernatural, I thought it would be in God's hands.' Sherwood's speech from the dock began: 'With the increase in evil in the world, the deliverance from evil through exorcism is becoming more and more important.'

It was a sentiment that would be echoed more than a decade later, on the other side of the planet . . .

The 'deliverance' of Joan Vollmer

It was on 22 January 1993, in the hamlet of Antwerp, near Melbourne, that Joan Vollmer's 'deliverance' began. For all practical purposes it was an exorcism but to the Vollmers, being charismatics, it was a deliverance. Her ordeal would last until

Saturday the 30th, climaxing with – so the exorcists claimed – the expulsion of evil spirits. The only problem was that in getting rid of the demons Mrs Vollmer died; and not only did Mrs Vollmer die, but she died in acute agony.

Ralph and Joan Vollmer had been married for four years, but they had lived together for some time before that. Ralph was a fifty-four-year-old pig farmer, and the couple had lived in Antwerp for five years. The Vollmers were devoutly religious, Ralph almost to the point of fanaticism. Around 1990, fifty-year-old Joan had been admitted for treatment to the Lakeside Psychiatric Hospital at Ballarat. When she was discharged Ralph Vollmer suggested that she submit to a 'deliverance'; in fact he mentioned it several times. Sensibly, Joan's view was that if the hospital had discharged her she was in no need of exorcism. (Here we have one of those tragic cases where mental illness and infestation by demons are perceived as being inseparable.)

At this time Ralph Vollmer was a salvationist, but he began to attend 'home church' meetings at the house of John and Leanne Merlyn Reichenbach, who had gathered around them a dozen or so like-minded charismatic Christians. It was the Reichenbachs and members David Andrew Kligner and Matthew Nuske who would assist Ralph Vollmer in the deliverance.

On 22 January 1993 the ritual began. Because, according to Ralph, his wife had started 'behaving strangely', she was not consulted on the matter and was simply tied to a kitchen chair at the Vollmer home. While Leanne Reichenbach pushed against Joan's stomach and chest, twenty-two-year-old Matthew Nuske, who seems to have been in charge of the proceedings, ordered the demons to leave immediately 'in the name of Jesus Christ'. When the spirits proved stubborn, the treatment was tried again and again with increasing brutality. When she was not being pummelled and pushed, Joan Vollmer was having uplifting texts from the scriptures read and sung at her. 'When you are being led by the Lord,' John Reichenbach said later, 'you feel at peace about it and you act.' An identical attitude to that displayed by Anthony

Strover in the case discussed above: 'I thought it would be in God's hands.'

The end of Mrs Vollmer's torture came on the afternoon of 30 January. This is how Ralph Vollmer described the climax: 'It was just the last few moments before the evil spirits released their hold on Joan's tongue. By this time they were on the tongue, there was a hissing and frothing of the mouth, and then a groan when they finally released her.' It is worth adding that the spirits were described as manifesting themselves as a pig, a dog, a man, and two females calling themselves Princess Joan and Princess Baby Joan. The demons may have departed, but so had Mrs Vollmer's life.

Undeterred, the assembled exorcists received a message from God (oddly enough over the telephone) saying that Joan would be resurrected. And over the next couple of days, as the charismatics prayed, and the summer heat soared, the exposed body lying on a mattress in the back yard began to putrefy. According to Ralph Vollmer it became very smelly, and 'there were a lot of blowflies and things around'. Quite how long the earthly remains of Joan Vollmer would have been left awaiting resurrection is anybody's guess, had Ralph not received another telephone instruction from God – telling him to notify the authorities!

And that is how the Homicide Squad from Melbourne became involved. According to the press reports Ralph Vollmer was charged with manslaughter. Then on 8 September 1995, the Brisbane *Courier Mail* reported that thirty-two-year-old Leanne Reichenbach and thirty-year-old David Kligner, who had been freed on bail while awaiting appeal in the Supreme Court, lost their appeal against conviction and against sentence.

JESUS-AMEN MINISTRIES

The woman who didn't speak to people

According to United States police reports dated March 1995, five members of the Christian sect the Jesus-Amen Ministries beat to death a Korean woman during an exorcism. Twenty-five-year-old Kyung-A Ha met her fate in the cult's headquarters at Emeryville, California, following a report by her sister, Kelly, that Ha was possessed by devils. Kelly Ha explained in a statement to the police that the tell-tale signs were: 'She couldn't sleep at night. She didn't talk much to people. And sometimes she was aggressive.'

The five cultists, all women, were named as Eun Park, the founder, her fifty-two-year-old mother Hwa Ra, twenty-two-year-old cult 'director' Jung Sin, and two teenage Bible college students from Russia. It later transpired that during an all-night prayer meeting Kyung-A Ha had been struck at least one hundred times and suffered ten broken ribs. Eun Park did not report the death to the authorities immediately because she appears to have fervently believed that the woman's spirit would return from her 'journey to heaven'. Like the Strover/Sherwood case and the Vollmer exorcism, the belief in some kind of resurrection was undisputed.

All five members of the Jesus-Amen Ministries were charged with murder. In conversation with detectives, Eun Park insisted that the sacrifice was 'a victory for Jesus Christ'.

EXORCISM IN THE
MUSLIM FAITH

Kusor Bashir and the djinn called John Wayne

In the spring of 1991, twenty-year-old Kusor Bashir became depressed. It was not simply a momentary fit of despair with her life, but something deeper; somebody suggested that her failure to pass her driving test was the final straw. At any rate Kusor's parents, devout Muslims, decided that she had become inhabited by *djinns*, and that was very bad news indeed.

Djinns – some of which are benevolent, and some downright wicked – are believed by Muslims to be invisible spirits 'created by smokeless flame', and although many in the Asian community have departed from such superstition, even some less orthodox Muslims believe in the djinns and in the power of the holy Koran to dispel them. The more fanatical among the religion's believers are convinced that stronger measures are necessary to rid the body and soul of the unwelcome demons. Such believers were Mr and Mrs Bashir.

Consequently, the Bashirs called in the local Muslim *pir*, or holy man, in the person of sixty-three-year-old Mohammed Nurani, who introduced his assistant to the proceedings, a 'priest' named Mohammed Bashir (no relation to Kusor). Between the holy men and the family a decision was made to exorcise Kusor of the djinn called John Wayne!

In the trial of Mohammed Bashir, which opened at Manchester Crown Court in April 1992, Mr Richard Henriques QC, Crown prosecutor, told the court that an orgy of violence took place over the succeeding eight days. First Nurani visited the family at

267

Oldham and placed Kusor Bashir inside a circle drawn with chalk and forced her to inhale the fumes of burning mustard oil. Then the exorcism began. Deprived of food and sleep for the following week, Kusor was repeatedly beaten with heavy sticks and was subjected to having hot chilli powder forced down her throat to expel the djinn John Wayne. When the spirit refused to leave quietly, Kusor Bashir was kicked, stamped on and jumped on.

Perhaps that did the trick; perhaps it was the last straw for John Wayne and he fled. We will never know, because after eight days of torture Kusor Bashir died when one of sixteen fractured ribs perforated her lungs. When her body was eventually examined by a pathologist he found, apart from these injuries, a fractured breastbone, extensive bruising to the victim's arms and legs and lacerations across her face, head and breasts.

The Mancunian jury, who had sat horrified by the descriptions of this outrageous ritual, returned an unsurprising verdict of 'guilty of murder' against holy man Mohammed Bashir. His spiritual leader, the pir Mohammed Nurani was convicted of 'plotting to cause grievous bodily harm'. They were given, respectively, life imprisonment and five years.

Perhaps the saddest epitaph is that Kusor Bashir's family, distraught at her suffering, had repeatedly been told 'the girl is not in pain; it is the djinn who feels the pain' – and they believed it.

WITCH CULTS

Witchcraft is a difficult cult subject to discuss in the context of this book, because the activities of the stereotypical witch of the seventeenth century were so vastly different from those of the twentieth-century witch. Clearly the witch trials that took place under purges such as the Inquisition were so corrupt as to make no distinction between those who practised sorcery and those who were merely old and eccentric or the victims of family or neighbourhood feuds. However, it is unwise to dismiss the possibility of 'bewitching to death'. Cases abound – not in old grimoires, but in medical and psychological journals. In some areas of Africa there is still a strong belief in the power of the witch doctor to cause death in the apparently healthy; as there is in parts of South America. Similar ritual killing among the Aborigines of Australia is called 'pointing the bone'. The voodoo priests of Haiti are reputed to be able either to cause death or to induce a state of catalepsy for the purpose of creating zombies.

Therefore, while there is no suggestion that the modern witch coven is a killing machine, there is little doubt that in former times the local 'wise woman' may well have been tempted by requests for certain sorts of potions – for poison has always been more reliable than chanting mumbo-jumbo round a cauldron of bats' wings and frogs' legs.

A short note on witchcraft

Witchcraft and some form of magic are as ancient as humankind.

It is believed that palaeolithic man was engaging in rudimentary magic in some of his cave markings. It is also universal. Witchcraft and sorcery traditionally differ from other forms of spell-casting in that they always involve an evil intent put into practice by supernatural means. One definition, though it is contentious, is that witches are always evil and sorcerers only occasionally. One might think that it depended upon the individual.

In medieval Europe villages frequently had a 'cunning man' or 'wise woman' in the community (the equivalents of shamen or witch doctors). Most of the day-to-day activities of these witches were curative, and they were looked upon as being privy to the secrets of herbal medicine.

Local groups of witches, called covens and generally consisting of thirteen, met at weekly Sabbaths (from the Hebrew for seventh day) for group rituals. However, there were a number of Great Sabbaths, which marked the seasons: winter (Candlemas, 2 February), spring (23 June), summer (Lammas, 1 August) and autumn (21 December). Walpurgis Night (Walpurgisnacht) and All Hallows' Eve (Hallowe'en) were also important events on the witches' calendar.

Although details differed from coven to coven, country to country, the broad form of the Sabbath was this: they would begin with a ritual of homage to the devil followed by the initiation of new recruits. This formality over the revels began, and there was much eating, drinking and dancing. There was also a great deal of sexual activity. At Great Sabbaths it was not uncommon for the devil himself to appear – or, rather, a man who had probably inherited the right to play the part. He wore a mask painted with a demon's face strapped to his backside beneath an animal's tail. This had to be kissed by all the celebrants before the ritual copulation took place. As a precautionary measure, the devil carried a carved horn phallus with him. Sex-magic has always played a big role in witchcraft, and it is difficult to tell whether it was because it was just plain enjoyable or because Christians so frowned on it. The magical force, or energy, generated by this lascivious activity was usually directed to some communal evil purpose, though some have claimed it could be for good. (There is a legend that all the covens in England combined their energies to raise the storm which led to the defeat of the Armada.)

WITCH TRIALS

Although there is evidence of strict laws governing the practice of witchcraft in England from early Anglo-Saxon times, the concept of its evil was based on the purely practical expedient of punishing crimes against man and against his property. However, the spread of the Church of Rome throughout western Europe ensured that witchcraft would eventually be seen as a heresy and an offence against God, and the suppression of heretics – real or imagined – became a crusade. The Spanish Inquisition was established in Castile with royal assent in 1478, with Thomas de Torquemada as Grand Inquisitor. Aimed especially at the Jews and the Moors, its initial mandate was the eradication of all heretical beliefs and practices. By a Bull of Pope Sixtus V in 1585, the Inquisition was enabled to eradicate all forms of sorcery.

In 1486 Jakob Sprenger and Heinrich Kramer composed the terrifying treatise on 'Witchcraft, Its Discovery, Treatment and Cure' called the *Malleus Maleficarum*, a practical handbook on each step in the denunciation, trial and execution of 'heretics'. It is impossible to compute the numbers of the Spanish Inquisition victims, but in 1481 it is said that 3,000 were burned in Andalucia alone, and 17,000 others tortured.

A Day in the Life . . .
(Translation of a report made by the overseer of a torturer responsible for 'questioning' a suspect witch at Prossneck, Germany, in 1629)

1. The hangman bound her hands, cut off her hair and placed the woman on a ladder. He poured alcohol on her head and set it afire in order to burn the hair to the roots.

2. He placed strips of sulphur under her arms and around her back and set fire to them also.

3. He tied her hands behind her back and hoisted her to the ceiling by a pulley; she was left hanging there for about three or four hours while the executioner was away at breakfast.

4. On his return he threw alcohol over the woman's back and set fire to it; he attached heavy weights to her body and drew her up again to the ceiling. After that the hangman put her back on the ladder and placed a very rough plank full of sharp points against her body. Having thus arranged her, he jerked her up again to the ceiling.

5. Afterwards he squeezed her thumbs and big toes in a vice, and trussed up her arms with a stick; in this position he kept her hanging for about a quarter of an hour, until she fainted away several times. Then he squeezed the calves and the legs in the vice, always alternating the torture with questioning.

6. The hangman then whipped the woman with a raw-hide whip which caused the blood to flow out over her shift. Once again he placed her thumbs and big toes in the vice and left her thus in agony on the torture stool from ten in the morning till one o'clock after noon while the court officials and the executioner took sustenance.

7. In the afternoon a functionary arrived who disapproved of this harsh procedure. But they whipped the suspect again in a frightful manner to conclude the first day of torture.

The next day they started all over again, but without quite such savagery as the previous day.

The witch hunts in Britain

At first the insular nature of Britain protected it in large measure from the worst excesses of the Inquisition; although 'sorcery' was still legislated against, penalties were mild – one has only to recall the penalty meted out to one William Byg who, for using a crystal ball, was sentenced merely to appear in public with a notice on his head inscribed *Ecce sortilegus* ('Behold the fortune-teller'), and compare it with the many thousands of 'sorcerers' across the channel in France who had already been put to the fire.

Witchcraft first became a heinous crime in England under a 1563 statute of Queen Elizabeth I, arising in part from political insecurity and in part from pressure from the clergy. This Act of Elizabeth made the invocation of spirits 'whereby any persons shall be killed or destroyed, or wasted, consumed or lamed in his or her body or matter' an offence punishable by death. The steady growth of superstition during the queen's reign is amply exhibited by the spectacular nature of some of the contemporary trials – at Chelmsford in 1566, the first major witch hunt in England; at St Osyth in 1582; and the extraordinary trial of the Warboys Witches at which, in 1593, three completely innocent people were executed as the result of the caprice of five children.

In 1604 James I increased the severity of the punishments for all kinds of witchcraft, and the eastern counties trembled before the name of Matthew Hopkins, self-styled Witchfinder-General of England, responsible for the executions of more than a hundred so-called witches and the imprisonment and torture of countless others. Hopkins masterminded the lurid trials of the Manningtree witches in 1645 and the Bury St Edmunds witches in the same year (see below).

Earlier, a number of notable local witch hunts had resulted in the executions of the witches of Northamptonshire on 22 July

1612, and the deaths of many of the Lancashire witches tried in August of the same year.

Of the many pamphlets, broadsides and chapbooks recounting the trials and executions of the witches in England, the most remarkable – for its style, its accuracy and detail and its retention of atmosphere – is *The Wonderful Discovery of Witches in the County of Lancaster*, written by Thomas Potts, clerk to the Lancaster court, and published in London in 1613. The book is uncommonly long and recounts many instances of 'bewitching to death' or murder by witchcraft. In all, ten of the witches were hanged, and the one called Old Demdike died in gaol before trial.

The last witch to hang in England was Alice Molland at Exeter in 1684, though with the restoration of the Stuart line in 1660 there were few executions, and most indictments for witchcraft were charged only with the more serious crimes of murder and destruction. The last recorded witch trial was in 1712 when Jane Wenham was convicted at the Hertford Assizes but not executed.

Dates for the rest of Europe are: Netherlands 1610, Scotland 1727, France 1745, Germany 1775. In America 1692.

OBSERVATIONS FOR THE DISCOVERY OF WITCHES

The following 'rules' derive from *The Laws Against Witches and Conjuration*, published in London in 1645.

1.   These witches have ordinarily a familiar, or spirit, which appeareth to them; sometimes in one shape, sometimes in another, and in the shape of a man, woman, boy, dog, cat, foal, fowl, hare, rat, toad, etc. And to these their spirits they give names, and they meet together to Christen them.

2.   Their said familiars hath some big or little teat upon their body, where he sucketh them; and besides their sucking, the Devil leaveth other marks upon their body, sometimes like a blue-spot, or red-spot, like a flea

277

biting, sometimes the flesh sucked in and hollow, all which for a time may be covered, yea taken away, but will come again to their old form. And these Devil's marks be insensible, and being pricked will not bleed; and be often in their private parts, and therefore require diligent and careful search.

3. They have often pictures of clay or wax (like a man, etc. made of such as they would bewitch) found in their house, or which they roast or bury in the earth, as the picture consumes, so may the parties bewitched consume.

4. There are other presumptions against these witches; as is they be given to usual cursing, and bitter imprecations, or some other mischief presently followeth.

5. Their implicit confession, as when any shall accuse them for hurting them or their cattle, they shall answer, 'You should have let me alone then', or, 'I have not hurt you as yet': These and the like speeches are in a manner of a confession of their power of hurting.

6. Their diligent inquiry after the sick party; or coming to visit him or her unsent for; but especially being forbidden the house.

7. Their apparition to the sick party in his fits.

8. The sick party in his fits naming the parties suspected, and where they be or have been, or what they do, truly.

9. The common report of their neighbours, especially if the party suspected be of kin, or servant to, or familiar with a convicted witch.

10. The testimony of other witches, confessing their own witchcrafts, and witnessing against the suspected, and that they have spirits, or marks; that they have been at their meetings; that they have told them what harm they have done, etc.

11. If the dead body bleed upon the witch's touching it.

12. The testimony of the person hurt, upon his death.

13. The examination and confession of the children (able and fit to answer) or servants of the witch; especially concerning the first six observations of the party suspected. Her threatenings and cursings of the sick party; her inquiring after the sick party; her boasting or rejoicing at the sick party's trouble. Also whether they have seen her call upon, speak to, or feed any spirit or such like; or have heard her foretell of mishap, or speak of her power to hurt, or of her transportation to this or that place, etc.

14. Their own voluntary confession (which exceeds all other evidences) of the hurt they have done, or of the giving of their souls to the Devil, or of the spirits which they have, how many, how they call them, and how they came by them.

15. Besides, upon the apprehension of any suspected, to search also their houses diligently for pictures of clay or wax, etc. hair cut, bones, powders, books of witchcrafts, charms; and for pots or places where their spirits might be kept, the smell of which place will stink detestably.

The torture of Johannes Junius, burgomaster of Bamberg

The case of burgomaster Johannes Junius is remarkable for two things. First, the fact that in areas of the most intense persecution, even civic dignitaries fell victim to the witch hunt. Second is the letter that Junius wrote to his daughter Veronica, and had smuggled out of his death-cell by a gaoler. The letter survives to this day, and stands as one of the most moving documents in the history of the witch persecutions.

Johannes Junius had served as a burgomaster to the principality of Bamberg, in northern Bavaria, from 1608 until he was arrested in 1628, in his fifty-fifth year. His wife had been executed as a witch the previous year. Among the 600 individuals who were burned alive during the same purge were another four burgomasters and the Chancellor of the principality.

At his trial on 28 June 1628, burgomaster Junius protested his innocence despite the accusations of several fellow-citizens. Following extensive torture during the first week of July, Johannes Junius finally concocted a confession. Following his conviction, he was burned at the stake on 25 July 1628.

LETTER FROM JOHANNES JUNIUS TO HIS DAUGHTER

Many hundred thousand good-nights, dearly beloved daughter Veronica. Innocent I have come into prison, innocent I have been tortured, innocent I must die. For whoever comes into the witch prison must become a witch or be tortured until he invents something out of his head and – God pity him – bethinks him of something. I will tell you how it has gone with me. When I was the first time put to the torture, Dr Braun, Dr Kotzendorffer, and two strange doctors were there. Then Dr Braun asks me, 'Kinsman, how come you here?' I answer, 'Through falsehood, through misfortune.' 'Hear, you,' he says, 'you are a witch; will you confess it voluntarily? If not we'll bring in witnesses and the executioner for you.' I said, 'I am no witch, I have a pure conscience in the matter; if there are a thousand witnesses I am not anxious, but I'll gladly hear the witnesses.'

Now the Chancellor's son was set before me who said he had seen me. I asked that he be sworn and legally examined, but Dr Braun refused it. Then the Chancellor, Dr George Haan was brought, who said the same as his son. Afterwards Hoppfen Ellse. She had seen me dance on Hauptsmorwald, but they refused to swear her in. I said: 'I have never renounced God, and I will never do it – God graciously keep me from it. I'll rather bear whatever I must.'

And then came also – God in Highest Heaven have mercy – the executioner, and put the thumb-screws on me, both hands bound together, so that the blood spurted from the nails and everywhere, so that for four weeks I could not use my hands, as you can see from my writing. Thereafter they first stripped me, bound my hands behind me, and drew me up on the ladder. Then I thought heaven and earth were at an end; eight times did they draw me up and let me fall again, so that I suffered terrible agony. I said to Dr Braun: 'God forgive you for thus misusing an innocent and honourable man.' He replied: 'You are a knave.'

And this happened on Friday, June 30, and with God's help I had to bear the torture. When at last the executioner led me back into the prison, he said to me: 'Sir, I beg you, for God's sake confess something, whether it be true or not. Invent something, for you cannot endure the torture which you will be put to; and even if you bear it all, yet you will not escape, not even if you were an earl, but one torture will follow after another until you say you are a witch. Not before that,' he said, 'will they let you go, as you may see by all their trials, for one is just like another.' Then came George Haan, who said the commissioners had said the Prince-Bishop [Johann George II] wished to make such an example of me that everybody would be astonished.

And so I begged, since I was in wretched plight, to be

given one day for thought and a priest. The priest was refused me, but the time for thought was given. Now, my dear child, see in what hazard I stood and still stand. I must say I am a witch, though I am not, must now renounce God, though I have never done it before. Day and night I was deeply troubled, but at last there came to me a new idea. I would not be anxious, but, since I had been given no priest with whom I could take counsel, I would myself think of something and say it. It were surely better that I just say it with mouth and words, even though I had not really done it; and afterwards I would confess it to the priest, and let those answer for it who compel me to do it . . . And so I made my confession, as follows; but it was all a lie.

Now follows, dear child, what I confessed in order to escape the great anguish and bitter torture, which it was impossible for me longer to bear:

[The gist of this confession is much as it was presented to the court, see below]

Then I had to say what people I had seen [at the witch Sabbath]. I said that I had not recognised them. 'You old rascal, I must set the executioner at your throat. Say, was not the Chancellor there?' So I said yes. 'Who besides?' I had not recognised anybody. So he said: 'Take one street after another; begin at the market, go out on one street and back on the next.' I had to name several persons here. Then came the long street. I knew nobody. Had to name eight persons there. Then to the Zinkenwert – one person more. Then over the upper bridge to the Georgthor, on both sides. Knew nobody again. Did I know anybody in the castle – whoever it might be, I should speak without fear. And thus continuously they asked me on all the streets, though I could not and would not say more. So they gave me to the executioner, told him to strip me, shave me all over, and put me to the torture. 'The knave knows one in the market place, is with him daily, and yet won't name him.' By that they meant Dietmeyer: so I had to name him too.

Then I had to tell what crimes I had committed. I said nothing. . . . 'Draw the rascal up!' So I said that I was to kill my children, but I had killed a horse instead. It did not help. I had also taken a sacred wafer and had desecrated it. When I had said this, they left me in peace.

Now dear child, here you have all my confession, for which I must die. And it is all sheer lies and made-up things, so help me God. For all this I was forced to say through fear of the torture which was threatened beyond what I had already endured. For they never cease with the torture till one confesses something; be he never so good, he must be a witch. Nobody escapes, though he were an earl. If God send no means of bringing the truth to light, our whole kindred will be burned. God in heaven knows that I know not the slightest thing. I die innocent and as a martyr.

Dear child, keep this letter secret so that people do not find it, else I shall be tortured most piteously and the jailers will be beheaded. So strictly is it forbidden. . . . Dear child, pay this man a thaler . . . I have taken several days to write this: my hands are both lame. I am in a sad plight. . . . Good night, for your father Johannes Junius will never see you more.
July 24 1628.

[In the margin was added]
Dear child, six have confessed against me at once: the Chancellor, his son, Neudecker, Zaner, Hoffmeister Ursel, and Hoppfen Ellse – all false, through compulsion, as they have all told me, and begged my forgiveness in God's name before they were executed. . . . They know nothing but good of me. They were forced to say it, just as I myself was.

CONFESSION OF BURGOMASTER JOHANNES JUNIUS

After losing a considerable sum of money as the result of a

lawsuit, the burgomaster was brooding in his orchard when a young woman approached him. Having seduced the good fellow to do her will, the maiden in an instant transformed into a goat. 'Now you see with whom you have lain. You must now be mine.' Then the spirit transformed again and gripped the terrified Junius by the throat, demanding that he should renounce God. Instead, the pious burgomaster cried aloud 'God help me'. Which invocation dispatched the demonic vision. But the devil returned, this time accompanied by a horde of demons. So frightening were they that Johannes Junius was obliged to recite: 'I renounce God in Heaven and all the heavenly host, and will henceforth recognise the Devil as my God.' After which he was baptised by the Devil.

As a reward, the new convert was provided with a succubus called Vixen, who promised to provide him with money and to escort him to the sabbats. His mode of transport to such occasions was a black dog which could fly.

Immediately following his seduction by the succubus, she had insisted he kill his youngest son, Hans. And gave him a powder for the purpose. However, this was asking too much, and Junius poisoned his horse instead. Then the succubus urged him to kill his two daughters. He flatly refused and was savagely attacked by a gang of demons for his disobedience.

Once, he was ordered to present his succubus, with whom he had been enjoying sexual union, with a holy wafer, which she desecrated. This, with minor embellishments was the confession of Johannes Junius which was read to the court, and ratified by him.

The trial of the Bury St Edmunds witches for murder

At the Bury St Edmunds spring assizes of 1662, Rose Cullender and Amy Duny, two elderly widows of Lowestoft, stood indicted before Mr Justice Matthew Hale with bewitching seven children aged between several months and eighteen years, one of them to death. In addition they were charged with a variety of other acts of sorcery.

It all started when Mrs Dorothy Durent asked her neighbour, Amy Duny, to babysit her child William. Although warned against it by the mother, Amy Duny, in order to quieten the restless infant, gave it her nipple to suck on. When she admitted as much, Mrs Durent became quite abusive, and in her own turn Mother Duny offered the mother a mild curse as she stamped out of the house. That evening baby William fell sick, and when he failed to recover after some days, Mrs Durent called in a Dr Jacob of Yarmouth, celebrated in the county for 'helping children that were bewitched'. The good doctor advised Dorothy Durent to suspend the blanket in which little William slept in the chimney-corner by day, and to wrap the mite in it by night. However, if she were to find 'anything' in the blanket, Mrs Durent was immediately to throw it in the fire. Sure enough that night, as she prepared to lay young William down, what should hop out of the blanket but a large toad. Fortunately, Mrs Durent's fright was eased by the presence of a neighbour's son whom she asked to catch the toad and burn it, which the lad did.

Next day Mrs Durent learned that Amy Duny was in 'a most lamentable condition', being burned on the face, arms, legs and thighs. The implication was obvious, if rather silly. Intrigued, and perhaps gloating more than was seemly, Dorothy Durent went to see for herself. She asked Mrs Duny how she came to be in such a state, and the latter was unwise enough to give air to yet another curse: 'You will live to see some of your children dead, and yourself upon crutches.'

Two years later, Mrs Durent's ten-year-old daughter Elizabeth was taken sick in much the same way as her brother William. Returning from the apothecary where she had been to purchase medicine, Mrs Durent found Amy Duny in her house. When asked to explain herself, Mother Duny replied that she had just given Elizabeth some water. When Mrs Durent became angry, Duny

285

spat back: 'You need not be so angry, your child will not last long.' Despite careful ministrations the girl died three days later.

Other children, more fortunate in that they survived their alleged 'bewitching', were paraded before the court at Bury 'and were in reasonable good condition. But the morning they came to the Hall to give instructions for the drawing of their Bills of Indictment, the three persons (Ann Durent, Susan Chandler and Elizabeth Pacy) fell into strange and violent fits, screeking out in a most sad manner so that they could in no wise give any instructions in the court who were the cause of their distemper. Although they did after some certain space recover out of their fits, yet they were every one of them struck dumb so that none of them could speak neither at the time, nor during the Assizes until the conviction of the supposed witches.'

Mother Durent claimed that not long after the death of her daughter, she had fallen lame in both legs and could not walk without crutches. What more proof were needed, she asked the judge, than that Amy Duny was a witch?

And so Mr Justice Hale, in his wisdom, ordered Amy Duny to approach the Pacy child and touch her, 'Whereupon the child without so much as seeing her, for her eyes were closed the while, suddenly leaped up and catched Amy Duny by the hand, and afterwards by the face; and with her nails scratched her till the blood came . . .'

Mother Duny's fate, it seems, was sealed.

Elizabeth Pacy's father, Samuel, a local merchant, gave evidence that his two daughters (Deborah was too ill to attend court) had become badly afflicted the previous year after Mother Duny had come to buy herrings from him and had been turned away. Between their fits the children would cry out: 'There stands Amy Duny and Rose Cullender', and claim that the apparitions of the two women took form before them 'to their great terrour and affrightment'. The spirits, they claimed, threatened that if the girls said anything to anyone their torment would increase tenfold. The court next heard evidence on the charge relating to the bewitching of Ann Durent. When her father had refused, like

Mr Pacy, to sell Mother Cullender some herrings (remember Lowestoft was at that time the centre of the east coast herring fishing fleet), the old woman had gone off muttering angrily. Days later Ann 'was very sorely afflicted in her stomach, and felt great pain like the pricking of pins, and then fell into swooning fits, and after the recovery from her fits, she declared that she had seen the apparition of the said Rose, who threatened to torment her'.

The mother of Susan Chandler gave evidence that Samuel Pacy had been granted a warrant for a group of women to physically examine Rose Cullender for evidence that she was a witch. Mrs Chandler was one of the women who went to Mother Cullender's 'and asked whether she was contented that they should search her? She did not oppose it, whereupon they began at her head, and so stripped her naked, and in the lower part of her belly they found a thing like a teat of an inch long. They questioned her about it, and she said that she had got a strain by carrying water which caused her that excrescence. But upon narrower search, they found in her privy parts three more excrescences or teats, but smaller than the former. This deponent further says that in the long teat at the end thereof was a little hole, and it appeared to them as if it had been lately sucked, and upon the straining of it, there issued out white milky matter.'

On the day following the examination Susan Chandler fell sick and complained of seeing apparitions of Rose Cullender. Her condition developed into fits so violent that her mother needed help to restrain her.

Further evidence brought against Rose Cullender did not include bewitching to death, but nevertheless emphasised the gross ignorance and superstition of the time as regards witches and enchantment. For example, in his testimony against Mother Cullender 'one John Soam of Lowestoft, yeoman, saith that not long since, in harvest time, he had three carts . . . And as they were going into the field to load, one of them wrenched the window of Rose Cullender's house, whereupon she came out in a great rage . . . And so they passed on into the fields and loaded all three carts. The other two carts returned safe home and back again twice loaded that day. But as to this cart that touched Rose Cullender's house, it was overturned twice or thrice that day.'

Later, Robert Sherringham gave evidence against Mother Cullender that 'about two years since he was much vexed with a great number of lice of an extraordinary bigness. And although he many times shifted himself [changed his clothes], would swarm again with them; so that in the end he was forced to burn all his clothes – being two suits of apparel – and then was clean from them . . .'

Thus did a rickety cart and an evidently unhygienic man help lead to the deaths of two old ladies whose only fault was a short temper.

Sir Matthew Hale did not sum up the evidence, but simply asked the jury 'whether or no these children were bewitched? Secondly, whether the prisoners at the bar were guilty of it?' He did, however, take the opportunity to air his own views: 'That there are such creatures as witches, I make no doubt at all. For first, the scriptures have affirmed so much. Secondly, the wisdom of all nations has provided laws against such persons, which is an argument of their confidence in such a crime. And such hath been the judgement of this kingdom, as appears by that Act of Parliament which hath provided punishments proportionable to the quality of the offence. I desire you strictly to observe the evidence and that the great God of Heaven will direct your hearts in this weighty thing you have in hand. For to condemn the innocent and to let the guilty go free are both an abomination to the Lord.'

On Thursday afternoon, 13 March 1664, after a retirement of just thirty minutes, the jury returned a verdict of guilty on all thirteen counts, and three days later Amy Duny and Rose Cullender were hanged.

Appendix: Matthew Hopkins, Witchfinder-General

A failed lawyer from Essex, Matthew Hopkins was to become one of the most feared men in the eastern counties of England. He was responsible for the trial of the Chelmsford Witches and the Bury St Edmunds trials; indeed, at his death in 1646 it was estimated that he had been responsible for the execution of several hundred people in one year alone.

The following is just one instance of the corrupt ways in which Hopkins made sure of earning his 'one pound a head'. It was also one, the sheer wickedness of which, began his downfall.

It should be mentioned here that Matthew Hopkins did not work alone. At first he employed an assistant, a sort of Witchfinder-Lieutenant, named John Stearne. Then, to search women's bodies for marks of the devil, he employed two female assistants (Privates, perhaps). Finally he recruited two men who would help out with heavy duty jobs such as 'walking' – of which more later.

Hopkins and his ruffianly band had reached Brandiston, in Suffolk. Now it happened that the town's vicar, John Lowes, a pious if irascible octogenarian, had fallen out of favour with his parishioners. They suggested he might make way for a younger and more efficient shepherd of their souls. Lowes, rightly or wrongly for he had held the living for upwards of fifty years, refused.

Enter the Witchfinder-General. Hopkins was accustomed to finding many of his 'clients' as the result of feuds among families or neighbours. One of the sides would approach him and denounce their adversary as a witch. Hopkins made his £1, the complainant was rid of an irritating sister or a disagreeable neighbour. So it was that a group of Brandiston's parishioners casually mentioned to the General that parson Lowes engaged in witchcraft. Lowes, understandably, vehemently denied the charge, and Hopkins was obliged to resort to other tactics to earn his blood money.

The tactic he chose was 'walking'. The Witchfinder had his cronies stalk old Lowe and as soon as he looked as though he might go to bed demanded entry to the house (a privilege of the witchfinders when on business). According to a contemporary written account:

[They] ran him backwards and forwards about the room until he was out of breath. Then they rested him a little and then ran him again. And thus they did for several days and nights together, till he was weary of life and scarce sensible of what he said or did.

Exhausted beyond endurance and unable to put thoughts together, John Lowes agreed that five years previously he had made a pact with the devil, who presented him in return with four familiars which he sent out to cause mischief and misery in and around Brandiston. Despite the fact that the vicar, when he had recovered from his ordeal, retracted this absurd confession, he was sentenced to death and hanged. Another twenty shillings in the purse of the Witchfinder-General.

The confession of Mother Lakeland of Ipswich

The following text was taken verbatim from the pamphlet 'The Laws against Witches and Conjuration and Some brief Notes and Observations for the Discovery of Witches – Being very useful for these Times wherein the Devil reigns and prevails over the souls of poor Creatures, in drawing them to that crying Sin of Witchcraft'.

The said Mother Lakeland hath been a professor of religion, a constant hearer of the Word for these many years, and yet a witch (as she confessed) for the space of near twenty years. The devil came to her first between sleeping and waking, and spake to her in a hollow voice, telling her that if she would serve him she would want nothing. After frequent solicitation she consented to him; then he stroke his claw (as she confessed) into her hand, and with her blood wrote the covenants. (Now the subtlety of Satan is to be observed, in that he did not press her to deny God and Christ, as he useth to do to others; because she was a professor, and might have lost all his hold by pressing her too far.) Then he furnished her with three imps, two little dogs and a mole (as she confessed) which she employed in her services: her husband she bewitched (so she confessed) whereby he lay in great misery for a time, and at last died. Then she sent one of her dogs to one Mr Lawrence in Ipswich, to torment him and take away his life: she sent one of them also to his child to torment it and take away the life out of it, which was done upon them both: and all this (as she confessed) was because he asked her for twelve shillings that she owed him, and for no other cause.

She further confessed that she sent her mole to a maid of one Mrs Jennings in Ipswich, to torment her and take away her life, which was done accordingly: and this for no other cause but for that the said maid would not lend her a needle that she desired to borrow of her, and was earnest with her for a shilling that she owed the said maid.

Then she further confessed she sent one of her imps to one Mr Beale in Ipswich, who had formerly been a suitor to her grandchild; and because he would not have her, she sent and burned a new ship (that had never been at sea) that he was to go master of; and sent also to torment him and take away his life; but he is yet living, but in very great misery, and as it is verily conceived by the doctors and surgeons that have him in hand, that he consumes and rots, and that half of his body is rotten upon him as he is living.

Several other things she did, for all of which she was by law condemned to die, and in particular to be burned to death, because she was the death of her husband, as she confessed; which death she suffered accordingly.

But since her death there is one thing very remarkable, and to be taken notice of: that upon the very day she was burned, a bunch of flesh, something after the form of a dog, that grew upon the thigh of the said Mr Beale ever since the time that she first sent her imp to him, being very hard but

291

could never be made to break by all the means that could be used, brake of itself, without any means of using. And another sore, that at the same time she first sent her imp to him, rose on the side of his belly in the form of a fistule which ran and could not be healed by all the means that could be used, presently also began to heal, and there is great hope that he will suddenly recover again, for his sores heal apace and he doth recover his strength. He was in this misery for the space of a year and a half, and was forced to go with his head and knees together, his misery was so great.

(Published in London, 1645)

'La Voisin' at the court of the Sun King

There lived in Paris, towards the end of the seventeenth century, a certain widow named Catherine Deshayes, who had forsaken the menial occupation of the midwife for the more profitable one of fortune-telling. We know little of Deshayes' early life, but for the fact that she claimed to have recognised her 'powers' in childhood. Those powers would soon extend their malignant influence to embrace the French Court, and even to threaten the 'Sun King' Louis XIV.

It so happened that Madame's specialty was the prophecy of death. More specifically, the death of husbands. This being so, it was not unnatural that she should attract to her by no means modest cottage at Villeneuve-sur-Gravois a number of discontented wives, anxious to learn the worst. And it is a remarkable thing that by looking into a crystal ball, or consulting the cards, without any intimate knowledge of her subject, her predictions were unerring. She would simply concoct some innocent-looking philtre intended to, for example, make the husband blind to the lady's amorous indiscretions, instruct her client to administer it, and remark: 'The cards foretell your husband's death within the week.' Pure magic. As one great literary mind described it: 'Madame Voisin's [the name she adopted] clients were generally in a hurry and so were willing to take any little trouble or responsibility necessary to ensure success. They had two qualities which endear customers to those of La Voisin's trade; they were grateful and they were silent.'

To cut a long story short, word of Madame's high rate of success soon spread outwards and, more importantly, upwards. So that soon the very rich and the very powerful were also beating a path to her door – the Duchesse de Bouillon, for example, and Olympe de Mancini, the Comtesse de Soisons, and her most illustrious client of all, Françoise-Athenais de Rochechouart de Mortemart, Marquise de Montespan, mistress of King Louis XIV. A woman who, with no difficulty, overshadowed both the queen, Marie-Thérèse, and Louis' other mistress, Mademoiselle de la Vallière. Sadly the Marquise, apart from being exceedingly beautiful, was also exceedingly paranoid, and not content to overshadow she desperately wanted to *eliminate* all possible rivals. So very soon the Marquise was on the old fortune-teller's doorstep. It is true to say that the royal mistress fell totally for La Voisin's hocus-pocus, and was a regular customer for the philtres and potions with which Madame had so long ensured the accuracy of her predictions. Some say that one of these deadly cocktails was meant for the king himself, but was eventually used to dispose of La Vallière. But the more deeply she became involved in her own mischief, the more excessive did de Montespan's demands become. It is a matter of record that she paid vast sums of money to have special rituals enacted which would ensure her supreme control over the king; black masses performed by the defrocked hunchback Abbé Guilbourg.

But in this the Marquise was not alone, for many of society's brightest stars were thought to be involved in similar necromantic practices – at some of which, it was rumoured, children were sacrificed. Guilbourg himself later described one such ceremony, and it was later confirmed by La Voisin's daughter Marguerite:

He had bought a child to sacrifice at the mass, said on behalf of a great lady. He had cut the child's throat with a knife, and drawing its blood, had poured it into the chalice; after which he had the body taken away into another place, so that later he could use the heart and entrails for another mass. He said this second mass in a hovel on the ramparts of Saint-Denis, over the same woman, and with the same ceremonies. The body of the child would, he said, be used to make magic powders.

Such was the scandal that swept through the French Court over its members' involvement in black magic, witchcraft and poisoning that for a while even Louis' own reputation seemed at risk. Many arrests were made in high places in an attempt to stifle the almost rampant spread of sorcery and murder, and many cases came before the so-called *Chambre Ardente* (similar to England's 'Star Chamber'). After that, Police Commissioner Reynie – in charge of the cleaning-up process – turned his attention to the little band of dedicated sorcerers and poisoners who were servicing the lucrative trade. During the purge there were 319 arrests, of which 104 were later convicted and sentenced – thirty-six to death, four to slavery in the galleys, thirty-four to banishment and thirty were later acquitted.

Among those sentenced to death was La Voisin. In February 1680 she was dragged to a public square in the centre of Paris and burned alive at the stake.

SELECT BIBLIOGRAPHY
AND WEBOGRAPHY

A note on websites

An increasing number of people now have access to the Internet, and it is proving to be one of the most important research tools of modern times. For that reason it was decided to append to the more familiar bibliography a list of websites which proved invaluable in the compilation of this book. Most of the references given are to key 'home pages', or indexes, which will lead readers electronically to different aspects of the same subject or other related subjects.

It is not necessary to understand what the letters and symbols mean, but it is essential that they are keyed in correctly, otherwise the location of the page will not be recognised.

Killer cults in history
Judaeo-Christian cults

Baron, Salo Whittmayer, *A Social and Religious History of the Jews*, London and New York, 1952–80

Cohn, Norman, *The Pursuit of the Millennium*, Temple Smith, London, 1957

Middle Eastern cults

Falconet, Camille, 'A Dissertation on the Assassins', in J. de Joinville, *Memoirs*, Paris, 1807

Franzius, Enno, *History of the Order of Assassins*, Funk and Wagnalls, New York, 1969

Hammer-Purgstall, Baron Josef von, *History of the Assassins*, London, 1835

Willey, Peter, *Castles of the Assassins*, Harrap, London, 1963
Indian cults
Bruce, George, *The Stranglers*, Longmans, London, 1968
Hervey, Charles Robert West, *Some Records of Crime*, Sampson Low, London, 1892
Sleeman, Captain W. H., *The Thugs, or Phansigars, of India*, Carey and Hart, Philadelphia, 1939
Russian cults
Conybeare, Frederick C., *Russian Dissenters* (Harvard Theological Studies), Harvard University Press, London, 1921
Sitwell, Sacheverell, *Roumanian Journey*, Batsford, London, 1938

Twentieth-century Christian cults
Yahwehs
http://www.yahwehbenyahweh.com/index.html

Armageddon cults
Branch Davidians
Leppard, David, *Fire and Blood*, Fourth Estate, London, 1993
ftp://think.com/pub/waco
http://lycos-tmp1.psc.edu/cgi-bin/pursuit?query=Waco&first=191&maxhits=10&minterms=1&minscore=0.01&terse=standard
The People's Temple
Melton, J. Gordon, *The People's Temple and Jim Jones*, Garland, New York, 1990
http://www.scimitar.com/revolution/by_topic/express/religion/jonestown
Aum Shinri Kyo (Supreme Truth Sect)
Kaplan, David E., and Marshall, Andrew, *The Cult at the End of the World*, Hutchinson, London, 1996
http://www.smn.co.jp/PICS/sarin_map-e.jpg
http://www.tezcat.com/octopus/Aum/
Church of Jesus Christ of Latter-Day Saints (Mormons)
Lindsey, Robert, *A Gathering of Saints*, Corgi, London, 1990
Naifeh, Steven, and Smith, Gregory White, *The Mormon Murders*, Sphere, London, 1989

Sasse, Cynthia Stalter, and Widder, Peggy Murphy, *The Kirtland Massacre*, Zebra True Crime, New York, 1992
http://www.tcd.net/~garn/polygamy.html
http://www.sas.upenn.edu/~dbowie/dispute/dispute.html
Order of the Solar Temple
Huguenin, Thierry (with Lionel Duroy), *Le 54e*, Fixot, Paris, 1995
http://www.anatomy.su.oz.au/danny/usenet/aus.religion/archive/march-1995/0100.html

Eastern and Asian cults
Hare Krishna (International Society for Krishna Consciousness)
Hubner, John, and Gruson, Lindsey, *Monkey on a Stick*, Onyx (Penguin Books), Harmondsworth, 1990
Bhagwan Shree Rajneesh
Carter, Lewis F., *Charisma and Control in Rajneeshpuram*, Cambridge University Press, Cambridge, 1990
The Rajneesh Times (newspaper, British edition), Rajneesh Foundation International, London, 1984
http://earth.path.net/osho

Satanism
Churton, Tobias, *The Gnostics*, Weidenfeld and Nicolson, London, 1987
LaVey, Anton Szandor, *Satanic Bible*, Avon, New York, 1969
Parker, John, *At the Heart of Darkness*, Sidgwick and Jackson, London, 1993
Terry, Maury, *The Ultimate Evil*, Bantam Books, New York, 1989
http://www.earthlight.co.nz/users/spock/satan.html
http://ourworld.compuserve.com/homepages/blacksun/homepage.htm
http://www.contrib/andrew.cmu.edu/~shawn/occult//
http://webpages.marshall.edu/~allen12/links.html

Political and social cults
Ku Klux Klan
Tarrants, Thomas A. III, *The Conversion of a Klansman*, Doubleday, New York, 1979

http//www.danger.com/kkk.html
Death Angels
Howard, Clark, *The Zebra Killings*, New English Library, London, 1980

Voodoo cults
http://www.nando.net/prof/caribe/Gods.html
Voodoo
Deren, Maya, *The Voodoo Gods*, Paladin, St Albans, 1975
Metraux, Alfred, *Voodoo in Haiti*, André Deutsch, London, 1959
Oke, Isiah, *Blood Secrets*, Berkley, New York, 1991
http://www.vmedia.com/shannon/voodoo/voodoo.html
Santeria (Path of the Saints)
Brandon, George, *Santeria from Africa to the New World*, Indiana University Press, Bloomington, 1993
Efundé, Agún, *Los Secretos de la Santería*, Ediciones Cuba-mérica, Miami, 1983
http://www.seanet.com/~efunmoyiwa/ochanet.html
http://www.nando.net/prof/caribe/santeria.html

Cult exorcism
Baker, Roger, *Binding the Devil: Exorcism Past and Present*, Arrow, London, 1975
Storm, Rachel, *Exorcists: the Terrifying Truth*, Fount, London, 1993
Watkins, Leslie, *The Real Exorcists*, Futura, London, 1984
http://www.linknet.it/Spirit/new-exorcism.html

Witch cults
Crow, W. B., *A History of Magic, Witchcraft and Occultism*, Abacus, London, 1972
Robbins, Rossell Hope, *Encyclopedia of Witchcraft and Demonology*, Spring Books, New York, 1968
Seth, Ronald, *Stories of Great Witch Trials*, Arthur Barker, London, 1967
Valiente, Doreen, *An ABC of Witchcraft*, Robert Hale, London, 1973
Wallace, C. H., *Witchcraft in the World Today*, Tandem, London, 1967

http://www.ucmb.ulb.ac.be/~joan/witches/index.html

General reference books
Allen, John, *A Book of Beliefs*, Lion Publishing, Tring, 1983
Boyle, James J., *Killer Cults*, St Martin's True Crime Library, New York, 1995
Freedland, Nat, *The Occult Explosion*, Michael Joseph, London, 1972
Galanter, Marc, *Cults*, Oxford University Press, Oxford, 1989
Godwin, John, *Occult America*, Doubleday, Garden City, 1972
Goldberg, B. Z., *The Sacred Tree*, Jarrolds, London, 1931
Gratus, Jack, *The False Messiahs*, Gollancz, London, 1975
Lane, Brian, *Chronicle of Twentieth Century Murder*, Virgin, London, 1993
Lane, Brian, and Gregg, Wilfred, *The New Encyclopedia of Serial Killers*, Headline, London, 1996
Larsen, Egon, *Strange Sects and Cults*, Arthur Baker, London, 1971
McConnell, Brian, *Holy Killers*, Headline, London, 1994
Melton, J. Gordon, *Encyclopedic Handbook of Cults in America*, Garland Publishing, New York, 1992
Melton, J. Gordon (ed.), *Encyclopedia of American Religions*, Garland Publishing, New York, 1993
Newton, Michael, *Raising Hell*, Avon Books, New York, 1993
Streiker, Lowell D., *The Cults Are Coming*, Abingdon, Nashville, 1983
Wilson, Colin, *The Occult*, Mayflower, St Albans, 1976
Wilson, Colin and Damon, *World Famous Cults and Fanatics*, Magpie, London, 1992

General reference websites
http://www.contrib.andrew.cmu.edu/shawn/occult/
http://lycos-tmp1.psc.edu/cgi-bin/pursuit?query=religious+cults
http://faraday.clas.virginia.edy/~jmb5b/syzygy.html
http://virtumall.com/mindcontrol/main.html

INDEX

300

Baldock, Edward 191
Bamberg, Bavaria (witch) 280–84
Bar Asher ha-Levi, Rabbi Isaac 7
Bar Jacob, Hillel 9
Barnett, Governor Ross 217
Barton, Blanche 151
Bashir, Kusor 267–8
Bashir, Mohammed 267–8
Basic Teachings and Beliefs (Church
    of Satan) 152
Beach, Henry L. 226
Beale, Mr 291–2
Beechook, Mirella 240–42
Beechook, Ravi 241–2
Beechook, Sabrina 241–2
Beechook, Tina 240–42
Bell, Mabel 154
Bellow, Shamira 249
Berkowitz, David ('Son of Sam')
    63–7, 171, 173–4, 179–80, 182
Bhagavad Gita (holy book) 132
Bible, Book of Revelation
    Chap 5, quoted 62
    Chap 16, quoted 57–9
    Chap 20 59
Biggs, David 106
Bin Sabbah, Hasan 16–18
Bing, Norman 181–2
Birth of a Nation, The (film) 200
Black Muslims 42
Black Thai (Vietnam) 142–3
Blois, France 9
Blood Atonement (Mormons) 98–9,
    108
blood sacrifice 150, 158–60, 239,
    244, 246, 252–4
Bogomilism 28, 149
Boilard, Solange 116–17
Bolton, K. 148
Book of Mormon (Smith) 97, 104
Book, The (Africa) 229
Booth, John Wilkes 199
Boppard, Germany 7
Bouillon, Duchesse de 293
Bowen, Daniel Paul 156–8
Box Canyon, California 40–41
Branch Davidians 61–82
Brand, Richard 108
Brandiston, Suffolk 289–90
Braun, Dr 280–81
Breault, Mark 74
Breslin, Jimmy 164

Brethren of the Cross 150
Britain, witch trials 276–9, 284–92
British National Party 203
Broderick, Judge 162
Broer, David 227
Bugliosi, Vincent 176
Buksh, Khoda 23
Burnt River, Ontario 115–17
Bury St Edmunds witch trial 276,
    284–8
Bush, George, Vice-President 244
Byg, William 276

Ca Van Liem 142
Caldwell, Phyllis 140
Candlemas 159
Candombe 247
Cannon, Mary Louise 154
Cannon, Ted 105
Carns, William 155
Carr, John 167, 173
Carr, Michael 167
Carr, Sam 165–7
Cartagena, Nilda 247–8
Carter, Leroy 245–6
Catherine II, 'the Great' 33–4
Catholic and Apostolic Church
    (Irvingites) 59
Central Intelligence Agency (CIA) 87
Centre for the Preparation of the New
    Age 120
Chamblee, John 216
Chandler, Mrs 287
Chandler, Susan 286–7
charismatic Christians 262–5
Cheiry, Switzerland 121–3
Chelmsford witch trials 276
Chivalric Solar Tradition, Inter-
    national Organisation of 120
Christensen, Steven 103–6
Christian cults 39–54
    see also Armageddon cults;
        Judaeo-Christian cults
    Christian Scientists 46–54
    Fountain of the World WKFL 39–41
    Yahwehs 42–5
Christian Ethiopian Orthodox Church
    53–4
Christian Identity Church 202, 226
Christian Patriots 201
Christian Science Monitor
    (periodical) 53

301